From Here
to
Economy

FROM HERE
TO
ECONOMY

A SHORTCUT TO
ECONOMIC LITERACY

Todd G. Buchholz

A DUTTON BOOK

DUTTON
Published by the Penguin Group
Penguin Books USA Inc., 375 Hudson Street,
New York, New York 10014, U.S.A.
Penguin Books Ltd, 27 Wrights Lane, London W8 5TZ, England
Penguin Books Australia Ltd, Ringwood, Victoria, Australia
Penguin Books Canada Ltd, 10 Alcorn Avenue, Toronto, Ontario, Canada M4V 3B2
Penguin Books (N.Z.) Ltd, 182-190 Wairau Road, Auckland 10, New Zealand

Penguin Books Ltd, Registered Offices: Harmondsworth, Middlesex, England

First published by Dutton, an imprint of Dutton Signet,
a division of Penguin Books USA Inc.
Distributed in Canada by McClelland & Stewart Inc.

First Printing, May, 1995
10 9 8 7 6 5 4 3 2

REGISTERED TRADEMARK—MARCA REGISTRADA

LIBRARY OF CONGRESS CATALOGING-IN-PUBLICATION DATA:
Buchholz, Todd G.
    From here to economy : a shortcut to economic literacy / Todd G. Buchholz.
       p.   cm.
    "A Dutton book."
    Includes bibliographical references and index.
    ISBN 0-525-93902-4
    1. Economics.   I. Title
    HB171.B862   1992
    330—dc20   94-35228
                                                                   CIP

Printed in the United States of America
Set in Garamond Light
Designed by Eve L. Kirch

For Debby and Victoria . . .

CONTENTS

Part Four. Making a Buck: Business Finance and Personal Investing

Part Five. A Tourist's Guide to the History of Economic Thought

ACKNOWLEDGMENTS

Frankly, I used to skip over acknowledgments—until some of my friends started writing books, and I began looking for my name within their pages. So let me thank some terrific people. First, my wonderful wife, Debby, and adorable daughter, Victoria. While I would not necessarily recommend writing a book during the first year of your first child's life, Debby's warmth and wise counsel made it a joy. And Victoria cooperated in her own special way, which involved a lot of angelic smiles and some 3 a.m. consultations. Thanks to my parents, who taught me many lessons about economics over the years, especially ideas about sacrificing so your children can attend good schools to enhance their intellectual capital. And with my mother's wit, they taught those lessons without sounding preachy.

While many economists praise entrepreneurship, few get a chance to prove their talent. My business partner David Sawyer taught me about the entrepreneurial spirit, his tireless energy pushing the G7 Group ever forward. My talented colleagues at the G7 Group—Tim Adams, Jonathan Symonds, Kim Willis, Blaise Antin, Mike Jones, John Griffen, Rebecca Archer, Bart Kaplan, Jane Hartley, and Bill Eville—may recognize some of the examples in this book from our daily debates on international economic policy. And of course, I've learned tremendously from smart and savvy clients like Julian Robertson and John Griffin.

My agent, Susan Ginsburg of Writer's House, pushed me along in this project, with enthusiasm and prudent advice, helping me conquer the many distractions. Though politics and academia often have the reputation for pettiness and selfishness, friends and colleagues like Marty Feldstein, Michael Moohr, Larry Lindsey, French Hill, Rob Dugger, and Clayton Yeutter have shown that good, supportive people can move in these arenas.

INTRODUCTION

Most people respond to economists the way Henry Higgins reacted to women: "I'd be equally as willing for a dentist to be drilling . . . I'd prefer a new edition of the Spanish Inquisition." Yet most of us find we can no more avoid economics than Henry Higgins could avoid women. Turn on the television, and you will have to do some very aggressive channel-surfing to escape a story about the budget deficit, the trade wars, the unemployment rate, or the stock market.

Even sports shows get intertwined with economics, since broadcasters cannot avoid talking about the multimillion-dollar incentive clause in some athlete's contract. Inevitably, the football or basketball game's color commentator will discuss something green. During the 1920s, Babe Ruth joked that he earned more than President Hoover because he had a better year. Today, some sports superstars earn not only more than the president, but more than every senator combined! Many of these athletes are forced to learn economics just to protect their fortunes from all the "advisers" eager to help them "double their money in no time."

So why does economics suffer from such a dreary reputation? The reputation goes back a long way. Thomas Carlyle inflicted the lasting insult, calling the practitioners of economics "dismal scientists" in the 1800s. Many modern economists do deserve the tag. They certainly look the part. Tweedy, beady-eyed, and bow-tied, they are virtual mascots for sleep aids. And their dull appearance is often accompanied by teaching methods that consist mostly of scribbling graphs on a blackboard. Even the most witty economists sometimes fall into this soporific mode. John Maynard Keynes, who could conduct a fascinating conversation on everything from modern art to Newton's physics, bored Franklin Roosevelt, leaving the befuddled president with a "whole rigamarole of figures." Roosevelt's typical reaction to economics reminds me of humorist Fran Lebowitz's advice to teens: "Stand firm in your refusal to remain conscious during algebra. In real life, I assure you, there is no such thing as algebra."

Yet *real life is about economics*. It is about finding a job, surviving a recession, battling inflation, saving for retirement, and investing in a mutual fund or playing the stock market. These days many thirty-year-old children are still living at home with their parents because they can't afford to buy or even rent a home of their own, and those same parents must also worry about who will care for their aging mothers and fathers. And if they're squeezing their savings to pay for kids and elderly parents, will there be any money left when they want to retire? We are all bounced around by seemingly abstract forces with names like "supply," "demand," and "productivity," and it helps to know which way you are about to bounce.

This book gives you the tools to chart your own course rather than remaining passive in the face of economic change. Even the superwealthy and superpowerful cannot fully escape these forces. George Bush was the most powerful man in the world in 1992; nonetheless, he could not adequately explain the wrenching change the American economy was going through. Bill Clinton won the right to sleep in the White House because his campaign kept the nation's attention on the sluggish job market. His campaign team's slogan—"It's the economy, stupid"—was meant to insure that they never lost sight of the prime issue.

Most people have found economics to be like a bad steak:

dry, tough, and tasteless. One of my goals in this book is to add sizzle, to make economics much easier to swallow. Following the approach of my first book, *New Ideas from Dead Economists,* I use contemporary examples to bring to life those dreary diagrams and graphs. Rather than encountering dusty examples involving antiquated goods like flax, you will find references to television shows and popular songs. After all, the biggest challenge is to make ideas worth remembering. Someone once said that even a parrot could be an economist—just teach it to say "supply and demand." These are among the few words students usually recall after a typical economics course.

Economists often lose their audiences when they fall into the language of theoretical models and start tossing around words like *parameters, constraints,* and *functions.* Since economists, unlike biologists, do not have the luxury of controlled experiments, they must resort to mathematical models that help explain behavior. Biologists can, for example, feed some rats water and others Kool-Aid to test whether red drinks make white rats turn color. Economists cannot so easily divide the country into two districts to perform similar tests. Instead, they gather statistics and estimate mathematical relationships, postulating for example that a $15 billion tax cut will send national income up by $30 billion. But this relationship, of course, depends on all sorts of other relationships and assumptions. For instance, what if people don't feel good about the economy and refuse to spend the money they get?

Noneconomists find it difficult to understand how economists, in reaching their conclusions, decide which factors are most important. Sometimes, for the sake of explanation, simplified models work best, but one can only hope that the simplified models come close to the truth. I'm reminded of the anecdote Noel Coward told about a picnic he attended, where a little girl asked him to explain what two dogs who were copulating in front of her eyes were doing. "Well, my dear girl," he replied, "the dog in front is blind and the one behind is just pushing her so she can get where she wants to go." While Coward's explanation certainly simplified the touchy issue, it did not come close to the truth.

There is a mistaken idea that economists never agree, and that any two in conversation inevitably break into the kind of bickering that brings married couples to marriage counselors. In fact, most of the principles that I will present in this book get almost unanimous support from professional economists. Most important for our day is the almost universal support among economists for free trade and opposition to tariffs and import quotas. Back in 1930, over a thousand economists signed a petition begging Congress not to pass something called the Smoot-Hawley Tariff Act. Congress didn't listen, and the oppressive tariffs ignited a worldwide trade war and helped twist a typical recession into the terrible Great Depression. In the more than six decades since then, the fortunes of American citizens have become even more tied up with the performance of our international trading partners, making protectionist policies even more lethal from the point of view of economists. This book should make the importance of these relationships clearer and more compelling.

Though economists do frequently agree on the most important policy matters, they've never come together to agree on a definition of economics itself. The great Victorian economist Alfred Marshall took the broadest view, saying that economics is the "study of mankind in the ordinary business of life." But as Marshall knew, economics is not just an academic study, but also a craft for practitioners. If economists did nothing but study events, they would be merely irrelevant. In fact, economists can be downright dangerous. The economist who gives the prime minister bad advice can bring misery and unemployment to the average family. Marshall's student Maynard Keynes recommended that economists take their responsibility more seriously and act less like ivory-tower philosophers and more like dentists who will hear the screams of their patients. To quote a noneconomist, Marlon Brando seemed to agree with Keynes's approach, once telling an interviewer that "Acting is a business—no more than that—a craft, like plumbing, or being an economist."

I see economics as the study and practice of making choices, in a world where people want to better themselves but cannot escape the reality of scarcity. Just as James Madison said we wouldn't need government if men were angels, we wouldn't need economists if the world overflowed with a limitless supply of time, money, food, clothing, shelter, and happiness. After all, we did not need economists in Eden. But ever since Adam bit a chunk out of that apple, people have had to worry about simple questions like, Do I use the plot of land to plant vegetables or raise cattle? Do I send my children to school or out into the workforce? Do I vote for lower taxes or do I vote for higher government spending?

I will try in this book to demystify economics by simplifying its key principles. I have divided it into four basic parts, with an added bonus at the end. Part One tackles the broadest issues, *macroeconomics*—how the economy as a whole moves through cycles of booms and busts, inflation and unemployment. These are the issues that dominate the congresses and parliaments of the world. Part Two looks at narrower issues, *microeconomics*—how companies compete with each other and how the government attempts to regulate businesses. In addition, in Part Two, we'll unpack the economist's bag of tools, so we can take apart and examine such issues as advertising, the environment, education, and health care. Once we understand how the economy works and how individual firms operate within it, we can move to Part Three and take a global view, exploring why countries trade with each other and how international currencies move up and down, as goods flow around the world.

Since many people want to learn economics because they want to help themselves perform better as investors, Part Four examines business and individual investment, employing the key economic ideas covered in Parts One through Three. In Part Five, I provide a short tour of the history of economic thought. After you have learned all the great ideas in the first four parts of this book, you may want to know who developed these principles and when they did it. For those who want to excel at cocktail parties, this last chapter also gives a briefing on the hottest new schools of economic thought.

Some of the examples used in this book come from my experience on the White House Economic Policy Council, as associate director for economic policy and deputy executive secretary. From 1989 until 1993, my office brought the president, his cabinet, and sometimes the chairman of the Federal Reserve Board together to debate and decide on economic policy. I had the fascinating and frustrating privilege of helping our highest officials struggle over difficult choices, choices that meant the difference between jobs and layoffs, inflation and price stability. As my tenure wore on, I became more and more convinced that politicians and even statesmen would make better choices if their constituents appreciated sound economic thinking. If there is no appreciation of good choices from government—no market for them—we cannot expect Washington to supply many. I hope I can make a contribution in this book toward boosting demand for sensible policies.

My current position as president of the G7 Group, an international economics consulting firm, is an adventure in entrepreneurship, as well as in understanding complex international financial markets. My experiences over the last few years especially support my discussions of currency trading (see chapter 6) and of personal investment strategies (see chapter 8).

I hope that this book serves not just to inform but to entertain as well. Economics is, of course, crucial to material success. Readers will learn the hardheaded theories behind everything from buying stocks to selling soap. But even that is not enough to sustain us. Woody Allen once mused, "Why does man kill? He kills for food. And not only food: frequently there must be a beverage." The theories and stories in this book should provide not only sustenance in material quests, but also a splash of fun.

PART ONE

HOW'S THE ECONOMY DOING? MACROECONOMICS

1 The Big Picture

- *What Is a Business Cycle?* • *What Caused the Downturn in 1990?* • *How Are Unemployment Rates Determined, and What Do They Mean?* • *Do Most of the Jobless Face Short-term or Long-term Unemployment?* • *Why Are Economists Sheepish About Unemployment Insurance?* • *What Is Inflation, and Why Is Everyone Afraid of It?* • *Why Do Most People Hate Inflation?* • *What Is Bracket Creep?* • *What Is Hyperinflation?* • *What Causes Hyperinflation?*

In the 1992 presidential campaign, whenever President George Bush tried to change the topic to foreign affairs, Clinton reminded him that the economy was in the doldrums, and that American workers had seen their paychecks shrink. While in retrospect 1992 was a decent year for the economy, at the time the word *sluggish* seemed to accompany every description of the marketplace. Pollsters asked their favorite, big-picture question—"Is the U.S. headed in the right [or "the wrong"] direction?"—and reported that voters were dazed and confused.

Macroeconomics is the study of the big picture: Which way is the economy headed? Is inflation creeping up? Is unemployment dropping? While our discussion of microeconomics in chapter 3 will look at individual firms and household decisions as if through a microscope, macroeconomics takes what you might call an aerial view of the market. As we will see, the picture can be pretty (we call that a "boom") or ugly (a "bust"). The toughest challenge for macroeconomists is to get a clear view through the clouds.

What Is a Business Cycle?

A few years ago I saw some graffiti in a New York subway station announcing that "Boomerangs are coming back." The pun fits all sorts of natural and unnatural phenomena, from lunar cycles to a nostalgic yearning to see Elvis again. Almost every academic and pseudoacademic discipline speaks of cycles or pendulums. Arthur Schlesinger keeps writing about cycles of history, while New Age psychotherapists rhapsodize about biorhythms.

Economists also talk about cycles—sometimes the economy is booming and sometimes it's busting. A boom brings more jobs, higher wages, and smiles to the faces of politicians, who inevitably take credit for the success. A bust brings frowns and scapegoating. In 1988, presidential contender (and Massachusetts governor) Michael Dukakis claimed that he was responsible for the "Massachusetts Miracle" that drove down that state's unemployment rate and drove wages up so high that McDonald's franchises in Boston were bussing in workers from outlying regions and paying them twice the minimum wage. Unfortunately, the Massachusetts Miracle turned into a muddle, with massive layoffs, especially in the high-tech sector, and a hemorrhaging state debt. Once the public realized that the miracle had evaporated, Governor Dukakis reversed tactics and claimed that Ronald Reagan was actually responsible for the economic state of the state.

Economists have been trying to figure out how the business cycle works ever since Joseph told Pharaoh to expect seven fat years, followed by seven lean years. Suffice to say, no one has proved as reliable a forecaster as Joseph. In fact, economists have proved notoriously inept at predicting upturns and downturns.

But perhaps Joseph got us started on the wrong track, for booms and busts do not appear in regular patterns. Recessions are not like swallows returning to Capistrano. They are more like pigeons deciding to flock overhead and release their droppings on the economy. We do not know when they will come or how long they will stay. For example, the U.S. economy hit bottom in 1961, 1970, 1975, 1979, 1982, and 1991. During these intervals, hucksters released books with titles like *Survive and Win in the Inflationary Eighties* and *The Great Depression of 1990*.[1]

Business cycle prophesies often take on a mystical tone. Even a serious economist like William Stanley Jevons (1835–1882) implored his colleagues to believe in regular boom-and-bust patterns. Why? Jevons, one of the first and best statisticians among British economists, had concluded that sunspots, which occur in 10.44-year patterns, cause economic cycles that last precisely as long.[2]

Now, Jevons was not a ninny; he put forth a theory behind the coincidence: "If the planets govern the sun, and the sun governs the vintages and harvests, and thus the prices of food and raw materials and the state of the money market, it follows that the configurations of the planets may prove to be the remote cause of the greatest commercial disasters."[3] In short, Jevons thought that sunspots stunted harvests in India, driving up prices in England and driving down the economy. Though Jevons's theory was more than half-baked, it needed more time in the oven, since he forgot to calculate that poor harvests in Asia would hit England only after a time lag. Thus, England and sunspots would not follow the identical 10.44-year cycle.

After Jevons's struggle with the business cycle, nearly every top economist tried to figure out why economies seem to ride on bouncy roller-coaster tracks rather than follow smooth, seamless trajectories. Some pointed to waves of innovation that shake up the manufacturing sector, while others said that bankers just get too loose with their loans, inciting bankrupcies and downward spirals.[4]

Herbert Stein, who served his country as chairman of the Council of Economic Advisers under President Nixon, and, more successfully, as a droll wit, posits Stein's first law of economics:

If something cannot go on forever, it must stop. Is an economic boom an unsustainable trend? Must rising wages and expanding production hit a brick wall, leading to layoffs and falling output? Is it really true that what goes up must come down? Or could an economy just keep growing?

It's hard to say. We have never seen a perpetual boom or an infinitely long slump. But we cannot prove that it is impossible. Likewise, doctors cannot prove that our neighbor won't live forever, even though no one so far has turned out to be immortal. U.S. business cycles come in many varieties. We have seen shallow, short-lived economic recoveries, sturdy, eight-year booms, temporary slowdowns, and deep depressions. To paraphrase T. S. Eliot, our booms tend to end not with a bang but with a whimper. And then everyone looks around and asks, "What happened?" There is usually plenty of blame to go around, for so much can go wrong.

Here is a list of the usual suspects that can incite an economic roller-coaster ride:

> *Policy mistakes:* The Federal Reserve Board bungles the money supply; Congress bobbles its spending policies.
>
> *Structural adjustments:* Waves of optimism or pessimism shake consumers and producers; geopolitical tumult changes foreign policy priorities and military spending policies.
>
> *External shocks:* Foreign entities drive up the prices of raw materials.

What Caused the Downturn in 1990?

The recent recession and sluggish recovery, which started in 1990, illustrate a variety of forces that can stymie the economy. By the end of the 1980s, the U.S. economy had concluded the longest peacetime expansion in history, creating 18 million new jobs in eight years. The unemployment rate hovered at 5.5 percent, the lowest in about fifteen years. But the party came to an end, and President George Bush was banished from the White House because he couldn't keep the band playing and the crowd rejoicing. What went wrong?

First, the Federal Reserve Board grew nervous about inflation and tried to engineer a "soft landing" for the economy by jacking up interest rates and by printing less money. As we'll discuss in the next chapter, the Fed forms the center of the U.S. banking system, sets short-term interest rates, and decides how much money should circulate in the economy. The Fed figured that with fewer dollars circulating and higher interest rates, Americans would slow down the national shopping spree that began in the early 1980s—it's harder to go shopping if your mortgage or car loan payments start climbing. Rather than trigger a recession the Fed hoped merely to tame the economy's growth. This was a delicate maneuver that might have worked, except for all the other forces slapping the economy in the face.

At the same time as the Fed was reining in the money supply, Congress, responding to the enormous and embarrassing costs of the savings and loan bailout of the 1980s, sicced the regulators on the banks, demanding tighter lending requirements, under the Financial Institution Reform, Recovery, and Enforcement Act of 1989. Meanwhile, banks had to comply with a 1988 international agreement called the Basle Accords, which had the effect of pressuring U.S. banks to lend more to the federal government and less to private borrowers. As a result of these measures, banks grew more stingy, touching off the "credit crunch" that shocked the financial system after the bonanza of real estate lending during the 1980s.

The White House was flooded with calls and letters from small business–owners who claimed that they could no longer get loans from their banks to support their businesses. The banks, in turn, claimed that their hands were tied by federal regulators who discouraged them from lending. The White House called Fed chairman Alan Greenspan to a meeting with the president, at which Greenspan argued that consumers and businesses had simply borrowed too much in the 1980s, and that the economy would not turn around until individuals and firms felt comfortable with their balance sheets. I recall watching the amateur sailors among the cabinet members nod when Greenspan described the economy as heading into fifty-mile-per-hour head winds. When Bush pushed Greenspan on the issue of federal regulators, Greenspan admitted that some of them might have been too aggressive and intimidating for the bankers. He ended up calling them all to Washington to urge prudence in the lending system, not pyromania.

Then the Soviet Union collapsed, leading policymakers to tear up their spending plans for the Department of Defense. Defense spending by the U.S. government shrank from about 6.5 percent of the national economy in 1986 to about 5 percent in 1990, and the unemployment rate in defense-intensive states like California, Massachusetts, and Connecticut shot up by over 4 percentage points. Employees at defense-related firms dramatically cut back their household spending, fearing pink slips. While a smaller defense budget helps the economy in the long run, the short run has been bloody, especially for Southern California.

When the Iraqis invaded Kuwait in August 1990, their aggression sent the price of oil skyrocketing to about double its pre–Gulf War level. And while the price of oil looked like a gusher, consumer and business confidence fell down the well. Though the Iraqis were repelled by early 1991, they had attacked at a time when the world economy was vulnerable.

While oil prices soared into the stratosphere, Washington raised taxes on gasoline, luxury goods, and upper-middle-class incomes, further sapping the economy's vitality.

Our largest trading partners suffered from similar maladies. The Bank of Japan and the Ministry of Finance drove up interest rates in order to burst fantastic real estate and stock market price bubbles, while Germany struggled to pay for the costs of reunifying. Prior to the bubble popping in Tokyo, that city's real estate was "worth" more than all U.S. real estate combined! No wonder Japanese executives gobbled up, sight unseen, tracts of lush Hawaiian swampland which appeared incredibly cheap to them.

But wait, there's even more than the forces listed above! How about the pigheaded real estate developers who kept building and building office and residential space without stopping to think where the new tenants would come from? A depressed California developer came to my office in 1992, furious with President Bush. "Todd, two years ago, I was worth thirty-five million," he told me. "Now, most of that is gone." Gee, I thought, he may be down to his last $17 million. Who is at fault here? Didn't he notice that the baby boom was petering out, and that California taxes and employment costs were driving businesses out of state? Did he want George and Barbara Bush to move into one of his housing projects? Well, it's true that just a few months later, they were looking for new accommodations.

During this excruciating period of flux, politicians and economists tried to forecast when the economy would bounce back. But just about no one got it right. From 1990 through 1993, the business climate just felt—well, depressed, as if it had caught a common cold and could not shake it. Instead of bouncing back in 1991, as the overwhelming number of business economists forecast, the economy took what morbid Wall Street players call a "dead-cat bounce," that is, it stuck to the bottom of the charts. Treasury Secretary Nicholas Brady exhausted his kit of metaphors to encourage business confidence. At one point, he proclaimed that "the robins were on the lawn." At another point, he told Congress that America's automobile tires were bald, and that a buying spree would soon begin. Then he announced gleefully that light bulb orders had jumped, suggesting that factories were working overtime. These leading indicators proved false. And by then the Bush administration's credibility took a dead lame-duck bounce.

Looked at in retrospect, the economy did start recovering in

1991 and grew at a respectable rate in 1992, but it did not create many new jobs, nor did it generate an atmosphere of optimism and revival. This was not a "normal" business cycle downturn. The forces at work, each in its own way, pummeled consumer and business confidence. Further, the unraveling of communism in the Soviet Union proved to be not just an epic political event, but an epic economic event as well. The former West Germany, often the driving force behind Europe's economy, had to transfer billions of dollars each year to its East German neighbors. And the vast labor force behind the Berlin Wall broke free, bolstering the supply of labor in the world and dampening the prospects for higher unskilled wages in the West. The world economy could not swallow this upheaval so easily. The economy had not just a passing cold but a bad case of the flu.

As the economy travels up and down through business cycles, it carries with it the mood of the population. These factors reinforce each other. A rising economic tide lifts not just spending but spirits, while a receding tide depresses people. In turn, pessimism makes recessions worse by scaring households and businesses into risk-averse, introverted spending patterns.

While Herb Stein's law states that unsustainable trends must end, Buchholz's corollary says, People don't believe Stein's law till it's too late. They believe that the current stage of the business cycle—whether boom or bust—will go on forever. During the 1980s boom, New York real estate developers kept pouring cement and piling bricks up until nearly every street corner was adorned with a skyscraper. They could not imagine a time when rents would fall. As late as 1987, the Japanese bought the top two thirds of the Citicorp Center, convinced that they could jack up rents in a market that had already begun to teeter. Then, in the recession of 1991, these same businessmen could not imagine that the economy would ever recover.

Likewise, the Japanese investors who sent the Nikkei stock market average through the roof in the 1980s thought that Japan would spend the rest of the twentieth century flat on its back, unable to resuscitate itself from the economic wallop of the early

1990s, when the Nikkei lost over half its value, a collapse rivaled in the U.S. only by the Wall Street market crash of 1929.

Naturally, stock market crashes and recessions end up tossing businesses into bankruptcy court and throwing people out of work. You might be surprised to hear it is difficult to count how many.

How Are Unemployment Rates Determined, and What Do They Mean?

Many economists avoid talking about unemployment in public, adopting a rather sheepish tone when forced to confront the issue. Why? First, they do not want to give their employers any ideas! Second, since they are suspicious of government programs to help the unemployed, they are afraid of sounding callous. Among themselves, economists usually agree that welfare payments and unemployment insurance make getting a job less attractive. But before explaining this analysis, we should define that heralded statistic, the unemployment rate.

In 1976, Jimmy Carter dethroned President Gerald Ford because Ford had presided over a lousy economy. Carter concocted a clever marketing toy called the "misery index"—the inflation rate plus the unemployment rate—and denounced Ford for allowing the highest level of misery since the Great Depression. By 1980, when Ronald Reagan tried to deploy that same rhetorical weapon to show that Carter had made the country even more miserable than Ford, the former Georgia governor dismissed the idea of the index.

But the unemployment rate cannot be escaped. Every month, the Bureau of Labor Statistics surveys about sixty thousand random adults throughout the U.S., asking whether they are working or not. If not, the surveyors ask whether they are actively looking for work. People without jobs who admit they are not seeking jobs do not count as unemployed. They are considered out of the workforce. *Only those jobless who are actively searching count in the unemployment rate.* This distinction causes some controversy and confusion. While it may seem fair to ignore those who are not looking, what if they are not looking because they are too discouraged by a weak economy? Quite often, critics of incumbent politicians will scoff at a low official unemployment rate and try to add these "discouraged workers" to the ranks of the unemployed. Trouble is, we cannot tell who is truly discouraged and who is truly not interested in putting in a day's work. In fact, incumbent politicians often rebut their opponents by arguing that many of the officially unemployed are lying to the surveyors when they report that they are actively seeking work.

It is tough to interpret the unemployment rate without knowing more details. Remember that the jobless include not just people who were fired, but people who stomped into the boss's office and yelled, "I quit!" Quitters, or people who fired their bosses, made up about half of the unemployed during the recession of 1991.[5] The average American worker holds ten different jobs over his lifetime, usually by choice. Think about your own career. You have probably resigned from more jobs than you have been fired from. The Japanese, who until recently clung to the romantic but sometimes serflike idea of "lifetime" employment, find these statistics astounding. While the Japanese question the American worker's loyalty, the Americans wonder about Japanese flexibility.

To understand the unemployment rate, we also need to know how long the jobless have been without jobs. Do the jobless have marketable skills or obsolete training? Are they concentrated in specific geographic regions or certain failing industries? With Congress slashing Pentagon spending over the past five years, it is easy to see why engineers who design missiles are facing bleak employment prospects. While the Bible speaks of beating swords into plowshares, these days it takes more than a little tinkering in the toolshed to pick corn with a surface-to-air missile.

Do Most of the Jobless Face Short-term or Long-term Unemployment?

That depends on your perspective, of course. If you love to work, then just one day of unemployment seems dreadful—especially if it is spent watching soap operas on television. The fact is that half of all unemployed Americans find new jobs in less than seven weeks. Only a few of the jobless (about 15 percent) face unemployment spells that last over six months. The American economy is among the most fluid in the world. Each day people switch jobs and move in and out of the workforce. Just because the overall unemployment rate stays steady for a year, at say 6 percent, does not mean that the same individuals are without work day after day.

Why Are Economists Sheepish About Unemployment Insurance?

Economists are sheepish because they think of themselves as generally mild-mannered and kind. Yet deep down they think unemployment insurance and welfare payments drive up the official reported unemployment rate.[6] How? First, in order to collect government help, the jobless must at least claim they are actually looking for work. Studies show that there is a lot of fibbing going on. Harvard professor Lawrence Summers, who currently serves as Undersecretary of the U.S. Treasury, found that this requirement boosted the reported unemployment statistic by .5 to .8 of a percentage point, which translated into about 600,000 to 1 million fibbers. No wonder daytime television generates such high ratings—an extra million people are channel-surfing, rather than knocking on doors and interviewing for jobs.

Certainly, most unemployed workers legitimately cannot find

work at the wages they are accustomed to. A rising unemployment rate does not mean that employees are suddenly less interested in working hard; more likely, it means that the overall economy has come on hard times, or at least some sectors of it have. And by collecting unemployment compensation, laid-off workers can continue spending, keeping the overall economy from slumping further.

Still, government programs do make sitting at home relatively more attractive. If you reward people to hang out, the amount of hanging out will go up. In economists' terms, government programs raise each individual's "reservation wage," that is, the minimum wage a jobless person will insist on before accepting a job. And if we add in the federal and state taxes, it is no wonder that Summers and his coresearcher Kim Clark conclude that ditching unemployment insurance would send the unemployment level falling by over 600,000.

Let's take an example. Suppose Vanna just lost her $9.00-an-hour job as a cosmetologist. Government assistance gives her about $4.95 to stay at home working on her own nails and hair. At first, that looks like a big drop in pay. But do not forget that when Vanna was working, she would make Social Security contributions of 7.5 percent on top of an average 18 percent in federal and state taxes. So her take-home pay as a working cosmetologist was only about $6.70 an hour. While on unemployment she does pay federal and state taxes, but she no longer sends 7.5 percent to Social Security. Her stay-home pay, then is about $4.05.

The upshot of this arithmetic: Vanna earns only an extra few dollars per hour if she goes to work. And don't forget that staying home saves on commuter and wardrobe expenses. Summers and Clark also discovered that unemployment insurance roughly doubles the number of people who stay unemployed for more than three months.

Of course, at some point, usually twenty-six weeks, the unemployment compensation runs out. What happens to those few who have not yet found jobs? They find them quick. Northwestern University economist Bruce Meyer discovered that the likelihood of getting a job actually triples during the last month of unemployment benefits.

Rather than dragging out the unemployed period and driving up the Nielsen ratings for daytime television, we might do better to offer ambitious unemployed workers the alternative of a lump-sum payment at the start of their unemployed period, which they must use as "seed capital" to start up a business.

Though economists tend to agree that the U.S. unemployment compensation system keeps workers on the sidelines, Europe presents a bigger mess. The government in France, for example, subsidizes unemployment by paying people almost 100 percent of their "lost wages." Even recent university graduates who never worked are getting paid, because they have lost their hypothetical jobs. This is a dire issue for the European Union (EU), which risks further economic stagnation if it cannot cut off the compensation for hypothetical work and instead start producing real things.

The EU's sad predicament reminds me of comedian Jackie Mason's routine about Hollywood, where no one works but everyone claims to be a producer. And they all have business cards that say PRODUCER. Have they released any films? Nah, they're working on some deal, or another deal just fell through, or they're about to start . . . After all the bluffing, what do they produce? Just business cards that say PRODUCER.

Admittedly, unemployment insurance is not the key perpetrator of unemployment. Naturally, most people thrown out of work do not like it and suffer psychological stress. Abstract concepts like supply and demand end up smacking not at all abstract individuals and hurting families. Rather than taking the callous view that the jobless should sink or swim, most economists favor government programs to help retrain workers for new jobs. And, of course, they believe that the government should try to avoid recessions—a tough task, but a worthy goal.

When firms lay off workers and start shutting factory doors, the macroeconomy starts to sound like an old steam engine grinding and sputtering to a stop. It's a sad noise. But what happens if instead of slowing down, the steam engine starts picking up speed at a dangerous pace, careening down the tracks? To an economist that sounds like inflation.

What Is Inflation, and Why Is Everyone Afraid of It?

Simply put, inflation means that prices go up, and money is worth less. Almost everyone deplores inflation, especially retirees who have fixed incomes that do not keep up with rising prices. Senior citizens cannot just call their banks and say, "Hey, I need more money 'cause the cost of my arthritis medicine has doubled." People who cannot afford to pay higher prices are forced to cut back on their spending, but that's not always so easy. When the Hollywood director Cecil B. De Mille was told that the cost of producing his movie *The Ten Commandments* was spiraling out of control, he responded, "What do you want me to do? Stop now and release it as *The Five Commandments?*"

For such an unpopular phenomenon, the world sure sees a lot of inflation. It is not a modern invention. Ancient economies were routinely ravaged by high inflation, which almost always shakes the political structure until its leaders tumble down. From ancient Rome to the Weimar Republic to the Carter presidency, regimes have been rotted by the monetary cancer called inflation. When citizens woke up to find the value of their coins had been slashed, they looked at the face of the emperor on the coin and decided to do their own slashing.

Governments measure inflation by going shopping. Each month U.S. Bureau of Labor Statistics (BLS) bureaucrats grab shopping carts, figuratively, run up and down the aisles of supermarkets and department stores, load up on goods, and then add up the prices. The next month, they pick up the same goods and recheck the prices. The rate of change is the Consumer Price Index (CPI), the most commonly quoted inflation statistic.

As the government bureaucrats race through the aisles, private investors and others stand outside the stores biting their fingernails, for the figures the bureaucrats tally up shake financial markets and shape the decisions of households. Investors in the bond market (see chapter 10), for instance, worry that if the numbers show rising inflation, their bonds will be worth less. Lenders will require borrowers to pay them higher interest rates to make up for inflation. Many employees have contracts that specify *cost of living allowances* (COLAs) based on the CPI. So, if the CPI climbs 5 percent, their bosses may be obliged to give them 5 percent raises to maintain their standard of living.

Though many people focus on the results of the CPI survey, the truth is that it's a sloppy system. First of all, the bureaucrats shop like robots, not like human beings. They buy the same basket of goods regardless of price discounts, coupons, special giveaways, and all the other promotions that vendors hold out to authentic consumers. Robotic bureaucrats do not look through the Sunday shopping circulars to find the lowest prices. Most shoppers know that only cave dwellers would pay the list price for electronics goods, for example. Recently, the list prices for breakfast cereals have skyrocketed. Yet studies show that the bulk of cereal buyers have been handing over to cashiers discount coupons worth 20 to 30 percent of the "regular" prices.

Second, the robotic bureaucrats are not flexible. They do not adjust their shopping list to take advantage of price fluctuations among competing products. For example, suppose Bernie from the BLS finds in his instructions a shopping list of ingredients he'll need to make a salad for the secretary of labor. He must buy a head of iceberg lettuce, a red pepper, a red onion, and some parsley. Bernie takes his bland government sedan to the local grocery store and trundles his way down the fresh produce aisle. Next to him, with a similar shopping list, is Tim, a househusband shopping for his family. Bernie grabs each of the items on his list, not even noticing that the price of the iceberg lettuce has jumped fifty cents since last month, the red peppers are bruised and blackened, the red onions cost twenty-five cents more, and the parsley looks like cigar ashes. No matter, Bernie will toss this ugly salad. When he figures out the CPI, he'll tally up huge price increases for fresh produce.

Tim is not so dumb. He sneers at the iceberg lettuce and instead reaches for a head of Boston lettuce, which is actually twenty-five cents cheaper than last month. Likewise, his shopping cart glides right past the bruised and blackened red peppers and instead stops at the green peppers, whose price is the same as last month. Instead of higher-priced red onions, he grabs a Bermuda onion. Finally, he skips the ashen parsley, figuring that since most people discard the garnish anyway, he'll just pick some crab grass from his lawn instead.

By showing some flexibility, Tim has not only avoided higher prices, he has avoided spoiled food and found substitutes that are better and will give him a delectable and interesting salad. While Bernie's official CPI will show a jump in produce prices and the secretary of labor will face a lousy salad, Tim's family budget will not budge.

Television reporters who talk about inflation usually have no more economics training than television weathermen have meteorological expertise. A common mistake: they forget that *inflation is a story about overall prices, not just the prices of a few items.* They will discuss inflation in women's wear, as if controls on that sector would cure overall prices. But at any point in time, some prices will be climbing while others will be slipping. That is how the market eases shifts in supply and demand. If blue jeans become more popular, prices should rise to encourage the clothing industry to start pumping out more denim. If virgin wool sweaters go out of style because they itch too much, their prices should fall, so that both manufacturers and sheep get the message: stop making so much.

Instead of tracking these individual sectoral shifts, macroeconomists focus on the overall price level. Why? Because true inflation hurts. It snatches the value from savings and robs people of their confidence in government. John Maynard Keynes wrote that the quickest way to destroy a country is to "debauch the currency."[7] Instead of *debauch,* Keynes could have used the word *debase.* In conversation we use the word to mean degrade, injure, or destroy. In fact, the origin of the word *debase* actually explains inflation. Back in ancient times, when coins contained precious metals, the government could not mint more coins unless it discovered more gold or silver. Since this limited the number of coins in circulation, it kept a lid on prices. Merchants could not, after all, boost prices if households did not have more money in their pockets. But sometimes unscrupulous leaders added coins to the money supply by minting new coins that contained less gold and silver. They added "base metals," like bronze or copper. The result: more coins snuck into circulation, driving up the prices of goods. Each existing coin was worth less. By adding base metals, the leaders *debased* the currency, hurting its value, and fueling inflation.

Why Do Most People Hate Inflation?

People hate inflation for the same reasons that Brooklyn Dodger fans hated the New York Yankees: the Yankees were annoying, and they "stole" awards that the Dodgers should have had. Inflation is annoying. It makes it difficult if not dangerous for businesses and households to plan ahead. For instance, how much should the parents of a newborn start saving to pay for her college education? If inflation averages 2 percent, prices double every thirty-six years. But if inflation creeps up to 8 percent, prices double every nine years. A Harvard education that currently costs $100,000 could cost half a million dollars for an infant born today. To plan for college, does a young couple invest in a ten-year U.S. Treasury note that pays 7 percent interest annually? If inflation picks up, that may be a bad deal. And don't forget, if the couple is in the middle class, they will pay about a third of that income to the government in taxes.

Millions of workers who retired with pensions during the 1960s and 1970s found that inflation pushed up costs far beyond their expected expenses. Many had to reenter the workforce just to make ends meet. And just when they thought the ends met, somebody in Washington moved the ends.

Businesses too cannot perform well if they must worry about unexpected price hikes. Suppose a corporation is deciding whether to sign on to a deal to build a new U.S. manufacturing plant to compete with the French. Typically, the firm will spend a huge sum of money on consultants, who will calculate and weigh the costs versus the expected benefits. While their estimates might look great at first, if U.S. inflation starts roaring ahead, the firm may not be able to match its competitors' prices, and the plant could go bust.

Inflation also squeezes businesses by raising what economists call *menu costs,* the cost of changing price tags or posted prices. We have all had a laugh—or a cry—when we've come across old advertisements that display incredibly cheap-sounding prices. In the early 1970s, Ford introduced a rickety compact called the Maverick. The car was not memorable, but the $1,995 price now sounds incredible. Today, some automobile stereo systems cost as much. A club soda was once called a "two-cents plain." Now a cup of ice will cost more than that.

Imagine how many times restaurants and merchants had to change their posted prices during the inflationary 1970s, when prices almost doubled. Certainly, the printing companies liked the constant business. No surprise though that by the 1980s, more restaurants started calling themselves "bistros" and scrawling the choices and prices on blackboards rather than pre-printing menus. While these "menu costs" might seem modest for restaurants, consider the hassle and expense of adjusting parking meters or coin-operated telephones.

Besides menu costs, economists also discuss *shoe-leather costs,* because inflation makes people run around more, wearing down their soles. Why? If inflation is high, interest rates will usually rise to compensate people for lending their depreciating currency. With higher interest rates, people have an incentive to keep money in the bank, not in their pockets. Remember, money in pockets earns no interest. In an inflationary climate, you actually lose wealth if you keep it in your pocket, almost as if your pocket had holes in it. The upshot: people end up running to the bank more, and keeping less in their pockets. As we said, running around wears down shoe leather.

Despite this harangue about inflation's costs, some ivory-tower economists scoff. Stop foaming at the mouth, Buchholz, they would say. If everyone expects an inflation rate of 10 percent, the economy will adjust very smoothly, for wages will go up 10 percent to compensate workers, and interest rates will go up 10 percent to compensate lenders.[8] But I would keep foaming. This cavalier attitude assumes that people know how much inflation to expect. Truth is, nobody knows. From 1978 to 1979, the inflation rate leapt by about 50 percent. People who signed contracts in 1978 to deliver goods at a certain price in 1979 got taken, not by their buyers, but by the government, which permitted higher inflation. Not only is it tough to predict changes in the inflation rates, but once inflation starts getting out of control, it becomes even less predictable.

The bottom line: economies get more efficient and countries get wealthier when businesses and households can depend on the currency to hold its value. That is why the decade of the 1970s has such a poor reputation among economists and historians—not to mention fashion critics, who watched polyester leisure suits expand at dangerous rates.

Though inflation in the 1970s hurt most people, one guy got lucky: Uncle Sam. Why? As we will see below, more money started pouring into the Treasury Department's coffers.

What Is Bracket Creep?

I am tempted to say that the commissioner of the Internal Revenue Service is *the* bracket creep, but it's not his fault. With a progressive tax system—meaning that people who make more money pay a higher percentage of their income in taxes—when inflation pushes wages up, families pay more in taxes even though they are not actually any richer. Again, the 1970s illustrate the dreadful problem. A middle-class family earning a combined income of $20,000 in 1970 landed in the 25-percent tax bracket. That same family, with the exact same buying power, would have been forced into the 40-percent bracket by 1980. Their tax burden jumped about 50 percent, just because of inflation. Similarly, lower-income families earning just $10,000 in 1970 found themselves moving from the 15-percent bracket to the 25-percent bracket by the end of the decade. People not only felt poorer, they *were* poorer, in terms of take-home income.

Though the Economic Recovery Act of 1982 under President Reagan eliminated bracket creep from personal income by "indexing" the tax schedule for inflation, President Clinton's 1993 Budget Act essentially restores bracket creep for upper-income Americans. While the U.S. government has addressed bracket creep for personal income, people still pay taxes on inflated gains when they sell assets like stocks, bonds, or real estate. For example, if Maury bought stock worth $1,000 on the New York Stock Exchange in 1970 and sold it in 1983, he would get about $2,000 and pay taxes on his $1,000 "profit." Yet during this same period, inflation had doubled the price of nearly everything, so his $2,000 in 1983 merely kept him even with the value of his $1,000 in 1970. After he forked over his taxes, he is much worse off than he was in 1970, despite "doubling" his money in the market.

As you can see from this example, by turning even savvy investors into saps, inflation and bracket creep sap an economy of its strength and confidence.

Though Ronald Reagan's advisers cringed at the challenge of fighting back the double-digit inflation they inherited in 1981, they had it easy compared to leaders who faced *hyperinflation.*

What Is Hyperinflation?

A frenzy. A mad scramble. When hyperinflation strikes, everyone has paper money, but paper money is useless. Prices skyrocket, so that price levels must be written in scientific notation. For instance, from the summer of 1922 to the fall of 1923, German prices soared by about 1×10^{10}, over 300 percent per month. It took about 1,800 printing presses working overtime to supply all the cash.[9] Since prices moved more quickly than paychecks could be written, employers paid their workers twice a day, so that they could shop during their lunch breaks. Restaurant patrons surely asked for the check at the beginning of the meal, and bar patrons ordered by the pitcher, since beer got stale more slowly than prices rose. For buyers at the market, haggling over prices for more than a second probably cost them more, for each tick of the watch brought prices higher.

Under these conditions a "five-and-dime" becomes a millionaire's club, but millionaires are poor. While the German episode has received the most attention from historians, the Hungarians outdid their neighbors after World War II, when prices jumped almost 20,000 percent per month! People spoke of "nonillions"—a *1* followed by thirty zeroes. This book is not big enough to waste extra space writing out such a number.

Naturally, a hyperinflationary environment destroys trust in government and in business dealings. Imagine the investors who held German bonds that paid only 5 percent per year. Their bonds might as well have been written with disappearing ink. The hyperinflation of the 1920s ravaged the stable working classes in Germany, eventually making Nazi propaganda more appealing.

What Causes Hyperinflation?

Governments permitting printing presses to spin out of control, pumping out so many bills that consumers bid up the prices of goods in a frenzied auction atmosphere. The atmosphere only intensifies, as the public realizes that it must buy now, since prices will be rising again very soon. The time period defined by "soon" starts shrinking. "I'll wait for next week, thank you" quickly turns into "Hand it over now, bub." Eventually money becomes worthless, and people are forced to barter or substitute with other sorts of currencies, like cigarettes.

A common joke was told about a German woman who ran to the market carrying a straw basket full of bills. She put down the basket to get a look at some fish. When she reached for the basket, it was gone. But the thief had left the worthless money.

A government can stop hyperinflation only by blowing up the printing presses. Frequently, the government will simply announce a new currency and guarantee that currency with something of value, like gold. In late 1923, the German government unveiled the *rentenmark,* and promised that it would only print so much as it had gold in its vault to back the new notes. This kind of step usually does the trick, though the government must usually work hard to earn back its credibility.

International lenders are often suspicious that governments in debt will resort to hyperinflationary policies. Why? Let's say that Bolivia owes Helen's Bank of California a billion bolivianos, worth, say, $200 million dollars. A quick way for Bolivia to ease its foreign debt burden would be to make a billion bolivianos worth ten dollars. So it prints up a few hundred billion bolivianos, drives up prices, ignites hyperinflation, and pays back Helen's Bank with some worthless paper. No more debt burden. In fact, in 1985 Bolivian inflation ran over 12,000 percent.

To avoid this disaster, international lenders will often force an unreliable government to denominate its bonds in a stable currency, like the dollar. That way, Bolivia would owe Helen's Bank a million U.S. dollars, even if that now translates into a nonillion bolivianos.

Now that we have an idea how hyperinflation gets started we can look at the causes of run-of-the-mill inflation. This takes us to the next chapter's discussion of monetary policy and the banking system.

If macroeconomics concerns the big picture, it must also concern the biggest player, the government. We'll now look at the many roles of Uncle Sam, including his performances as the world's biggest debtor and as the manager of the U.S. business cycle.

2 Uncle Sam the Debtor

DEFICITS AND FISCAL AND MONETARY POLICY

• *Why Doesn't the Government Balance Its Books?* • *What Is the Difference Between the Federal Deficit and the Federal Debt?* • *What Is the Difference Between the Cyclical, Structural, Unified, and Primary Deficits?* • *How Big Is the U.S. Debt?* • *How Can Deficits Affect the Economy?* • *Will Our Deficits Punish Future Generations?* • *Is It Possible People Save More to Make Up for Tomorrow's Debt Reckoning?* • *What Is Fiscal Policy?* • *What Was the Phillips Curve, and Where Did It Go?* • *What Is Monetary Policy?* • *How Does Monetary Policy Work?* • *What Is Money?* • *How Does the Fed Create Money?* • *How Is the Fed Structured?*

A Mexican and an American are lying on the beach in Acapulco discussing wine, women, song, and the U.S. budget deficit. "How big is the U.S. debt?" the Mexican asks. "About three trillion dollars," the American responds. "How much would that be in pesos?" he asks the Mexican. "Oh, that would be all of them."

For the past fifteen years, Americans have been assaulted by two annoying trends: higher deficits, and pundits sounding the alarms and telling us we cannot sleep well until we solve the crisis. The Chicken Little chorus, led most recently by Ross Perot, warns us that we are heading toward a dark abyss filled with red ink. Unless we swerve soon, we will drown.

During the first half of the 1980s, these cries actually put people to sleep. The deficit and the national debt appeared to be MEGO issues—"my eyes glaze over." More recently, though,

Perot's populist squawking, and best-selling books like John Figgie's *Bankruptcy 1995,* have shown that America's eyes may be widening, not glazing over. Still, most people cannot make much sense of the debate. Discussants frequently confuse the federal deficit with the national debt, ignore the underlying causes, and claim that there are pain-free solutions. My aim in this chapter will be to straighten out the rhetorical mess. In addition, we will look at how the federal government, through the budget, the tax code, and the banking system, tries to keep the economy flying straight.

Why Doesn't the Government Balance Its Books?

For a clue to the answer, let's rephrase this question just a little: Why doesn't the government balance *your* books? Most congressmen keep their personal finances in pretty good shape—though the House of Representatives banking scandal of a few years ago might give us pause. Those who fall deeply into personal debt become vulnerable to unflattering press reports. They could have trouble fund-raising. Their kids could have trouble qualifying for college loans. And they could be rejected by fancy golf clubs.

But they do not face the same punishment if they permit *your* debt—that is, the government's—to climb skyward. In fact, the federal budget is designed to deflect responsibility away from politicians. That is why some people have compared the federal government to an infant: it has a limitless appetite at one end and no sense of responsibility at the other. The taxpayer finds himself in the position of the parent, constantly scrambling to feed one end while struggling to control the mess at the other. But the mess keeps getting bigger and bigger. Washington has managed to balance the federal budget only twice since 1960, the last time in 1969. And at this point not even the most optimistic swamis are predicting a balanced budget until well into the twenty-first century.

Congress avoids responsibility by decentralizing the budget process. No one really is in charge of the overall spending. If you traveled to Washington in search of the man, woman, committee, or cabal that decides, you would find yourself like Kafka's Joseph K., who was unable to find or respond to the bureaucracy. The Kafkaesque budget process involves dozens of committees in the Senate and in the House, all wrestling over funds. You could knock on the door of the Agriculture Committee to discuss food stamps and farm price supports, but then you would have to trot over to the Ways and Means Committee to deal with Medicare. But to figure out the Medicare problem, you'd also have to find the door marked ENERGY AND COMMERCE, since that committee shares jurisdiction over Medicare with Ways and Means.

This decentralized fiasco creates what economists call a "tragedy of the commons." While this kind of tragedy has no Hamlet, it does show why the state of Denmark can look pretty rotten. Back in Hamlet's day, many shepherds shared grazing pastures. While the prince was seeing ghosts in the castle, the shepherds were seeing ghostlike, skinny cattle, rather than the hearty, beefy kind seen on private fields. The problem? Every shepherd had an interest in feeding as many cattle as possible. Since the pasture was held in common, no one had responsibility for controlling the number of grazers. The entire benefit of adding another animal went to the individual shepherd, but the cost of wearing and tearing the pasture was "commonized."

Each congressman is like a shepherd who wants to feed as many constituent needs and special-interest wishes as possible. Some industry group wants a subsidy, others want money for a bridge, still others want a tunnel. The common pasture is trampled and overgrazed. While some special interests get fat, the average taxpayer gets stuck cleaning up the manure and feeling pretty frail. Naturally, the congressmen, Hamlet-like, refuse to

follow Polonius's advice: "Neither a borrower nor a lender be."
Why should they? They do not have to repay the debts.

The trick is to make representatives more responsible or to
put in place automatic restraints on spending. It seems obvious
that the committee system should be revamped to cut back the
number of subcommittees, and to limit the reign of chairmen.
Longtime chairmen like Congressman John Dingell of the Energy
and Commerce Committee exerted control over almost half of
the legislation that crawled through Congress. Furthermore,
Congress should have incentives to cut back spending rather
than to spur it on. At the end of each year, representatives of
federal offices run around trying to distribute all of the extra, un-
spent funds. Why? They are afraid that if anyone finds out about
the leftovers, Congress will shave back their allocation for the
next year. Wouldn't it make more sense for individuals to receive
bonuses for returning money to the kitty?

As for automatic restraints, Washington has tried the so-called
Gramm-Rudman-Hollings Act, which Senator Warren Rudman
called "a bad idea whose time has come." The Act *would have*
forced across-the-board cutbacks if the federal deficit grew too
high. I emphasize the tense because Congress has the habit of
letting itself off the hook when convenient. In 1990 and again in
1993, Congress and the White House agreed to budget packages
that promised $500 billion in deficit reduction. Note though that
these sums represented cuts "from the baseline." This means
that spending continues to rise, but at a slower pace than had
been previously planned.

Here is one way to think of the baseline: Suppose Harry eats
doughnuts each morning while watching the aerobics channel
on cable television. Harry adjusts his meal schedule by the cal-
endar year, so that in each of the past five years, he has raised
by one the number of doughnuts he eats every day. So last year
he ate five per day, this year he is eating six per day, and next
year he expects to eat seven per day. But after admiring slim
bodies at the beach, he finally makes a New Year's resolution to
slim down. Instead of eating the expected seven doughnuts—his

baseline—per day in the next year, he eats only six. Will Harry get thinner? It turns out that the baseline has little effect on his actual waistline.

Such promises by the federal government do not count for much either, unless incentives are reversed. Most of the deficit reduction in the heralded 1990 and 1993 budget bills came either from tax hikes, which do not slow spending, or from promises for the long run. Even though, with the economy improving, the deficit dropped significantly in 1994, the Clinton administration foresees a big deficit upturn at the end of the decade. While Maynard Keynes did say that "in the long run, we are all dead," he should have added that the deficit, like Dracula, lives on.

What Is the Difference Between the Federal Deficit and the Federal Debt?

The deficit is a short annual story, while the debt is an epic, generational tale. In other words, the government runs a *deficit* when it spends more in any given year than it collects in revenue. For 1993, the number was about $200 billion. The government's *debt,* on the other hand, adds up all the borrowing over the years in the form of Treasury bills, notes, bonds, and U.S. savings bonds. In 1993, this total debt surpassed $3 trillion.

To quote the late Senator Everett Dirksen, "A billion here, a billion there, and pretty soon you're talking about real money." But if Dirksen knew that we would have to amend his line and say "trillion" instead of "billion," the imposing statesman would have cried. Though these are big numbers, the story is not over, and the plot has some more twists. In fact, the deficit and the debt cannot be bandied about in debate so freely. We have several ways of defining these concepts, each of which has a different effect on the size of the problem.

What Is the Difference Between the Cyclical, Structural, Unified, and Primary Deficits?

Just when you thought you understood the annual deficit, economists throw in a few more options, like the cashier at Burger King, who keeps peppering you with questions after you have ordered your hamburger. "Would you like ketchup on that? How about mayonnaise? A pickle? Onion? Lettuce? Mustard? Tomato? Relish . . ." For God's sake, just gimme my burger, you think.

Well, the *unified* deficit is the Whopper. It includes all cash payments by the government, and all cash receipts. The *primary* deficit tries to look more narrowly at the current year by asking if this year's programs are covered by this year's revenues. It asks the question, Does the current year make the situation better, by paying down some debt, or worse, by piling on even more? It, therefore, excludes old liabilities such as this year's interest payments to holders of Treasury bonds. After all, the government issued those bonds in prior years. *The government can, therefore, run a balanced primary account but a deficit in the unified account.* How? If, for example, this year's taxes can pay for this year's programs, but cannot completely cover interest payments on bonds issued in prior years, the primary deficit is said to be balanced.

We can also ask whether the deficit is *structural* or *cyclical*. We do not have to worry so much about a cyclical deficit, which means that a recession has temporarily slowed tax collections and spurred social spending. In fact, these reactions can help the economy recover and are known as *automatic stabilizers*. But structural deficits should worry us. Basically, a structural deficit means even if the economy were healthy, we would be short of bucks. We cannot blame it on a temporary downturn in the business cycle. Unfortunately, the U.S. has blown up its structural deficit, so that even in the boom years of the 1980s, we piled on more federal debt, which grew from about 22 percent of GDP to about 38 percent.

How Big Is the U.S. Debt?

Very big. Even bigger than Orson Welles in his later years. Once again, we have numerous ways to add it up. The most sensible method compares the debt to the size of the economy. The Gross Domestic Product measures the size of the economy by adding up the value of all the goods and services we produce. With the debt at about $3 trillion, and the economy at about $6 trillion a year, the debt/GDP ratio comes to just over 50 percent. Is 50 percent a passing score or a failing score? If misery loves company, we can take comfort, since 50 percent is average for industrialized countries.

More important, though, we must ask whether the situation is getting better or worse. The debt/GDP ratio peaked at over 100 percent during World War II, when the U.S. borrowed massively, including selling all those war bonds hawked by Bob Hope and his leggy accomplices. After falling steadily to about 25 percent in the mid-1970s, the debt has climbed steadily and unchecked toward 50 percent. At this point, if you divided the federal debt by the U.S. population, each of us would be tagged with over $10,000 of debt.

While this sounds awful, keep a few things in mind before jumping out the window to avoid your share of the debt. For one, it is unfair to look only at the liability side of the ledger. Like businesses and households, the government has assets as well. Even the most wealthy moguls and healthy corporations will take out loans or mortgages to finance homes and equipment. When Mr. Movie Mogul lounges around the swimming pool of his $10 million Malibu estate, we do not think of him as a pauper just because he is writing monthly mortgage checks to his bank. The real question is whether Mr. Mogul's next movie will get a thumbs-up from the public and make the bucks to keep him in Malibu. As for the government, it owns valuable assets too—assets like highways, buildings, parks, waterways, and minerals. These assets contribute to national income.

A more sophisticated way of assessing federal debt would be to try to compute our net worth by subtracting debt from assets. Robert Eisner of Northwestern University claims that this calculation leaves the debt picture looking less desperate.[1] Before we blithely accept Eisner's optimism, though, note that even using Eisner's charitable method to figure the debt, it has ballooned in the last decade. So clearly the problem was getting worse, even if it didn't start out very serious. To implement Eisner's system and treat the federal government like a business, we'd have to figure out how much Mount Rushmore is worth, and how much we should depreciate it each year to account for wear. All the king's accountants would have trouble with that assignment.

Though Eisner's contention that we must consider government assets makes analytical sense, it makes for dangerous politics. Why? Politicians will almost always claim that their pet project represents an investment, an asset, not the wasteful, ordinary kind of spending program that drives up the debt. During 1993, President Clinton characterized all of his favorite spending programs as investments. The newspapers were filled with rhetoric applauding "investing" in food stamps, superconducting supercolliders, space stations, roads, welfare, etc. Eisner's method is too twistable to entrust to politicians.

How Can Deficits Affect the Economy?

Again, we must focus on structural, ongoing deficits, rather than temporary blips that naturally accompany recessions. A cyclical deficit is like Melvin, who, understandably, gets fat in the hospital, because he cannot exercise. A structural deficit means that he continues to pile on pounds after he leaves, because

Melvin eats Twinkies and does not exercise, even when he is "healthy." Bottom line: just as a structural eating disorder is hazardous to Melvin's health, a growing structural deficit is dangerous for the economy.

Let us take the Melvin metaphor further. Suppose that Melvin is at a buffet where there is a fixed amount of food, so that if Melvin gobbles up more than his share, others are left with empty plates. This is the sad portrait of the federal government as it gobbles up funds that could have been used by private businesses to build new plants or buy new equipment. When the federal government runs a deficit, it borrows the extra money by selling more Treasury bonds to the public. Remember, though, that firms also borrow money by selling bonds. Like Bigfoot, the bloated Uncle Sam stomps on Wall Street and starts grabbing the available funds, usually from private savings. Economists call this gluttony "crowding out." By gobbling and guzzling, Uncle Sam depresses private investment, which ultimately robs workers of potential tools that could lift their productivity and their wages. This may not show up right away, but over time, as Uncle Sam looks fatter America's economic might will look flimsier.

"Crowding out" makes long-term business projects less attractive. If interest rates are 4 percent, a firm that puts $1,000 in an idea must get back at least $1,800 in fifteen years, or the project "loses" money. But if government borrowing pushes rates up to 6 percent, that same $1,000 investment must now yield a minimum of $2,400. Clever inventions and innovations that merely double your money would not make the cut anymore.

This buffet nightmare assumes, of course, that the restaurant does not replenish the serving trays after Uncle Sam makes a pig of himself. Could the waiters and waitresses come up with more grub? That is, could the private sector find more sources of funds, other than U.S. savings? This is where foreigners come into the cafeteria and provide a partial solution. As we will discuss in chapter 6, the international finance market is growing more integrated, linking every country's stock, bond, and currency trading. When Uncle Sam eats too much, U.S. interest rates will tend to rise, since demand for funds is surpassing supply. Foreign investors will see these higher rates as a good opportunity to lend money and will buy U.S. assets, whether bonds or real assets like manufacturing plants.

By adding to the serving tray, foreign investors alleviate the shortages caused by Uncle Sam's binges. During the early 1980s, we saw net foreign investment in the U.S. jump from zero to about 3.5 percent of U.S. GDP. These foreigners do not, though, completely save the day and satisfy the U.S. hunger for funds. For the U.S. must pay back the foreigners, and when those funds flow back across the seas, they sap our economy. In sum, it is better to have willing foreign investors to help out, but it is even better not to need them and keep a balanced structural budget.

Will Our Deficits Punish Future Generations?

Despite the combined $1 trillion in "deficit reduction" claimed in the 1990 and 1993 budget agreements between Congress and the White House, the next century looks treacherous for taxpayers. Current estimates—which are vulnerable to massive revisions—project the federal deficit dipping for a few years from 1993's 5 percent of GDP but then soaring again to 12 percent in 2030, as so-called mandatory spending on Social Security, Medicaid, and Medicare squeezes taxpayers.

Who is going to pay this bill? Not today's retirees in Fort Lauderdale, not even the baby-boomers of President Clinton's generation. Today's children, sitting entranced in front of their television sets, have no idea how much fiscal pain they will have to endure. And it gets worse for tomorrow's tots. One recent study showed that the future toddlers of America will pay over 70 percent more to the government over their lifetimes than young workers pay today.[2] Just by looking at Social Security benefits, we see that people who retired in 1972 took out *in just the first year* over 28 percent of the total amount they paid in to the system. Their grandchildren who retire in 2012 will have paid in so much more that they will take out just 5.6 percent of it in the first year.[3]

Instead of merely calculating the deficit, economists have proposed *generational accounting* to estimate how big a burden government policies will place on old people, middle-aged people, young people, and future generations. This method adds some interesting twists to the typical deficit story. Programs that at first appear like gifts end up, under generational accounting, looking like heavy loads to carry. Suppose your favorite uncle proudly tells you that your birthday present is a subscription to the Salmon of the Month Club. He whips out a Norwegian fish and beams as he informs you that he has paid for . . . the first twelve months of a ten-year contract. Uh-oh. Suddenly your "gift" from the old generation weighs you down.

Likewise, during the 1950s and 1960s, even though the federal budget deficit looked like it was shrinking, your Uncle Sam spawned some big fish by building up civil service, military retirement, and Social Security programs. In contrast, the 1980s, which in some ways looked like a disastrous decade for the federal deficit, saw a few government policies that actually sliced future generational burdens, for example, by raising the Social Security retirement age from sixty-five to sixty-seven and taxing Social Security benefits. Further, by spending so much on defense in the early 1980s, the U.S. spurred the collapse of the Soviet Union, which should reduce future outlays on defense. A good investment, it seems, but a tough one for accountants to grapple with.

Generational accounting is as complicated as sorting out a family quarrel. But it can depict a clearer portrait of what the government is doing to—or for—our kids and our parents.

Is It Possible People Save More to Make Up for Tomorrow's Debt Reckoning?

This is the best-case, though unlikely, scenario for paying off future debts, which comes from the great David Ricardo via Harvard economist Robert Barro.[4] In the early nineteenth century Ricardo suggested that the current generation might bequeath to their children and grandchildren enough money to pay off the debt they leave them with. Hmm. Though Ricardo himself got along well with his dad, he was less optimistic about other families and suspected that many old-timers didn't give a hoot about the youth. After all, many people do not have children. Actually, recent studies show that private savings rates have not offset the ballooning U.S. deficit. Though there is still time for the Ricardian case to be proved right, to paraphrase Blanche Dubois, we are taking an awful risk when we depend on the kindness of strangers.

Government spending is not just about irresponsible generations ripping off their descendants or leaving their children broke. When Congress spends money today, it moves the economy today. We call that *fiscal policy*.

What Is Fiscal Policy?

Let's go back to Melvin's buffet. This time the other customers do not feel hungry. They are depressed and gloomy. Perhaps some have lost their jobs. Others just feel as though they have lost their confidence, that spring in their step that usually propels them to the serving trays. Further, pundits are prophesying doom and more job layoffs. Melvin, our metaphor for the government, starts worrying. If my neighbors stop eating, he thinks, the restaurant may have to close down, leaving more people on the unemployment lines, further depressing the place.

What can Melvin do? Waddle up to the buffet and pile on helping after helping, generating more demand for food to compensate for everyone else's being thrifty. Now that Melvin's bulking up, the restaurant can afford to stay open, and if Melvin eats enough, it may be able to hire more cooks and waiters. Melvin's deliberate binge can start to reverse the gloom. No use permitting the prophets of doom to wipe all the smiles away; Melvin can turn the depressed joint into a cabaret.

That, in effect, is fiscal policy; using the government's budget—Melvin's appetite—to move the economy. In Melvin's case, the government spurred the economy by spending more: *expansionary* fiscal policy. In the opposite situation, it could have slowed an overheated economy by cutting back on its spending: *contractionary* fiscal policy. In addition to adjusting government spending, Congress can also adjust taxes, either cutting them to push spending or hiking them to restrain the economy.

Though Thomas Malthus endorsed an activist fiscal policy at the turn of the nineteenth century, John Maynard Keynes gets the credit for bringing fiscal policy into the twentieth century and for giving it an analytical grounding. Keynes, a fascinating British intellectual, devised his most powerful ideas during the Great Depression, delivering his advice in many venues, academic and popular. In an article in *Redbook* magazine Keynes asked the question, Can America spend its way into recovery? Keynes's answer: "Why, obviously!"[5] Keynes begged the British Treasury and the U.S. government to pump up the economy, though the prevailing wisdom in London and Washington taught the treasuries to rein in the budget. In a letter to Franklin Roosevelt he advised "a large volume of loan expenditure under government auspices. . . . Preference should be given to those which can be made to mature quickly, on a large scale, as, for example, railroads. The object is to start the ball rolling."[6] Keynes was disappointed that Roosevelt, whom he characterized as a second-rate mind working behind a first-rate personality, did not take his advice seriously enough. Even the New Deal was too tepid for the Cambridge economist.

As we have pointed out elsewhere, today the economy automatically deploys fiscal stimuli when the business cycle winds down. How? Unemployment insurance keeps spending up during recessions, while tax collections fall, leaving a greater portion of funds in the hands of consumers. When this is not enough, many people argue à la Keynes for "discretionary" fiscal stimuli to "prime the pump," or "get the economy moving again."

The early 1960s showed such policy at its best. In 1964, Kennedy-Johnson advisers prescribed a shot of economic adrenaline for the sickly economy. They cut taxes by about $13 billion. Soon, all the vital signs improved, and Keynes looked like the hero of the century. Graduate students all over Cambridge, Massachusetts, which led the Keynesian battle from MIT and Harvard, wanted to put up statues of the witty genius.

But for the last twenty-five years, economists have criticized Keynesian stimuli the way pigeons criticize statues. Why does discretionary fiscal policy often fail? Let us count the ways: First, the government is very bad at forecasting; its ability to prescribe the right dose and kind of medicine is suspect (the 1964 episode might have been a lucky shot). Second, the government takes a long time to act. By the time proposals have meandered through committees, the government spending plan may come too late and end up overheating the economy's natural recovery. Moreover, the actual spending will be tilted toward groups that wield the most political power; Chairman Big Mouth will, no doubt, get a big bridge in his district. Third, as we pointed out above, new deficit spending "crowds out" private-sector investment by pushing up interest rates. Fourth, by pushing up interest rates, fiscal policy can push up the exchange rate of the currency. As we will see in chapter 6, a stronger dollar makes our exports seem more expensive to the rest of the world, depressing export jobs.

Fifth, fiscal policy can be flummoxed by people's expectations. For instance, if the government tries to stimulate demand by temporarily cutting taxes, households may save the extra dough rather than spending it. After all, most people base their consumption patterns on long-run goals and expectations, not jumpy blips on the screen.[7] For example, a temporary investment tax credit to spur business equipment purchases will merely lead firms to spend less later. In addition, as President Clinton learned when he proposed such a credit in 1993, firms will delay any purchases until the legislation actually passes Congress. Thus, Clinton actually saw firms *slowing* their equipment purchases in response to his ultimately failed initiative.[8]

Perhaps this harangue is what football players call "piling on." The historical lesson of activist fiscal policy is this: be modest about what we know and what we can achieve. Instead of fine-tuning, Princeton's Alan Blinder (currently vice chairman of the Fed, following a one-and-a-half-year stint on President Clinton's Council of Economic Advisers) advocated "coarse-tuning." If the economy is floundering and confidence has faltered, a burst of spending might do the trick in turning around expectations. Even the Bush administration, which usually claimed to have abandoned Keynesian precepts, ended up proposing a $5,000 credit for first-time home buyers and a bunch of other demand-side measures to pump up the languishing economy of the early 1990s. Congress rejected this program, and so Keynesians did not have much opportunity to show their stuff. Nor did they have much of a chance when President Clinton took over, for his administration was forced to spur the economy through lower interest rates, rather than through higher government spending.

A frequent debating topic between Keynesians and their critics is the Phillips curve, which for a brief time in the 1960s gave economists a false sense of confidence that they could neatly balance economic slowdowns and economic booms.

What Was the Phillips Curve, and Where Did It Go?

Economists love to discover new statistical relationships because it gives them the chance to achieve immortality. Thus, we have Harberger triangles, Okun gaps, Keynesian multipliers, and Phillips curves. Although like most of us, economists would rather reach immortality by not dying than through formuli, they settle for the latter. For about a decade starting in 1958, A. W. H. Phillips seemed to find an eternal place in economic history by pointing to a long-standing inverse relationship between inflation and unemployment, tracking the two figures from 1861 to 1957.[9] According to Phillips's charts, when unemployment was high, prices were low, and when unemployment was low, prices were high.

Phillips's analysis seemed to deliver a Chinese menu to policymakers, in which they could choose "one from column A," the unemployment rate, and "one from column B," inflation. Great Keynesian economists like Paul Samuelson could point to the high 6.5-percent unemployment rate in 1961 and prescribe that the government should drive down that rate to 5 percent, which would bump up prices by .5 percent, a reasonable Phillips curve trade-off.

Then the magic wore off the Phillips curve. Milton Friedman and Edmund Phelps persuaded the economics profession that the Phillips curve menu was only a temporary trade-off—that ultimately, government spending to cut the unemployment rate would only push prices up but not push unemployment down. In fact, with the stagflation of the 1970s, the Friedman-Phelps view destroyed the Phillips curve, which seemed to shift outward, meaning the U.S. and the U.K. suffered from both higher unemployment as well as higher inflation. Remember, Phillips said that if one went up, the other must go down. Indeed, following the deep recession of 1981–82, inflation collapsed and the unemployment rate began to drop, far faster than most economists had expected. The most dramatic rejection of the Phillips curve came from British prime minister James Callaghan, who headed the Labour government in the mid 1970s:

> We used to think that you could spend your way out of a recession and increase employment by cutting taxes or boosting government spending. I tell you, in all candor, that that option no longer exists, and that insofar as it ever did exist, it only worked by injecting bigger doses of inflation into the economy followed by higher levels of unemployment as the next step.[10]

In retrospect, the Phillips curve never reached immortality but merely enjoyed its Warholian fifteen minutes of fame. Though the Phillips curve debate seems over, a related debate rages on: How much power does the Federal Reserve Board have over the economy, and how confident can we be about the board's ability to wield it? This now takes us to the issue of *monetary policy*.

What Is Monetary Policy?

We all know that too much of a good thing is a bad thing. Even too much oxygen makes people hyperactive, until they eventually become less productive. But can there be too much money? Surely, as individuals we would welcome that knock on the door from Ed McMahon telling us that Publishers Clearing House has chosen us as the $10,000,000 grand prize winner, and that we would also get a new Jaguar convertible in the color of whatever stamp we'd licked and stuck on the entry form. But what if Ed McMahon knocked on every door in the U.S., distributing a $10,000,000 gift to the whole population? Would we all be rich? No. All those bills floating around would quickly overwhelm our capacity to produce goods. Instead of spurring more output and a stronger economy, those dollars would merely bid up prices. We could achieve the same effect just by having everyone add a bunch of zeroes to their salaries and to prices. As Adam Smith taught, the only way to measure wealth is by how many goods and services we can buy, not by numerals. Certainly, Japanese millionaires are not rich. It takes about 100 Japanese yen to buy one U.S. dollar.

Monetary policy is the effort to get the right amount of money into the economy: enough to buy all the goods and services produced, so everyone who wants a job has one, but not so much that prices jump. This is no easy trick. For one, the monetary officials must deftly gauge the country's productivity and ability to churn out goods and services. Gallons of ink have been spilled in academic journals and in newspapers over monetary policy. Several times each year, U.S. senators hold hearings to berate the Federal Reserve Board for mishandling monetary policy. It has become a sport in Washington, and Federal Reserve officials have developed the skill both to absorb the verbal blows, and to respond in long, windy paragraphs intended to fill up time but not say anything in particular. Fed Chairman Alan Greenspan's skillful pronouncements bring to mind Churchill's comment about Clement Attlee: that he had the ability to condense the least amount of thought into the greatest number of words. Generally, politicians believe that central bank officials are too stingy with the money supply and too concerned about inflation.

While the Senate can lambast the Federal Reserve, the central bank is relatively independent of Congress and of the White House. The president appoints and the Senate must confirm the Fed's seven-member board of governors, but neither the legislative nor the executive branch can force the Fed to push the money supply or interest rates in any particular direction. Under the Bush administration, Treasury Secretary Nicholas Brady continually fired off futile missives to Greenspan urging him to pump up the economy. Greenspan often answered in metaphors, explaining that the economy was running into "fifty-mile-per-hour head winds."

This independence from elected officials gives the U.S. central bank a great deal of credibility in world financial markets. Germany's Bundesbank enjoys similar standing. France only recently moved to depoliticize the Bank of France, its central bank, in an effort to boost the bank's credibility. Like the Supreme Court, central banks act most prudently when insulated from politicians, who usually clamor for them to inflate the economy, especially in election years.

How Does Monetary Policy Work?

The Fed sets monetary policy by controlling short-term interest rates and by trying to control the supply of money. When the Fed wants to speed up the economy, it can cut interest rates and/or get more money into circulation. These moves goad households and businesses into spending more on goods and services. Lower interest rates, for example, spur car loans and home mortgages. To combat the recent, deep German recession, the Bundesbank gradually sliced short-term interest rates from 8.75 percent in July 1993 to 4.5 percent in July 1994.

When the economy looks as though it may be overheating and spawning inflation, the central bank can either hike interest rates or slow down the growth in the money supply. Starting in February 1994, Alan Greenspan began pushing up short-term interest rates every few months or so, stating that he was moving from an overly "accommodative" monetary policy to a more "neutral" one. To the frustration of the financial markets, Greenspan refused to say in advance what level of rates would be neutral, leaving the markets constantly guessing what would be the magic level. In the meantime, car loan rates and mortage rates leapt, braking key sectors of the economy. A decade earlier, to tame double-digit inflation in the early 1980s, Fed chairman Paul Volcker jacked up interest rates and ordered the U.S. Mint to print less money. These actions threw the economy into a recession, but also tamed the inflationary monster.

Though the central banks wield enormous power, we should not overstate their ability to shape the economy in the long run. The central banks cannot do much to make factory management more efficient, or to make workers work harder, or to inspire inventors to invent more. The central bank merely supplies fuel to the economy's engine. It must figure out how much to give the engine without flooding the motor, and when and how much to ease off the gas without stalling. Just as the gas station cannot change the horsepower of the engine, the central bank cannot change the economy's productivity. This, too, brings great frustration to politicians. The central bank is often a terrific scapegoat but incapable of solving crises. For example, the Bundesbank got blamed for Germany's sluggish economy, even though this sluggishness came from forces the Bundesbank could not control, namely, the cost of reunifying Germany and the uncompetitiveness of Germany's high-wage industrial workforce.

These limits on the central bank's powers take us back to the Phillips curve controversy. Before Friedman and Phelps tore up the curve, economists assumed that the central banks could pump up the economy and drive down the unemployment rate beyond the "natural" rate determined by productivity and a variety of nonfinancial factors. But as Friedman and Phelps persuasively taught, monetary stimulation is just a temporary high that wears off, leaving the economy with higher prices, not lasting new jobs.

Now that we've covered monetary policy and seen how the Fed cranks out greenbacks, let's back up a moment to ask a more fundamental question: what do we mean by *money* anyway?

What Is Money?

At first, this sounds like a silly question, and one is tempted to respond as Louis Armstrong did when asked, What is jazz?: "Man, if you have to ask, you'll never know!" In fact, money is a tricky concept. So tricky that the government keeps track of several different money supply figures. After all, money does not show up in the chemist's periodic chart of the elements; it is not a pure concept. Monopoly game money could actually serve as real money, if a community agreed to it. In the 1980s cult movie *The Gods Must Be Crazy*, a Coca-Cola bottle falls out of the sky and is discovered by an African tribesman. The shapely bottle becomes a valuable, religious object for the tribe. Surely, Coke bottles can be traded as money. In prison camps, cigarettes frequently reach that status. To quote Groucho Marx—who probably contributed more to social welfare than his namesake Karl—"What is a thousand dollars? Mere chicken feed. A poultry matter." In fact, chicken feed can work just as well as greenbacks, though it would be tougher to catch when it poured out of a bank's automated teller machine.

While the Federal Reserve does not yet count chicken feed or Coke bottles, the bank does keep track of three different money supply definitions. Newspapers publish these figures regularly. The Fed terms the first, fairly narrow definition of the supply *M1;* to calculate it, money, coins, dollar bills, and checking account deposits are counted up. To arrive at M2 the search is widened by adding, for example, savings accounts and small CDs. To get M3 the Fed starts with M2 and adds, for instance, large CDs. In 1993, M1 equaled just over $1 trillion, while M3 came to over $4 trillion.

Incidentally, these money supply figures have nothing to do with gold. Not since 1971 has gold even partially backed the U.S. money supply. One book on the money supply suggests that readers who feel nervous about this, and therefore distrust their U.S. money, should send the authors the suspicious stuff.[11] I agree with this approach but send it to me, not them.

If gold does not back the money supply, what does? Credibility—namely, the credibility of the Fed, the U.S. government, and U.S. taxpayers. People all over the world accept the U.S. dollar, only because they trust that the government and the taxpayers will stand behind their debts and not fuel rampant inflation that would make the currency useless.

How Does the Fed Create Money?

Earlier we said that money does not show up on the chemist's periodic chart. Nor does it show up in the physicist's lab, since unlike matter, money can be both created and destroyed. Central banks can create money by getting private banks to lend more. The Fed uses three tools to achieve this. First, the Fed controls the proportion of deposits that each bank must hold back and not lend; this is called the *reserve ratio*. Suppose the Fed sets the reserve ratio at 20 percent, meaning that banks can lend 80 percent of each deposit they take in. Our friend Joan strolls into the bank and plops down $100 to open an account. This deposit counts as part of the nation's money supply. Joan happily walks out with a new blender. If Al then walks in to borrow $80 from the bank, that $80 gets added to the money supply, beyond Joan's original $100 deposit. According to the Fed's accounting rules, the money supply has already grown by $180. If Al deposits his $80 in a checking account, the bank can lend $64, and if Jill now borrows $64, that amount gets added as well. Each time someone borrows money from a bank, the money supply rises. Thus, Joan's initial $100 spurs a series of loans, each of which adds to the money supply. The smaller the reserve ratio, the bigger the *money multiplier*. If the Fed suddenly bumped the reserve ratio up to 50 percent, the banks would have to call in loans, shrinking the money supply and slowing the economy.

The Fed's second tool to fiddle with the money supply is the *discount rate,* the rate at which the Fed lends money to banks. If the Fed wants to jump-start private lending, it can slash the discount rate, which encourages banks to borrow from it and then loan more to the general public. The Fed may also adjust the discount rate to help out troubled banks that face fiscal emergencies.

Finally, the Fed plays with the money supply by buying or selling government bonds (these transactions are called *open-market operations*). The Fed can, for example, boost the nation's money supply by buying Treasury bonds from the private sector. How does this push up the money supply? In this deal, the Fed prints money and exchanges it for a private person's bond. Since the private person gets the cash, the cash counts in the money supply. Meanwhile, the bond that the Fed holds does not count as money. Likewise, the Fed can shrink the money supply by selling the public a bond. Since the public buyer gives up cash (or a check), the money supply contracts. The bond that the public takes in exchange does not count as money. The Fed's Open Market Committee (FOMC) handles these open-market operations.

By adjusting the money supply and interest rates, the Fed is also manipulating household *liquidity.* Every household wants to manage its spending and saving in a certain way, and to hold on to a certain amount of cash for near-term spending. They keep this handy money in their wallets, purses, checking accounts, or even cookie jars. By buying more bonds from the public, the Fed injects more cash than people had previously desired. What will they do with the "extra" money? Spend it. Thus, by increasing the amount of money circulating through the system, the Fed makes households more liquid, and more likely to spend.

While these tactics do not give the Fed direct control over the money supply, the Fed can try to tune the amount of bank reserves. By keeping tabs on bank reserves, the Fed can then use the money multiplier to calculate how much lending will eventually take place. These calculations are certainly not precise. In fact, sometimes banks seem more inclined to lend than at other times. During the 1930s, Keynes warned Franklin Roosevelt that pumping up the money supply could not drive the U.S. out of the Depression any more than buying a bigger belt could fatten up a skinny person.

Likewise, in the early 1990s the Fed worried about a "credit crunch" during which both banks and borrowers seemed reluctant to go about their normal lending and borrowing. Though the Fed pumped money into the banks, the money supply seemed not to budge much. At the same time, the different money supply measures—the Ms—seemed to split from each other, with M1 shooting upward and M2 lagging way behind. Economists still struggle to figure out why currency and checking account deposits moved, while CDs, for example, stayed stagnant. Certainly, the revolution in finance, with more people putting their savings in mutual funds and other nonbank entities, has complicated monetary relationships. In June 1993, Chairman Greenspan admitted to Congress that the Ms had become too unreliable to precisely guide his interest-rate policies. Instead of relying on a single measure to guide rates, the Fed has become more eclectic, looking at everything from wage agreements to the value of the U.S. dollar against other currencies. Nobel laureate Paul Samuelson has provided a metaphor for this new eclecticism and flexibility of the Fed: "Sometimes I blow on my soup to cool it, and sometimes I blow on my hands to warm them"[12]

Though the chairman of the Fed has a startling ability to shake—and to reassure—investors from Wall Street to Bombay, he cannot act alone. In fact, Congress organized the Fed to spread the power around, a bit.

How Is the Fed Structured?

The Federal Reserve Board's governors toil in an august, marble building on Constitution Avenue in Washington. Among a governor's perks is access to an outside balcony, which has a commanding view of the Fourth of July fireworks; an invitation to hobnob with Fed governors on the Fourth is coveted by Washington social climbers.

Congress created the Fed in 1913 with a desire to ensure geographic diversity and independence from politics. As a result, none of the seven governors can come from the same regional Federal Reserve District, of which there are twelve. Each district has a regional Fed bank, and if you look at a dollar bill, you will see the stamp of the Fed district that issued it. To preserve independence, Fed governors enjoy secure terms of fourteen years. In practice, most governors do not complete the whole term; many cannot pass up lucrative Wall Street careers for that long.

The chairman, appointed by the president of the United States, serves for four years, but this term does not move in sync with the presidency. New presidents, then, are stuck with their predecessor's choices for a few years. Just as Ronald Reagan inherited Jimmy Carter's choice of Paul Volcker, George Bush and Bill Clinton inherited Alan Greenspan. This situation can be touchy, since the financial markets usually like stability. President Bush, for example, was concerned that if he did not reappoint Greenspan, the stock and bond markets could tumble. No surprise, then, that Greenspan got the nod. Over the past decades, Fed chairmen have made good copy for reporters, with their idiosyncratic personalities and power over world markets. Little Arthur Burns puffed on a pipe in the 1970s and wore his hair parted down the middle, like a Smithsonian relic from 1910. Six-foot-seven Paul Volcker chomped on a huge stogie and dominated a room. With their circumspect locution, Burns and Volcker kept their real views to themselves and left financial journalists and senators alike with no choice but to try their hand at reading smoke signals.

The Fed governors do not make policy by themselves. They get help from the presidents of the regional Fed banks. The FOMC consists of the Fed governors plus five of the regional Fed bank presidents. While majority rules in Fed decisions, the chairman carries a lot of weight. In good old realpolitik tradition, the chairman controls the staff and the budget. Governors rarely buck their chairman and directly reject his recommendations. The governors will often give the chairman discretion to act on their behalf. In the spring of 1993, for example, the governors voted to give Greenspan *asymmetric* authority on interest rates. This is a fancy way to say that the governors told Greenspan he could boost rates a bit without their further permission, but he could not cut rates on his own.

Fed meetings are secret, to the annoyance of some congressmen, who want to expose the secrets of the temple on Constitution Avenue. Since the Fed's actions can push and pull the financial markets, a spy with inside information can make a fortune. Rumors about the Fed, or even the health of Fed governors, can move the market as well. During the summer of 1993, my office was peppered with questions from Wall Street asking whether Greenspan was truly ill or had canceled a trip to Scandinavia in order to stay home to raise rates. I called the Fed. Turns out Greenspan had been heard sneezing. No need for the market to catch the flu.

No matter what the Federal Reserve Board or the White House does to energize economic growth, it is the private sector that determines whether jobs are created. In the next two chapters we'll look at the everyday business and household decisions that actually make the economy go round.

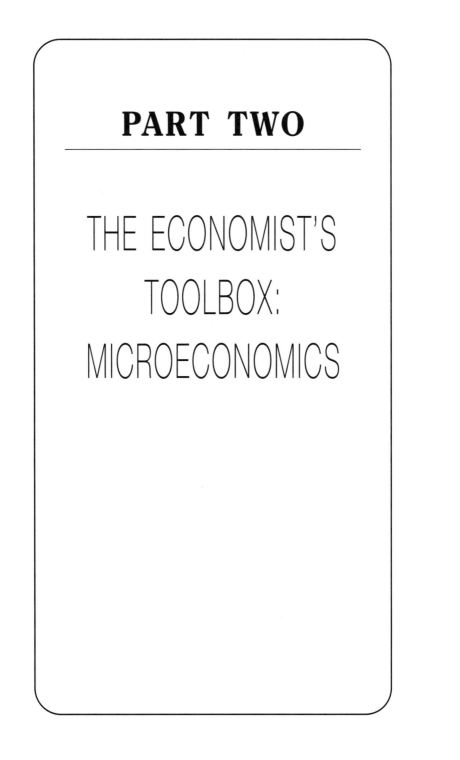

PART TWO

THE ECONOMIST'S TOOLBOX: MICROECONOMICS

3 The Very Model of a Modern Major Market:

MICROECONOMICS

• How Does the Free Market Work? • How Do Prices Keep the Market in Line? • Can the Market Work Without Complete Information? • What Is the Marginalist Approach to Economics? • How Does Marginalism Affect Supply and Demand? • What Is Elasticity, and Why Is It Important? • Has the Competitive Market Been Destroyed by Big Business? • How Do Monopolies and Oligopolies Lose Their Power? • What Is a Natural Monopoly? • What Is Antitrust Law?

"Communism is bad, man, it's like the phone company," said Lenny Bruce back in the sixties. Since the comedian's comment, both Bruce and communism have died, along with Ma Bell's monopoly over telephone service in the U.S. But Bruce's point lives on: market competition brings good things to life, while central planning inspires creativity only in those trying to get around it.

In this chapter, I'll explain how competition and its twin partners, demand and supply, bring consumers and producers together in the marketplace. Economists call the study of this *microeconomics,* for it focuses on the small-scale, individual decisions of households and businesses: "Do I need to buy another can of tuna?" "Should I manufacture another car?" "Can I cut my price to beat my competitor across the street?" As narrow and mundane as the questions may sound, they ultimately form the basis for modern society. In fact, when governments forget the principles of microeconomics, they often injure the common people. We will look at government's role in the marketplace and find some of these mistakes, as well as a few successes.

One popular blunder that almost every economist denounces is rent control. By keeping prices artificially low, rent control leads both to a shortage of units and to landlords skimping on maintenance. Even Vietnamese communist leaders have compared it to bombing as a means of destroying a city! In 1989, Vietnam's foreign minister Nguyen Co Thach said that "The Americans couldn't destroy Hanoi, but we have destroyed our city by very low rents. We realized it was stupid and that we must change policy."[1] Recently, the Vietnamese have begun to sound as if they have read Adam Smith, for they now seem to appreciate how competition, not government control, can make them better off. Then again, maybe they just discovered an old Lenny Bruce comedy album left by Yankee soldiers twenty-five years ago.

How Does the Free Market Work?

Our Sunday newspapers are stuffed with advertisements: "We've Slashed Our Prices!" "Holiday Price-Cutting!" "We Cut Out the Middleman, Passing Savings On to You!" "We'll Beat Any Price!" "Thirty-Day Price Guarantee: If You Find It Cheaper, We'll Double the Difference!" Who benefits from this kind of hand-to-hand wrestling among retailers and wholesalers? Consumers. Sellers don't like it much, but they must constantly struggle to cut their costs and keep down their prices. They are resigned to this battle. After thieves robbed $200,000 worth of suits from a New York branch of Brooks Brothers, one clerk quipped that if only the crooks had come during the sale two weeks ago, the store could have saved 20 percent.

Surely, this "buyers' market" does not prevail all over or all of the time. But compared to most of the world, the U.S. smolders with hot, intense competition. Meanwhile, consumers abroad are left to smolder themselves, as they pay far too much for food and clothing. England's cozy, sleepy retail sector has recently been shaken up by the invasion of U.S. discounters like Costco. For all their national wealth, the average Japanese consumer must work almost an hour to afford a plump cantaloupe. (A good thing, perhaps, since their tiny, overpriced refrigerators don't hold much more than a few pricey oranges.) Only recently did the Japanese government admit that its consumers get robbed—not by overly competitive firms, but by noncompetitive companies. While socialists love to call capitalists "greedy," we see far greater greed where competition does not prevail.

Let's go behind the political bumper stickers and the advertising slogans and look at an example of how free-market competition motivates a self-interested person to wake up in the morning, look outside, and produce from the earth's raw materials not what he wants, but what others want. Not in the quantities he prefers, but in the quantities others want. Not at the price he dreams of charging, but at a price reflecting how much his neighbors value what he has done.

Take Tom, who is a bit slow of mind yet determined to make some money as a carpenter. He wakes up and sips his tea while listening to an old Beach Boys album. He had heard that Reagan administration officials distrusted the Beach Boys. Could *Surfin' USA* refer to Khrushchev's threat to bury the U.S.?

Then it hits him—why not manufacture and sell surfboards? After all, the specially treated wood from Oregon would cost only $40 per board, and Tom can saw and sand one per week. He decides to sell the surfboards for $200 each and dreams of big profits, so he can afford one of those fast T-birds and a trip to the palmy beaches of Southern California.

That's the hitch. You see, Tom has never been to California. He lives in Iowa. Not much demand for surfboards there, but Tom is, as we said, slow to catch on.

He opens a surfer shop in Ames, Iowa, right down the street

from the tractor repair shop. His neighbors take a look and then giggle. High tide won't be coming to landlocked Ames soon. Finally, his devoted girlfriend offers $10 for one. Tom gives in— and goes out of business. Adam Smith's "invisible hand" (see chapter 8) gives a thumbs-up. Why?

Tom was too greedy, and not very perceptive. Instead of producing something his neighbors wanted, he dreamily sawed and sanded something utterly useless to them. Then he charged a ridiculous price. Of course, no one would pay him even the cost of the wood. Didn't Tom have to charge more than his costs? Well, yes, but that's not the point. The answer is not to charge more but to not make surfboards in Iowa. The invisible hand of the market cheered Tom's bankruptcy, because Tom wasted scarce resources that he sawed and sanded into planks of uselessness. Oregon only has so many trees, after all.

The market forces people to add value to raw materials, not detract from them. Tom took $40 worth of wood, chopped it, sawed it, sanded it, and came up with something worth less than the $10 his girlfriend offered. The invisible hand was tempted to show Tom its middle finger.

Back to the drawing board. Tom breaks his Beach Boys album in half and stares at his room full of surfboards. Inspiration strikes. Why not sell skateboards instead? Iowa may not have sandy beaches, but it does have blacktop. He finds a lumber mill and a metal shop that will sell him wood planks and wheels for $5 per skateboard. He can produce twenty per week, and he figures his time is worth $200 per week, based on his previous carpentry jobs. Adding in tools and rent, he calculates the total cost per skateboard at $20. Tom window-shops to check out the competition and discovers that other stores sell skateboards at $25 each. Not only will Tom be able to pay himself $200 per week, but he can also make a profit—if he sells enough skateboards every week, that is.

Tom has finally pleased the invisible hand by taking raw materials and producing something worth more than what he started with. The free market forces mortal men to act like alchemists; they must turn base materials into more valuable goods. Semiconductor chips in computers start as silicon, a fancy form of sand. Silicon Valley in California is filled with modern Merlins turning such common stuff into wondrous electronic brains. Scientists at General Electric in the 1950s actually figured out how to transmute common items like roofing tar and even chunky peanut butter into diamonds![2] In comparison, Tom's original surfboard shop was a reverse-alchemy laboratory, and reverse-alchemists go bankrupt. A man who can change peanut butter into diamonds, now there is a genius. Of course, the market smiles only if people demand such a skill. Certainly, if eight-year-olds ran the country, they would prefer that the GE whizzes keep their hands off their peanut butter sandwiches.

How Do Prices Keep the Market in Line?

Returning to Tom, suppose he wants to boost his profits, so he can afford to bring his girlfriend with him on his vacation to Southern California. Why not boost the price of his skateboards from $25 to $35? He can't. If Tom hikes the price, his profits will actually plunge rather than climb, because shoppers will simply bypass his store and instead buy from his competitors, who charge less.

Of course, all the skateboard sellers could get together and conspire to raise prices. But this seldom works. First, like any committee, these sellers would have difficulty agreeing. As the great diplomat George Kennan said, the probability of any committee agreeing decreases by the square of the number of participants. But even if they could agree, other self-interested people would probably see the excessively high profits in the skateboard industry and open up new shops of their own. These aggressive new businesspeople could earn huge profits by undercutting Tom's prices and stealing sales away from the cartel.

Prices and profits signal to entrepreneurs what to produce and what price they can charge. High prices and high profits quickly catch the ears of entrepreneurs, screaming at them to start manufacturing a certain product. When a company called Soloflex started racking up sales by hiring muscular young men to pose looking sweaty next to high-priced exercise equipment, a dozen new firms with similar products jumped into the market and drove down Soloflex's market share and profit margin. Suddenly, the firm looked flabby, and the corporate executives started to break out in a sweat. Just as high prices drag new firms into a market, low profits and losses grab the businessman by the shirt collar and shake him mercilessly until he stops producing or improves his product and pricing. During the last few years, several European automakers, including Peugeot and Sterling, drove out of the U.S. market because they could not take the tough competition.

Prices and profits are arid concepts, by themselves. But behind these economic tools lies something more basic. What does it really mean when profits are high? It means that people need or want a product. If consumers decide they want cars with airbags, demand will rise for such cars, and producers will be able to charge more. But manufacturers of cars without airbags will have to scramble and retool; they may shift workers from one factory to another; and the price will finally return to normal.

Over the past decade prices for electronic goods have plummeted, especially if you adjust for improvements in quality, and new features. Today's desktop computers pack more brain power than the mammoth-size computers used to guide the Apollo moon mission. (And they do it in tinier spaces. The early space launches may have been directed from Houston Control because Houston is such a big place.) If autos reflected such incredible progress in reducing the size and cutting price, today's Rolls Royce would be the size of a matchbook and cost about $10.

Prices on everything from computers to compact disc players

to portable telephones have dropped not only because firms have cut costs, but because so many high-technology manufacturers have crossed national boundaries to jump into the fray and compete for profits. In the long run, no industry should earn more than a normal profit. The free market automatically induces self-interested Toms, Dicks, and Harrys to satisfy the desires of strangers. No central planner need call, no taskmaster need coerce.

Can the Market Work Without Complete Information?

Yes. Economic theories sometimes confound common sense. While most people would agree that people should think about what they are doing, economists might not. The great Friedrich von Hayek argued, in fact, that civilizations advance when people can take action without knowing all the facts. The market permits people to make decisions and to act without going through the impossible task of collecting all the relevant information. How? Let's follow Hayek's piercing logic:

> Assume that somewhere in the world, a new opportunity for the use of . . . tin has arisen, or that one of the sources of supply of tin has been eliminated. It does not matter for our purposes—and it is very significant that it does not matter—which of these two causes has made tin more scarce. All that the users of tin need to know is that some of the tin they used to consume is now more profitably employed everywhere, and that in consequence they must economize tin. There is no need for the great majority of them even to know where the urgent need has arisen. . . . If only some of them know directly of the new demand, and switch resources over to it, and if the people who are aware of the new gap thus created in turn fill it from still other sources, the effect will rapidly spread throughout the whole economic system and influence not only all the uses of tin, but also those of its substitutes and the substitute of these sub-

stitutes, the supply of all the things made of tin, and their substitutes, and so on, and all this without the great majority of those instrumental in bringing about these substitutions knowing anything at all about the original causes of these changes?[3]

Hayek's most damning criticism of government intervention in the economy rests on this "ignorance argument"— governments cannot possibly gather enough information from throughout the world to intelligently choose whether the price of tin should be X or Y dollars. In contrast, market players do not need to know anything other than prices in order to make their choices.

We can see Hayek's idea behind not just commodities like tin, but even more tasty goods. Suppose Chef Troy makes a devastatingly delicious bouillabaisse, in which he can toss any number of ingredients, including, for example, shrimp, scallops, haddock, pollack, snapper, and halibut. Each morning Troy wanders down to the Fulton Fish Market on Manhattan's Lower East Side to inspect the daily catch. If the fishermen come up short on haddock and therefore charge a higher price, Troy can turn the other cheek and buy halibut instead. He does not need to interrogate the old salts on the dock to find out why haddock is high-priced. All he needs to know is that his customers will have to enjoy a bouillabaisse that is a little heavy on the halibut. Certainly, Troy has enough troubles in his life without worrying about haddock. The market lets him get on with his work.

Hayek borrows a provocative quotation from the philosopher Alfred North Whitehead to bolster his ignorance argument:

> It is a profoundly erroneous truism, repeated by all copy-books and by eminent people when they are making speeches, that we should cultivate the habit of thinking what we are doing. The precise opposite is the case. Civilization advances by extending the number of important operations which we can perform without thinking about them.[4]

Imagine trying to drive a car while also mentally focusing on the pistons firing in sequence, the spark plugs igniting, the tires rolling, the transmission shifting, and the maniac in front of you swerving into your lane. Whitehead and Hayek would agree that only the last item deserves your attention.

What Is the Marginalist Approach to Economics?

Since economics is a study of choices, it is time to ask, How do people choose? We started this chapter by describing microeconomics as the complex study of mundane questions like whether to buy another can of tuna. During the nineteenth century, economists refined their approach by developing the *marginalist* method. England's Alfred Marshall and William Stanley Jevons get the credit for bringing this new system into mainstream economics. Without their work, we might not be able to explain crucial issues like tuna.

The following three snippets, gathered from the worlds of literature and entertainment, can better explain marginalism than the dozen or so graphs that crisscross microeconomics textbooks.

The first example is found in Evelyn Waugh's novel *Scoop*. A British newspaper owner confronts an editor whose vocabulary consists of just two replies. If the owner says something true, the editor replies, "Definitely." If the owner says something false, the obsequious editor replies, "Up to a point":

> "Let me see, what's the name of the place I mean? Capital of Japan? Yokohama, isn't it?"
> "Up to a point, Lord Copper."
> "And Hong Kong belongs to us, doesn't it?"
> "Definitely, Lord Copper."

The old vaudeville comedian Henny Youngman, whose jokes have brought even more moans and groans than Borscht Belt cooking, also delivered many classic lines worthy of philosophy professors: when asked, "How's your wife?" he came back with, "Compared to what?"

In the movie Western *Shane,* the little boy beseeches his hero gunslinger, "Shane, come back! Come back, Shane!" But, alas, the cowboy must move on and cannot look back.

How do these anecdotes explain marginalism in economics? Imagine you are visiting a fantastic amusement park, filled with death-defying roller coasters, splashy log-flume rides, and the biggest miniature golf course you have ever seen. You begin by coasting down the log flume, which makes you laugh. Next you rocket through space mountain, which you enjoy more than any ride you have ever whizzed through. Your space trip cost $5 but gave you at least $100 of pleasure. You consider jumping onto the rotating teacup but you worry that it will disappoint you compared to space mountain. You usually prefer rocketing and rolling to swiveling. How do you decide whether to go ahead with the teacup or pack it in and go home?

First, consider Shane. Don't look back. Your fun on space mountain is in the past and irrelevant now. *Marginalism declares that the past is behind you.* The issue is whether to step forward, and the starting point is where you are now.

Second, remember Henny Youngman—please. What do you compare when choosing whether to jump into the teacup? You ignore the past pleasure on the log flume and space mountain. Instead, ask whether the benefits of the teacup outweigh the cost. If the teacup ride costs only $2 and will give you $3 of pleasure, go ahead. So what if the fun of the log flume outweighed the cost of it by tenfold? The issue at hand is whether to go forward. And you should continue moving forward if the benefits outstrip the costs, even if they exceed them by a lesser margin than before (assuming the rules don't allow you to jump on the same ride twice).

Third, recall the *Scoop* editor. Up to what point do you keep moving forward? You continue as long as the fun of another ride outweighs the cost of one more ride, until the *marginal benefit* equals the *marginal cost.* When a $3 ride gives you just $3 of pleasure, you rest. To keep going would be like the proverbial boy who says he can spell *banana* but just does not know when to stop.

One should not get carried away with forward movement. This is a lesson some businesses cannot seem to learn. They do not know when to stop expanding. In recent years, America's focus on healthy foods inspired the Conagra corporation to start up the Healthy Choice line of foods. Though Conagra started modestly with high-quality, low-fat frozen dinners, pretty soon they expanded their offerings to include everything from ice cream to liquid eggs. These tasty, yet healthy choices for the consumer seemed to multiply faster than Conagra's ability to test the market. Finally, its profits diluted by the far-flung ventures, Conagra wisely decided to shave back the number of products, until it could refine its corporate strategy.

The key to marginalism, then, is to focus on incremental steps. How do firms decide how many cars to produce? They continue to run the assembly line until the revenue they receive from welding together just one more car equals the cost of producing that extra car. Consider, the 1,999th car may have a higher profit margin than the 2,000th—if, for example, the 2,000th used overtime labor—but it's still worth producing the 2,000th as long as it still ekes out a margin of profit. The marginal revenue/marginal cost rule can be applied in and out of economics. Some students study all night for exams. But if at midnight the cost of staying up an extra hour (in terms of fatigue the next day) exceeds the benefits of cramming a bit more, it is better to be between the covers of a bed than the covers of a book.

Though marginalism agrees with *Scoop, Shane,* and Henny Youngman, it disagrees with many clichés that begin with phrases like "We've come this far . . ." and "Anything worth doing . . ." Not that economists celebrate mediocrity—though there are many mediocre economists—but they do cheer when people know when to stop.

Suppose Dopey City, Alaska, starts building a $100 million

domed stadium, because the city council, filled with Mensa rejects, believes that the Los Angeles Dodgers could be enticed to move to the least populous state in the country. After a year, the igloo-shaped stadium has cost the citizens $20 million in very cold cash. Economists would beg them to stop. What about the $20 million they have already invested? Forget about it. Just because there are "sunk costs" that cannot be recovered is no reason to add even one more icy brick. Why dig a deeper hole in the city's finances? Better to tear down the igloo and try to get a refund on the bricks.

Marginalism also applies to government tax policy. It warns policymakers not to get tangled up with averages but to focus instead on increments. For example, if the government considers cutting business taxes to boost investment, it should consider not the average investment rate but rather ask what the chances are that these extra, marginal dollars placed in the pockets of businessmen *will be spent on investment projects.*

How Does Marginalism Affect Supply and Demand?

Someone once said that parrots could be economists: just teach them to squawk, "Supply and demand." Let's return to the amusement park. Jack's demand for cotton candy is based on the additional pleasure that each "cloud-on-a-stick" gives him. Alfred Marshall called this *marginal utility.* Marshall claimed that the marginal utility of each sticky stickful of cotton candy Jack eats will slip. That is, the first stick might give him $1.00 worth of pleasure; the second, only 80¢; the third 30¢; and so on. Finally, the very thought of one more sweet and sticky mouthful would make him sick.

How does Jack decide how much to eat? He compares the price to the marginal utility. If the price were $1.00, he would only buy one (because a second stick would give him only 80¢ of fun). If the price were 30¢ Jack would grab three. Economists draw a downward-sloping demand curve that traces this "diminishing utility." At each possible price, Jack would compare the marginal utility (pleasure) to the marginal cost (price).

Alfred Marshall's law of demand declares that the greater the amount to be sold, the smaller must be the price.[5] Now before you assume that Marshall was obsessed with prices and exemplified Oscar Wilde's line about cynics, who know "the price of everything and the value of nothing," you should know that he admitted that several other factors helped to determine demand. Most important, the consumer's tastes, customs, and preferences. Marshall knew that a vegetarian would not eat venison even if it were free. If Jack, a professional baseball player, read that eating cotton candy would sharpen his eyesight, permitting him to hit that wicked slider, he would start salivating, and his tastes would change. Even if the price stayed the same, he would buy and eat more. Marshall also discussed the impact of the consumer's income, as well as the price of rival goods.

Economists use a similar framework to explain the supply side of the supply-demand equation. As a producer makes more goods, her costs tend to rise. Making more cotton candy requires buying a new, bigger machine. The law of supply is opposite the law of demand. Firms will invest more and bring more to market only if they get a higher price from consumers. The firm compares the marginal cost of producing one more unit to the price, which is the marginal benefit. (A supply curve slopes upward, whereas a demand curve slopes downward.)

Firms must also play the marginal game when they choose between, say, spending another dollar on human laborers and spending it on machines and robots. Manufacturers must ask, "How can we best use this additional money?" If the dollar brings more by spending it on worker retraining than on robot recalibrating, managers should bet the money on people. At *equilibrium* the marginal return from spending on machines (capital) equals the marginal return from spending on labor.

This delicate balance can be knocked awry. Assume the federal government passes a health care law that forces employers to spend an extra $2,000 per year per worker. Suddenly, capital looks cheaper and managers would substitute robots. Conversely, an electricity tax that makes robots more expensive would shift the balance in the other direction, back toward labor. Managers constantly struggle to perform this balancing act, not just with machines and humans, but with new machines versus secondhand machines, skilled labor versus unskilled labor, even with land. If the government levies a high tax on land, the government can look forward to taller buildings that have smaller "footprints" and take up less property.

Again, economists like Marshall do not argue that all producers act marginally or rationally all of the time. If the producer does not, her competitors will be more successful and ultimately eat her alive. Economic evolution favors the lean and mean over the fat and lazy. About 60,000 businesses go bust each year in the United States. Most of them should have spent some time with *Scoop, Shane,* and Henny Youngman before they launched their failures. A fat ego can blind a corporate executive to reality like a bad cataract.

What Is Elasticity, and Why Is It Important?

Like well-toned athletes and good musicians, economies work best when they are flexible and limber, rather than brittle and stiff. A running back will likely find his face in the mud if he cannot zigzag. A pianist cannot specialize in "slow" music just because it takes his fingers too long to plow through "The Minute Waltz."

But since economies do not have fingers or feet, what can economic elasticity mean? Elasticity measures responsiveness: whether firms and households can easily respond to price changes, or, like the football player above, they are stuck in the mud. Will football fans buy the same number of tickets if the team jacks up the prices? If they do, then demand is *inelastic*. If higher prices lead the fans to cut back their attendance, then demand is *elastic,* or sensitive to change.

Here again, Alfred Marshall led the way for economists and developed a simple formula to calculate elasticity—the percentage change in price divided by the percentage change in demand. If the National Symphony Orchestra hikes its ticket prices by 10 percent, and if patrons buy 12 percent fewer tickets, demand for its limber musicians is elastic. If patrons cut back their purchases by less than 10 percent, we would say that demand is inelastic.

Elasticity applies not just to consumer demand but to product supply as well. Suppose the symphony could get away with higher ticket prices because loyal patrons would keep buying. Would the symphony, then, decide to play more often, supplying more music to the community? Would higher prices induce a greater supply of music? If ticket prices fell, would the orchestra play less often? As we will see, elasticity shows up in almost every economic decision.

What determines whether firms, households, or symphony orchestras respond to price changes? First, the number of substitutes or alternatives. The more alternatives, the easier for consumers to switch and to avoid price hikes. The audiotape company Memorex used to advertise with a television commercial showing Ella Fitzgerald singing and then listening to a tape of herself. The advertising slogan was "Is it real or is it Memorex?" If consumers truly thought that listening to Ella on the tape recording was as good as hearing her sing in person (highly unlikely), then Ella might not be able to raise her concert prices much, since consumers might switch over and simply buy audiotapes instead.

Staying with the music metaphor, I confess that I often cannot tell the difference, either visually or audibly, between Michael Jackson and his sisters LaToya and Janet. If others shared my confusion—and indifference—Michael would not have been able to charge so much for his albums, or sell so many. In sum, the more substitutes, the more market power consumers have. Certainly, there is a high elasticity of demand at the fish market where our Chef Troy shops. If the price of flying fish jumps, Troy can pick up pollack, tuna, or even shark, if he's careful.

Second, we can be more elastic if we have more time. If the president of the United States unexpectedly arrives and demands a shredded fish pattie à la McDonald's, Chef Troy must quickly find that bland pattie. He does not have the time to search around the docks and wholesale fish markets. He must pay whatever the nearest fishmonger charges. But if the president makes his reservation a few weeks in advance, Troy can spend some time shopping around for a better deal.

The Organization of Petroleum Exporting Countries (OPEC) gave the world a dramatic lesson in elasticity by slashing oil output and shutting off oil shipments to the U.S. during the 1970s. The Arab sheiks who led the campaign in 1973 during their Yom Kippur War with Israel sent the world price of oil soaring from about $8 per barrel (42 gallons) to about $27 per barrel in 1974. At first, the U.S. continued to use roughly the same amount of oil. But after a few months, price sensitivity became the mother of invention: drivers bought smaller automobiles; homeowners switched to natural gas for heat; and, in a true display of concern for the bottom line, airlines even removed magazines to cut the weight of the planes and save fuel. *New York Times* columnist William Safire later wrote a witty essay on such OPEC shakedowns, profiling the Saudi oil chief Sheik Yamani. He entitled the piece "Yamani or Ya Life."

A second oil shock from OPEC in 1979 energized conservation efforts again. By 1987, U.S. homeowners had cut by about one third the energy needed to heat a square foot of space. Meanwhile, industry, too, had economized, with steel producers using about 20 percent less energy per ton. These oil crises showed elasticity of supply as well, for each shock brought new oil fields bubbling onto the market, from the North Sea to Mexico's Bay of Campeche.

Finally, elasticity depends on whether the product or service takes up much of the firm or household's income. Many families have tucked away in the back of a kitchen cupboard a small can of nutmeg, which they think of using once a year to sprinkle on eggnog. That nutmeg may have been bought fresh during the Eisenhower administration, but somehow it stays in the family. Nutmeg costs a tiny proportion of income, even for a poor family. If the greedy nutmeg makers raise the price, most of us will not notice or care. We will go on buying just as much or as little as we have all along. Our demand is inelastic.

Producers must ask themselves about elasticity whenever they consider changing the prices of their goods. Likewise, governments must figure out the elasticities before changing tax rates or prices for government services. In 1990, the federal government slapped a luxury tax on purchases of large boats, as well as of expensive cars, furs, and jewelry. Over the next two years, Congress learned that rich people do not have to buy yachts; their demand is elastic. As a result of the luxury tax and a "white-collar recession," fewer yachts were sold, and many lower- and middle-income boat builders lost their jobs. In the end, the tax brought in much less revenue than originally forecast. Yacht buyers proved that they were sensitive to both higher prices and their falling incomes.

My favorite elasticity discussion came a few years ago, when the Federal Aviation Administration was considering a new safety rule that would force parents to buy separate seats for infants who were traveling with them on airplanes. (Airlines permitted parents to hold babies in their laps, saving parents a lot of money.) The FAA discovered that parents had a highly elastic demand for airplane seats, and that forcing them to purchase extra seats for infants was likely to dissuade them from flying. Most families, they found, would choose to substitute automobile travel for air travel. Then the FAA realized that because auto travel had a higher injury rate than air travel, pushing the family out of the planes and into autos would actually raise the expected number of infant injuries. Thus, the FAA concluded that this proposed "safety rule" would actually make life less safe for little travelers! Air travel was not always safer than auto travel, of course. In 1910 Charles Rolls, founder of Rolls-Royce autos, had the ironic distinction of being Britain's first aviation fatality after crashing in a Wright biplane.

Has the Competitive Market Been Destroyed by Big Business?

Back in the 1960s and 1970s, many textbooks, after describing Adam Smith's model of competition, would sneer and announce à la Nietzsche that "the invisible hand was dead"—that the quaint idea of buyers and sellers jostling in the marketplace had been destroyed by gray-suited predators plotting in their modernist skyscrapers to rip off consumers. Critics of the Smithian-Marshallian approach would throw all sorts of statistics at the reader showing that just a few firms seemed to control the world. During the past twenty years, though, economists have reexamined the terrain and discovered that competition in most sectors remains quite brisk, and that the most persistent monopoly situations (post offices, electric utilities) arise from government policy, not from businessmen gobbling up their competitors.

Before looking at any elegant theories, we can start by just naming a few of the corporations that seemed to dominate the U.S. economy back in 1970 and ask, where are they now? Certainly, IBM seemed to walk like *Tyrannosaurus rex* in 1970. Today, it slinks along more like a herbivore than a carnivore, having lost market share to Intel, Apple, and all the other high-tech firms that have eaten into its profits. General Motors spent the last twenty-five years bleeding red ink and losing hegemony to both domestic and foreign competitors (though GM seems to be recovering now). Meanwhile, USX-U.S. Steel has shrunk itself while trying to fight off minimills in the United States, as well as steel firms all around the world.

This does not mean that monopolies and oligopolies do not exist today, but we should not underestimate what economist Joseph Schumpeter called the "gale of creative destruction" that tears apart seemingly stable, comfortable corporations. The Royal typewriter company thought it had a pretty good hold on the market, until the word processor and personal computer jolted its empire. Icebox makers and ice delivery men thought they could slide by until companies like Frigidaire started selling a lot of refrigerators. Today, U.S. telephone companies scramble to figure out how to survive the onslaught of cellular and wireless communications. Indeed, quite often companies develop monopolies not because they have swallowed up or stomped on their competition, but because they have leapt ahead through innovation. Magnetic resonance instruments (MRIs) can detect tumors better than old-fashioned X rays. Cancer patients would agree that it is better for firms like General Electric to have a temporary monopoly on certain MRIs than for us to be stuck with 1950s technology. And a monopolist named Isaac Merrit Singer probably did as much for poor people through his sewing machines, which made clothes cheap enough for the working class to own more than just one set, than just about any government assistance program.

Even where just a few firms dominate, we must ask, Can the government make the situation better or not? Certainly, the free market is not free of problems. Sometimes producers collude and consumers get ripped off. Other times, as "game theorists" like Nobel laureate John Nash teach us, they reach a stand-off; like lions sharing a cage, they refrain from attacking each other. But the medicine of government intervention can often make matters worse. That is the reason that since the Carter administration, the U.S. government has begun deregulating such industries as airlines, natural gas, trucking, electric utilities, and telecommunications.

How Do Monopolies and Oligopolies Lose Their Power?

A monopoly exists when one firm is the only seller of a good or service. An oligopoly exists in a market with just a few sellers. Though this kind of situation sounds dangerous, after a career of careful study, Nobel laureate George Stigler concluded that "economists might serve a more useful purpose if they fought fires or termites instead of monopoly."[6] Stigler had a way with words. He scoffed at the quaint idea of academia as a place where a professor and student can sit on a log in front of a fire and discuss great thoughts. Frustrated by his classes, he drolly suggested that it would be just as well for the professor to sit on the student and talk to the fire.

Stigler admitted that, theoretically speaking, monopolies were usually bad for society. Why? Monopolies tend to keep their prices and profits high by restricting the supply of a good. Consider the evil character Lionel Barrymore plays in the Christmas classic *It's a Wonderful Life,* a greedy banker who controls the lending in Bedford Falls.

So if Stigler admits the problem, why does he recommend that the government should usually stay away? First, Stigler believes that most monopolies that sell valuable products will not be able to keep their dominance too long—unless the government gives them special protection. The history of bank regulation suggests that Barrymore's bank probably received special licenses from the federal and state governments, which prevented competitors from opening up across the street. Until 1994, the federal McFadden Act of 1927 prevented banks from crossing state lines to open up new branches.

The first video rental store in your neighborhood had a monopoly, but pretty soon every supermarket and 7-Eleven offered video rentals. Second, temporary monopoly may be an appropriate reward for innovation. Xerox enjoyed a monopoly on plain paper copiers but then lost a big chunk of the business to Hitachi, Fujitsu, and Kodak. Third, government antitrust law moves so slowly to break up monopolies and oligopolies that the final results often arrive too late to make a difference. The Antitrust Division of the Department of Justice spent years suing IBM, only to give up the case in 1982—just as IBM saw its market share slipping away anyway.

The real question for market watchers is whether *other firms can enter the market and challenge the monopolist or oligopolists.* Thus, we must ask, What is keeping new competitors out of the market? Often the mere threat of new competition keeps prices down. Economists call this the "theory of contestable markets."[7] If our local 7-Eleven is the only place to rent a videotape, and if the owner starts price-gouging, you can bet that the local gas station or supermarket will get into the act. Of course, "getting into the act" may not be easy. Besides patents and government licenses, it may take an enormous investment to start up a company or take on a giant.

But despite the obstacles, we frequently see start-ups like Snapple beverages successfully challenging old-line firms like Nestlé. And do not forget the international sector either. Lazy American monopolists and oligopolists will often find their balance sheets attacked from across the seas. For years, Kodak's managers forgot to look in their rearview mirrors, so they failed to notice that Fuji was starting to sell bigger and bigger stacks of paper to professional photographers. Now the future of the photo business is completely in chaos, as firms like Kodak wonder whether customers in the twenty-first century will be more interested in looking at images on paper, laser discs, or computer screens. No one wants to have a monopoly in an unwanted product that has been surpassed. Somewhere there may still be a monopolist who makes steel tires for Model Ts, but I doubt that Goodyear, Bridgestone, Michelin, Cooper, and other tire manufacturers are worried.

Textbooks used to teach that consumer goods with well-known brand names were nearly invincible and able to get away with outrageous pricing. Again the record is spotty. If you walk down your local supermarket aisle, you will see many examples, from cereals to soaps, where the supermarket chain itself stacks the shelves with items bearing its own "private label," undercutting the prices of better-known firms. In many markets, Aunt Jemima and the Green Giant are running scared, chased by Safeway's and Ralphs' own brands. During 1993, these tight races shook Wall Street, where brand name stocks like Philip Morris and even Coca-Cola suffered, as investors lost confidence in their long-term ability to outpace lower-priced competitors.

What Is a Natural Monopoly?

In some cases, a monopolist may continue to grow more and more efficient—and thus less contestable—as it gets bigger. When a firm displays these *economies of scale,* we call it a *natural monopoly.* Consider your local sewer company. If the town splits the sewer company's system into two, the average costs will likely rise, since two sets of pipes and two processing plants will probably be more expensive. Most economists would favor leaving the monopoly in place but regulating the price of the sewer service, so that management does not gouge the customers, who have nowhere else to turn.

Over the past decade, though, more and more monopolies that had been considered "natural" have been proven otherwise. Old textbooks cited the telephone system as a natural monopoly, but the competition among various cellular and wireless technologies is now burning into the profits of the phone companies. In 1992, Congress passed a law making it easier for electric utilities to compete with each other, another attack on a classic textbook example. At the same time, large corporations are now generating their own power and completely bypassing the formerly dominant local utility. As technology leaps ahead, more monopolies will lose their "natural" status.

What Is Antitrust Law?

"If at first the market doesn't succeed, throw lawyers at them." That is the motto of antitrust enthusiasts. Ironic, since the legal profession in states like California and New York tries to limit competition within itself through excruciating bar exams. Antitrust law tries to stop cartels, conspiracies, and combinations that are, in the words of the pathbreaking Sherman Act of 1890, "restraints of trade." Most of us have read of Teddy Roosevelt's trust-busting jabs at the so-called robber barons of the nineteenth century, from John D. Rockefeller to J. P. Morgan. Since that time the Justice Department and the Federal Trade Commission have challenged everyone from the makers of breakfast cereals whose pricing looked too cozy to movie studios that owned movie theaters.

While judges used to jump at the chance to block mergers and tear up cooperative arrangements, over the past twenty years they have, at the urging of economists, taken a more lenient approach. The idea that "big is bad" has been blown away by empirical research showing that a market does not need hundreds of gladiators to be competitive. Antitrust officials used to routinely reject mergers that would grant the biggest four firms more than a 40-percent combined market share. These days a 70-percent share might pass muster, as long as the firms can convince the Justice Department and the Federal Trade Commission that they are not trying to fix or coordinate their prices. Though only a half dozen or so major carriers compose the U.S. airline industry, the cutthroat competition keeps their profits from flying anywhere near as high as their planes—in fact, the industry set records for losses during the early 1990s.

Before the federal government decides to block a proposed merger, it must figure out how to define the market in question. For instance, suppose Lassie, Inc., and Snoopy Corp., two of the leading canned dog food firms, decide to combine forces in the ready-to-eat slop industry. The Justice Department must consider whether dry kibble and those waxy, doggy burger meals provide direct competition with canned food. If so, then we do not have to worry about Lassie and Snoopy merging.

This brings us back to the elasticity question: are there easy substitutes for canned dog food? To answer the query, economists can deploy the *cross elasticity of demand,* which they use to calculate whether consumers will buy more of the potential substitutes if Lassie and Snoopy hike their prices. Mathematically, the cross elasticity would divide the change in the demand for kibble, say, by the change in the price of canned food. If the number is positive, meaning consumers can easily switch to other kinds of dog food, the Justice Department is more likely to let Lassie and Snoopy move in together.

Finally, note that U.S. industry has not grown more *concentrated*—meaning there are fewer firms accounting for more of the market—over time, even with more lax antitrust attitudes. More merging went on during the last two years of the Reagan administration than in the entire decade of the 1970s. And yet at the end of the Reagan term, the Fortune 500 held about the same proportion of U.S. corporate assets (about 45 percent) as they did in 1970. In fact, the twentieth century as a whole has not seen much change in the concentration of U.S. industry, despite waves of government activity. The only thing that has changed is the budget of the Antitrust Division of the Justice Department, which would make even a robber baron envious.

We have looked at some of the key principles that underlie microeconomics. They make up a good part of the economist's toolbox. In the next chapter we'll take these tools out of the box and apply them to some of the conceptually difficult questions that face policymakers.

4 Applying Microeconomics to Major Markets

ADVERTISING, EDUCATION, THE ENVIRONMENT, HEALTH CARE

● *Why Are We Bombarded with Advertising?* ● *How Do People Invest in Education and Human Capital?* ● *Do Economists Care About the Environment?* ● *Is Our Health Care System Sick?* ● *Does Health Care Cost More Than It Used To?* ● *What Kind of Perverse Incentives Drive Up Health Care Spending?* ● *How Does the Government Drive Up Health Care Costs?* ● *Should the Government Require Employers to Provide Health Coverage?* ● *Taking a Chance: Can We Make Life Less Risky?*

Nobel Prize–winning economist Milton Friedman once lamented that since everyone handles money, there are many know-nothings who think they understand economics. Just because you shop at the local indoor mall does not make you an expert on the retail sector of the economy. Nor does recycling your plastic bottles and composting your organic trash mean that you know a lot about the economics of the environment. To be fair, even economists did not know much about environmental economics until recently. However, during the past twenty years, economists have ventured not just into the forests, but into hospital rooms to understand health care, into the prisons to understand crime, and into the locker room to figure out why those grunting slabs of meat called offensive guards get paid ten times what pencil-necked economists make. This chapter examines key economic principles and explains how they can help us make sense of such common yet confusing topics as advertising, education, the environment, and health care.

Why Are We Bombarded with Advertising?

One of my favorite radio jingles urged Boston-area students to shop at Harvard's cooperative store: "You don't have to go to Harvard to shop at the Harvard Coop." The catchy tune seemed to imply that "Yes, we serve dumb people, too. You kids who couldn't get into Harvard, we'll do the math for you at the checkout counter." On the surface, though, the ad promised non-Harvardians that the university's prestigious gloss could rub off on them if they just strolled up and down the aisles. This kind of ad fits in the same category with those automobile commercials where beautiful women and handsome men stand around admiring some tinny car that looks like a four-cylinder can of tuna. Buy the car, become one of the beautiful people, the ad suggests. Other ads deliver strictly technical information, without the sizzle. Still others compare one brand to another, showing, for instance, that some ketchups are thicker than others or some diapers more absorbent.

While households today might feel as if they are the victims of the biggest public relations blitzkrieg since Lucy gave birth to little Ricky, advertising expenditures in the U.S. have remained a remarkably stable 2 percent of GDP ever since Franklin D. Roosevelt ran for president with the campaign song "Happy Days Are Here Again." Many of today's advertising tricks began at the turn of the century. Every time you see Michael Jordan's name on a pair of sneakers, remember that baseball Hall of Famer Honus Wagner endorsed Louisville Slugger bats back in 1905. Even fake personas like Aunt Jemima, the Cream of Wheat chef, and the Jolly Green Giant go back generations.

Developing a good advertising symbol is not enough, of course. Firms must find the right way to deliver their message. The outfield fences of baseball stadiums were once covered with ads for men's clothiers, shaving cream, and other products. Today, the Sunday morning public affairs programs on television feature slick pitches by industry groups that are trying to lobby Washington lawmakers. These firms know that congressmen and policy-minded voters watch those shows. Sadly, advertising posters in the New York subways have devolved so far that they feature cures for cockroach infestation and for such dreary ailments as anal warts. Perhaps this explains why so many subway riders prefer to remain standing.

Advertising used to make economic theorists uncomfortable. After all, the standard economic model of "perfect competition" derived from Adam Smith's philosophy assumed that all goods in a certain industry were identical. If we assume all beer is alike, all beer should sell for the same price, and no producer should have more market power than any other. This idealized model obviously does not match reality, except perhaps for a few commodities or raw materials (natural gas, for example).

During the early 1930s, economists Joan Robinson of Cambridge and Edward Chamberlin of Harvard argued that firms advertise to distinguish themselves from their competitors on trivial grounds, thus granting themselves some monopoly power. If Budweiser can persuade drinkers that it is "the king of beers," then perhaps the king can boost its prices without losing customers to Miller and Rolling Rock. This concept, called *monopolistic competition,* flustered many economists, who then worried that advertising was not just a waste of resources but also a tool for firms to hike their prices above competitive levels.

During 1993 and 1994, a number of firms tried to differentiate their consumer products by changing the color to "clear." We saw transparent colas, deodorants, and mouthwashes. A big failure, "clear" was soon dismissed as "last year's color," and the television show *Saturday Night Live* performed a spoof about "Crystal gravy—you can see your meat!"

While it is true that companies want to differentiate their products, more recent studies show that in fact advertising usually fosters more competition and, quite often, lowered prices. One classic study showed that eyeglasses cost significantly less in states that permitted advertising among optometrists.[1] The whole new industry of quick automobile "lube" jobs would not have emerged unless proprietors could advertise their substantial price savings compared with auto dealerships. In fact, we should be more suspicious of those industries where "competitors" agree not to advertise. Certainly, lawyers selling standardized, boilerplate wills for a lot of money had a cozy time while the lawyers' lobby was able to prevent advertising of legal services.

Brand names serve a useful purpose, not just for the producer but for the consumer as well. Because a respected brand name is a valuable asset, the producer has a tremendous incentive to protect the reputation. Coca-Cola would be wasting billions of dollars in potential sales if it allowed, say, poisoned water to seep into a production plant. But if all colas were generic, no consumer would know who was at fault, and producers would have less reason to prevent the contamination of their share of the total production. Marshall Goldman of Wellesley discovered this problem during a study of the Soviet Union, which banned such bourgeois totems as brand names in 1917.[2]

Consumers can take some comfort in brand names, which also save on "information costs." Suppose you were traveling to Boston two hundred years ago. If you arrived without a place to stay, you might have to choose between inns with names like the Boar's Breath and the Pig's Snout. You would have to speak with the locals or visit each one before you felt comfortable about your choice. Nowadays, the sign reading RITZ CARLTON or even HOLIDAY INN assures some level of quality (and at least a free vial of shampoo and a shower cap). Thus, visitors save on the costs of searching out good information. Again, the owners of these brand names have a strong incentive not to surprise you in an unpleasant way. One motel chain even uses the motto "Where the best surprise is no surprise."

Some years ago, when Hollywood producers were preparing to film a somber play called *Equus* about a boy and a horse, someone asked comic playwright Neil Simon how to guarantee an audience for this serious drama. Simon's advice: "Use *name* horses!" That is, audiences assume that a horse play starring Roy Rogers's Trigger assures a certain level of quality, just as Lassie would not star in any old dog movie.

These comments on advertising and product differentiation should not be interpreted as a wholesale defense of loud, annoying, or misleading ads. Surely there are abusive ads, and some contemporary versions of snake oil salesmen do show up on television with get-rich-quick schemes that work only for them. Still, most businesses in a modern economy depend on *repeat* customers—those who try their products and then return for more. Very few firms can turn a profit by selling just once and then scurrying out of town. That is why the goal of many ads is merely to get the viewer or reader to test-drive the car, or taste the spaghetti sauce before committing to a substantial purchase. Anyone who buys a car over the phone or orders a gross of spaghetti sauce from their living room deserves a lemon of a car and a sour stomach.

While advertising illustrates how businesses can employ microeconomic concepts, people also use microeconomics in their everyday lives, whether they know it or not. Though we often speak of firms investing in capital or goodwill, the next section shows us how individuals invest in capital as well.

How Do People Invest in Education and Human Capital?

The words *capital* and *investment* conjure up images of stockbrokers barking commands like "Buy! No, sell!" into telephones, and pinstriped corporate types posing for photographs at a groundbreaking ceremony for a new plant. Investments in stocks and in manufacturing plants pay off—one hopes—in the form of dividends or higher productivity. In fact, capital investment also comes in a warmer, fuzzier version: human beings. Every time a child learns something useful in school, she adds to her "human" capital. Whether she's learning calculus in math class or learning to be honest in Sunday school class, such lessons will yield dividends through, for example, higher future wages or a more fulfilling life.

While this lesson on human capital may seem better suited for a PTA meeting than an economics book, empirical studies do show that a society's economic progress depends just as much on education as on the chunks of machinery and plots of land that economists usually discuss. Countries do not compete well unless they develop their educational systems. One of the biggest mistakes a country can make is to bury education policy in a second-tier bureaucracy located several universes away from economic policy. Economic gurus tend to think of themselves as hard scientists, while caricaturing educators as limp, at best. In fact, nothing makes an economy limper than a soft school system.

The link between education and economic success has grown more and more important over the past thirty years. Prior to World War II, industrialized economies produced lots of high-paying jobs for ignorant people. The mining industry especially rewarded strong back muscles without much regard for smart minds. Even after World War II, with Europe and Japan devastated and out of the competition, the U.S. economy continued to reward brawn. Our gross domestic product was literally heavy, for it was dominated by coal, steel, iron, and grains.

Since the 1960s, though, as our trading partners have lifted themselves up and rebuilt their machinery, technology has permitted us to produce more goods with fewer muscular bodies. The workplace is far less dangerous than it was before, since machines have replaced men in the most treacherous jobs, for example, in the mines. At the beginning of the century, many male workers made their living by shoveling coal into factory furnaces, laying heavy railroad tracks and ties, or lugging sacks of grain from ship to shore.

On the other hand, the economy is far more dangerous for the uneducated, since they have fewer opportunities to sell their strength. The economy is literally lighter than it was earlier in the century. The valuable software developed by Microsoft weighs practically nothing, but it takes a lot of active brain cells to produce it. While in 1968 only 28 percent of highly skilled manufacturing workers had college degrees, that number has nearly doubled.[3] It is a sad scene to watch an uneducated person flip through classified ads that request résumés only from individuals who can put such initials as B.A., B.S., and M.B.A. after their names. Franklin Roosevelt obviously benefited from his elite, highly educated upbringing. He once suggested that "a man who has never gone to school may steal from a freight car, but if he has a university education he may steal the whole railroad."

One way to measure this trend toward more education is to compare the average wages of high school graduates to those of college graduates. Back in the mid sixties, male college graduates earned about 40 percent more than their friends who stayed behind. But now that premium has jumped to about 70 percent. For women, the story is even more dramatic. Female college grads today make more than twice as much as high school graduates. While the cost of college has obviously climbed over the past twenty years, the payoff has steadily climbed as well. This jump in the returns for education helps explain the widening gap between rich and poor in Western economies. While many pundits lambast the Reagan 1980s for purportedly tearing apart the middle class, the truth is that the decade saw a worldwide boom in the payoff for education. Even Sweden, despite its dedication to homogenous harmony, witnessed the same rift, as uneducated Swedes found fewer opportunities, and Volvo figured out how to build more cars with fewer muscles.

The challenge, then, must be to raise the education levels.

College is not the only answer. Indeed, many students seem to come out of college with little more than experience in how to mix drinks. That is why on-the-job training provides a valuable form of education. And certainly, the secondary school system needs a revolution, or at least some competition. Terry Moe and John Chubb of the Brookings Institution have argued that American schools suffer from too much bureaucracy, regulation, and complacency. Their solution: let parents and students choose their schools, spurring the institutions to compete for students by improving themselves.[4] School choice is an extremely controversial idea, since it fundamentally challenges the tradition of a single neighborhood school. Milwaukee is now experimenting with such a program, and social scientists await the long-term results. In the meantime, economists worry that the U.S. cannot have a grade A economy in the twenty-first century if we continue to send our youth to schools that fail them.

Do Economists Care About the Environment?

Of course! There are three caricatures concerning the environment that we must put to rest. First, there's the caricature of hardhearted economists whose favorite sound is the crunch of nonunion lettuce and favorite sight is a Greenpeace boat capsized after a crash with an oil tanker. In fact, economists have been developing tools to better understand and contribute to serious environmental debates.

Then there is the caricature that depicts pollution as a belch from a satisfied capitalist belly. In fact, as the Iron Curtain rose on Eastern Europe, the world squinted through brown soot to see how grimy and dangerous communism was for ears, noses, and throats. Several years ago the Russian city of Ufa was actually declared unfit for its one million citizens. We learned that automobile drivers kept their lights on even during the smoggy sunshine, while their eyes burned from acidic fumes.

And finally there is the caricature that depicts pollution in the West as having grown worse and worse, endangering more people each day. In fact, cleaner cars and smokestacks have brought dramatic drops in the levels of lead, sulfur dioxide, and carbon monoxide in the atmosphere. In the summertime, fish are jumpin' and anglers' spirits are high around lakes that were declared dead twenty years ago. I once saw a bumper sticker that read MICHIGAN, LAND OF 1,000 LAKES—AND ONE FISH. That fish has somehow multiplied many times over.

Economists begin to study pollution by asking the question that a third-grade teacher might ask a little boy who scrapes his muddy shoes on his classroom desk: "Do you scrape mud on your mother's furniture at home?" Other than smart-alecks who answer, "When she's not looking," most will sheepishly admit that they take better care of their personal property than their communal, school property. And that is the enduring problem. Even Aristotle complained that communal property always looked worse than private lands. Even if the community tries to organize a cleanup squad, some free-riders will shirk their duties, figuring others will take care of things. We have all been frustrated with such louts—and have probably even played the role ourselves, at times.

The atmosphere and the seas are, like the classroom, communal property without clear lines of ownership. Fishermen have an obvious incentive to net all they can, lest someone else grab all the fish. Compare a trout "run" to a trout farm. In a private farm, the owner knows that if he overharvests, he will not have any place to go for the next catch. The catch of the day would be the whole catch for the year.

This public-good problem is closely related to the problem of *externalities*. An externality arises when someone acts in a way that impacts other people who have no control over the situation. Suppose Winston Churchill and Luciano Pavarotti trundle into a restaurant and sit near you. Winnie whips out a stogie and starts puffing away, blowing smoke over to your table. Unless you like the scent, or what David Letterman calls the "brush with greatness," the stench would be a negative externality. Externalities can be positive experiences, as well. Suppose Pavarotti starts humming the theme from *The Beverly Hillbillies* and you like the tune. That would be a positive externality. If he switches to gangster rap, it could become negative. If he leans over to your table and steals a forkful of linguine from your plate, that would be a negative externality too.

Externalities bring trouble because people and companies do not, generally, pay for the costs they inadvertently impose on others. Though the smokestacks at Winnie's cigar plant may cost society by increasing the number of emphysema cases, that cost does not show up in Winnie's profit-and-loss statement. At this point, the government needs to step in and devise a way for Winnie to "internalize" the costs that it imposes on its neighbors. Governments have tried a number of ways to answer the problem. Europe has long followed the advice of Keynes's Cambridge colleague A. C. Pigou, who recommended externality taxes, which would require polluters to pay a fee equal to the amount of damage they do. Proponents of pollution taxes often point to success stories like Germany's Ruhr River, where people can safely go fishing in the shadows of industrial plants.

The crudest method to control externalities is to decree, "Thou shalt not pollute." Such blanket commands quite often do more harm than good. Every human activity has some risks (see "Taking a Chance," p. 104) and imposes some costs. There is no completely clean way of making insulin, which saves many lives each year. Sewage plants that turn sludge into safer materials certainly help the environment, but they do release some chemicals. Should we close down sewage plants because they are not absolutely perfectly clean? Economic logic tells us we should take action as long as we are helping society more than we are hurting it, and that requires weighing the extent and danger of the pollution. Sweeping thou-shalt-not rules also overlook the different costs of complying. One plant can clean up its act with, maybe, a $500 filter; another would require a $500,000 overhaul to achieve the same improvements. It would make more sense to induce the first plant to buy a few $500 filters than risk a shutdown and job layoffs at the second plant. Except for emergency situations, direct pollution controls have a fairly poor track record.

A better approach springs from our $500 filter example. In the 1990 Clean Air Act, the U.S. Congress introduced "tradable emissions permits" to address pollution. The key is this: *he who can come clean cheapest should have an incentive to do so.* The tradable emissions concept supposes that each region of the country is enclosed by a bubble. Our lungs do not care who is doing the polluting within each bubble; all they care about is limiting the total amount. Likewise, those windbags in Congress should not legislate who can and cannot release pollutants; they should just make sure our lungs are safe. Suppose Winnie's cigar plant can cut back its emissions at a cost of $5 per ton, but that it would cost Luciano's pasta plant across the river $100 per ton to cut back. If we deployed the crude thou-shalt-cut-emissions-by-100-tons rule, it would cost Winnie just $500 but bankrupt Luciano, costing him $10,000.

A better way would allow them to come to the following deal: Luciano would pay Winnie to cut back by an extra 100 tons, which would cost another $500 but save Luciano and his employees from the poor house. The net impact on the bubble is the same; emissions have dropped by 200 tons. Yet the net improvement costs society just $1,000—Winnie cutting back 200 tons at $5 per ton—rather than $10,500—Winnie cutting back 100 tons plus Luciano cutting back 100 tons at $100 per ton. This deal saves the environment, while also saving jobs.

The tradable permit approach has launched a new industry that brokers deals between firms. Business newspapers sometimes carry advertisements in which companies offer to sell their emissions permits. This concept can also be applied to the problem of fishing in common waters discussed above. In 1992, the federal government proposed tradable permits for fishing, in which the government would assign fishermen the right to catch a certain number of fish. More efficient fishing boats could buy the right to fish from the less efficient, thereby ensuring that boats are running at full capacity (cutting water pollution). Even more important, this would preserve the number of fish left in the sea to breed for the next season.

This flexible tradable system would work much better than thou-shalt-not approaches. In the early 1990s, Alaska tried a thou-shalt-not program: it chopped back the halibut season from four months to just two days. The result: a massive, frenzied harvesting of halibut that had to be frozen and showed up as stiff, tasteless patties in fast-food restaurants, rather than flaky, fresh meals. An indignity for the noble halibut and a waste of natural resources.

Government giveaways to special-interest groups often hurt the environment as well. Because Congressional programs effectively keep out sugar from the Caribbean and Latin America, U.S. sugar growers overproduce, injuring Florida's everglades. Generous federal subsidies actually encouraged farmers to plant rice paddies in naturally dry parts of California—this despite perennial drought emergencies throughout the state! Likewise, bad tax laws can foul the environment. The Clinton administration recently attacked the tax subsidies that make it more attractive for employees to drive their cars and park at the workplace rather than take public transportation. Still, Congress has been slow to take up arms against foolish laws that promote pollution.

Just as environment issues challenge economists to strike a balance between public and private good, health care provides another opportunity for microeconomists to show how government policies can make difficult situations better or worse.

Is Our Health Care System Sick?

According to grade school lore about Eskimos, they sent their old people off into the wilderness with maybe a few days' worth of raw fish, never to return. Thus old people preserved their dignity; the community preserved its scarce resources for the young. Today our more affluent senior citizens can afford to make their way to retirement homes in warm climes, where they play bridge, square-dance, and attend spring training baseball games. (The less privileged seniors have to stay up north, but many still benefit from subsidized housing and medical care.) Eventually, they all die, the lucky ones without spending time in a nursing home. In comparison, the Eskimos got off cheap, though in a brutal way.

We can debate health care reform till the North Pole melts, but we cannot escape this enduring dilemma: keeping people alive longer costs a lot of money. Individuals and the government spent much less on hospital care in 1900 when most people died before the age of forty and barbers performed dental surgery, extracting teeth in between haircuts. The more successful we are at extending longevity, the more it will cost us.

People over age eighty-four use medical services 2.5 times as much as people in their late sixties. And individuals in their sixties and seventies use them about 3.5 times as much as young and middle-aged people.[5] Between 1970 and 1990, the number of Americans over age seventy-five almost doubled, to over 13 million. Once you accept this problem, you can dismiss the demagogues who offer magical plans that will cut the percentage of GDP we spend on medicine. For years, some pundits and Congressmen have urged the U.S. to adopt a nationalized health care system, similar to that of the U.K. or Canada, in which the government takes over the system and allocates spending. While these systems have some virtues (for example, universal coverage), such radical surgery would not change the basic prognosis that we will continue to spend huge sums on medicine. Sure enough, over the past thirty years, health care spending in those countries has climbed at roughly the same pace as in the U.S. (though U.S. spending per capita has almost always been significantly higher).

That does not mean we should just shrug our shoulders and keep handing over ever-increasing shares of our national income to hospitals and doctors. Even without the "problem" of people living longer, the U.S. health care system suffers from perverse incentives that drive up spending.

Does Health Care Cost More Than It Used To?

We are serving more people than ever before, and so the total health care cost to the economy is higher than it has ever been. We spend about 13 percent of our GDP, compared with just 5 percent in 1960. The U.S. health care system can, like a McDonald's franchise, proudly post a sign that says OVER 200 MILLION SERVED. But we cannot figure out whether the cost of each "servicing" has gone up. Consider: McDonald's can easily compare the price of a burger in 1975 to one in 1995. Just as a "rose is a rose," a Quarter Pounder is a Quarter Pounder. But how do you compare open-heart surgery over that time period? Surgeons did not have the same fiber-optic tools and diagnostic equipment. Surgery patients today spend much less time in the hospital. Operating rooms come equipped with lasers and computers, not just the scalpels and saws of yesteryear. And far more delicate procedures are being performed in the doctor's office, bypassing the hospital completely. In 1989, gall bladder patients spent six excruciating days in the hospital; now laparoscopic surgery sends patients walking away after just one.

But while more sophisticated procedures may save time, they often rely on more expensive equipment. Still, despite the higher cost, most of us would not even consider choosing "old" medicine over "new" medicine. Back to the hamburger analogy. A fresh beef burger in medieval days would not have tasted too different from a fast-food burger today, although the bun would probably have been less stale. Yet medicine during that period was completely different, handled by leech-wielding doctors and medicine men. Has the price of heart surgery gone up in the last five hundred years? Or the last fifty years? Who knows?

Forget surgery for a moment. Even the cost of diagnosis has fundamentally changed. During the last ten years the number of hospitals with magnetic resonance machines has jumped about 500 percent, while the number of CAT scans performed has leapt 400 percent. Diagnosing ailments may have been cheaper in earlier days, but that is because many of the patients died before the doctors could figure out the problem! To compare the two eras would be like saying that exploring for oil has gone up in price, ever since psychics gave up their divining rods.

What Kind of Perverse Incentives Drive Up Health Care Spending?

We cannot avoid the human temptation to extend longevity, and we cannot reverse the aging process. Geriatric research aims for people to die young as late as possible. Nonetheless, our health system has structural flaws that make the demographic toll on social spending even worse. The basic problem is that *most people who receive medical treatment are using someone else's money.* While they are not stealing the money, they are using more of it than they would if they themselves had to weigh the costs and benefits. This is a problem found in most health care systems, whether funded through private insurance plans or government schemes. Since 1960 the share of health care spending that comes directly out of individuals' pockets has plummeted from 49 percent to only about 20 percent.

Consider Max, a senior citizen covered by Medicare who has an achy back. (Briefly, Medicare is the government-run program that provides medical benefits to Americans over the age of sixty-five regardless of income level; Medicaid provides medical benefits to lower-income Americans.) Instead of trying heat pads or some other simple remedy, Max runs to an orthopedic surgeon, who takes X rays and then charges his standard $125 fee to prescribe aspirin and some back exercises. While that sounds like a stiff fee, Max feels little of the monetary pain, since Medicare will pick up roughly 80 percent of the charge. In some nursing homes, podiatrists spend their days stopping in each room to clip toenails, for which Medicare—meaning the taxpayer—picks up the tab. This system obviously encourages overconsumption of health care.

The problem comes in private insurance plans as well. Suppose Jane, a flashy advertising executive, has a sore toe. She too does not hesitate to see her doctor, since her employer's insurance plan picks up the bill. Economists call this problem, which shows up in most insurance situations, *moral hazard.* Despite the term, it is not a moral issue, it is simply a question of economic incentives. A woman who insures her mink stole suddenly has less reason to watch it carefully when she goes to a restaurant.

Some people have trouble believing that insurance coverage makes a difference in how often people see their doctor or use health care services. To address this, the Rand Corporation performed a major five-year experiment to study the issue. The researchers gave one set of patients a policy providing basically free, unlimited care. Another set of patients had to pay just about all of their own bills, except in the case of catastrophically high-cost hospital stays. No surprise that the first set racked up about 45 percent more in medical bills than the second group, without any significant difference in their health. The experiment confirms basic economics: if you lower the price, people buy more; if you raise the price, they cut back.

Insurance companies have just a few ways to combat the moral-hazard problem. The first is to require patients to pony up more of the money themselves through high deductibles and copayments. The insurance firms also try to get more involved in the delivery of medicine, monitoring doctors to make sure they do not overprescribe drugs or overperform medical procedures. The goal of a health maintenance organization (HMO) is to more efficiently organize doctors and hospitals so that costs can be contained and the HMO can outcompete other systems. This aim naturally sends sparks flying, since doctors and patients alike tend to resent busybody bureaucrats who wants to know the intimate details of the diagnosis, treatment, and prognosis.

How Does the Government Drive Up Health Care Costs?

What drives up costs most unnecessarily are the various state mandates that require health insurance firms to cover certain benefits, even if the consumer does not want them. For example, Minnesota mandates that every insurance policy include toupees for people who go bald. Now, I admit that it can be chilly in Minneapolis and that most heat loss occurs through the head, but this kind of interference seems ludicrous. Californians must be covered for marriage counseling—this in a shaky state that does not require homeowners to take out earthquake coverage! And while California wants to send husbands and wives to therapists, Vermont demands that insurance cover visits to the clergy for counseling. Finally, Massachusetts requires insurers to keep a few vials handy at the sperm bank, just in case residents want to take advantage of the government-mandated "deposit" insurance for fertility purposes.

Even more important than these mandates, the federal tax code encourages overconsumption of health care because employees do not get taxed when their employers provide fringe benefits like insurance. If the Ace Co. gives Lori a $1,000 raise, she must pay income taxes on it. Yet if Ace Co. instead gives Lori insurance worth $1,000, she pays no tax. To invert a cliché, we get what we don't pay for. The tax system gives workers and their employers strong incentives to provide gold-plated health care rather than cash. No wonder most of the growth in employee compensation in the 1980s took the form of more generous health benefits; employees get a lot more bang for the same buck it costs employers.

A more efficient tax system would not discriminate between cash compensation and fringe benefits. If the tax code did not encourage overinsurance, individuals would have a stronger incentive to shop around for better but less expensive coverage. Studies suggest that this subsidy for health coverage keeps about $74 billion from the IRS each year, funds that could be used to cut overall tax rates or pay for health care coverage for the uninsured.

Should the Government Require Employers to Provide Health Coverage?

Because almost 60 percent of Americans already receive their insurance through their employers, politicians have frequently suggested that employers be forced to provide coverage. Most economists would disagree with this prescription. First of all, the mandate would look like a flat tax on each worker. And since this tax (equal to insurance costs) would be the same regardless of the worker's wage, it would hit lower-income employees hardest. Make no mistake: the firm must somehow pass along this new cost, more likely to the employee than to the consumer. And that means lower wages or fewer jobs. Despite its flaws, politicians find this nostrum beguiling, since the costs are hidden from the public. The slogan "Let the bosses pay" has a nice, 1930s rabble-rousing ring to it. Nonetheless, most economists find it as out of touch with reality as one of Trotsky's speeches in New York, which began, "Workers of the Bronx . . ."

A better approach would be to require *individuals* to get health insurance. Most people would still do so through their employers, but this system would give consumers a reason to care about costs. By cutting out the $74 billion tax subsidy for employer-provided coverage, the federal government could afford to help lower-income Americans to buy insurance. If people paid a bigger share of their own insurance costs, they would probably choose higher deductibles, which permit lower monthly premiums. Higher deductibles would lead individuals to use medical services less frivolously yet feel secure that their assets won't be wiped out by medical catastrophes.

Another innovative solution would encourage people to take the money saved on premiums and deposit them in "medical savings accounts," which would accrue interest tax-free, like individual retirement accounts, and could be used for retirement costs. The combination of higher deductibles and medical savings accounts would discourage unnecessary medical treatment and leave individuals with a nice nest egg to help them during those ever-expanding retirement days.

While implementing these improvements, the federal government could also outlaw insurance company discrimination against individuals who have "preexisting conditions"—for example, heart murmurs. Instead, insurance companies should spread this risk across all of their customers. This would make it easier for individuals to change jobs without the fear of having no health coverage.

Health care brings together some of the toughest issues in economics and brings to light some of the toughest choices for citizens. The topic cannot be intelligently discussed without admitting that incentives matter. Our current health care system is reckless because too few people have enough reason to care about the costs. How reckless is it? Imagine tossing the keys to a 300-horsepower rented Corvette to a seventeen-year-old boy who likes race cars. Would you expect him to poke along in the slow lane?

Taking a Chance: Can We Make Life Less Risky?

Yes, but let's not go too far. Life is risky, and even if you huddle under a blanket—stay away from an electric one, since some preliminary studies suggest it might raise the risk of developing cancer!—you could die of anything from inhaling poisonous microfibers from fabric to being hit on the head by a ceiling fan that shakes loose in an earthquake. The most dangerous thing most of us will ever do is ride in a car, especially in a taxicab driven by someone whose native country has not yet developed the traffic light. The death rate for riding in a car is even greater than the death rate from police work. Nonetheless, most of us step into automobiles daily without flinching.

Somehow, though, we expect the government to eliminate risks that are far more trivial than the everyday risks we blithely endure. And in trying to wipe out these risks, we actually create new risks. For example, the U.S. government banned a chemical called ethylene dibromide (EDB) because of a trace of a cancer risk. This chemical was used to kill a mold on peanuts that spawned deadly aflatoxins. Because of aflatoxins, a peanut butter sandwich now has seventy-five times the cancer risk of exposure to EDB. The most outrageous examples involve force-feeding massive doses of sugar substitutes to white laboratory mice, who eventually grew tumors. A human being would have to drink a Diet Coke reservoir the size of the Lincoln Memorial reflecting pool to ingest that kind of dosage, and even so, it would be less dangerous than stepping into a taxicab on Pennsylvania Avenue.

This fear of chemicals can be very dangerous. When the Peruvian government cut back the chlorine levels in its drinking water, relying on a U.S. report of cancer risks, about half a million people suffered from cholera, including 40,000 who died of the disease.[6] Again, the key question must be, What are the costs and benefits of avoiding the danger? The fear of chemicals can also delay new miracle drugs from entering the market. According to a Tufts University study, it takes an average of twelve years for a successful drug to wind its way from initial research to final government approval.[7] The slow-footed Food and Drug Administration kept beta blockers out of the U.S. a decade after these drugs had helped heart attack victims in Europe. Who knows how many people died while the FDA tested and re-tested? AIDS activists, wielding numerous studies on risk assessment, have pressured the FDA to speed up the drug approval process.

For markets to work well, consumers need access to adequate and accurate information. Given good information, consumers can send signals to firms to beef up the safety features. Over the past five years, automakers got the message that they must supply airbags and antilock brakes to satisfy buyers. While these safety features first showed up on luxury cars, the automakers devised inexpensive ways to equip economy cars with them as well. True, the government could have forced airbags into cheaper cars, but those new cars would no longer have been cheap, and poorer households would have been stuck driving older cars that also lacked the other safety improvements that have come along recently.

Despite all the talk about chemicals in our foods, make no mistake, life is much safer than it was years ago. People live twice as long as they did a century ago (which creates its own problems, including overcrowded geriatric wards). While pneumonia and influenza used to wipe out hundreds of thousands every year, the death rate is now one sixth as high as it was when the curtains closed on the nineteenth century. Despite the invention of the automobile, the overall death rate from accidents has plummeted as well. The one area we have not conquered is cancer. But since cancer tends to strike older people, the higher cancer rate comes partly from our success in extending life.[8]

The bottom line is that we can be proud of our achievements in medicine and consumer and worker safety, but we must also be modest about our ability to perfect the world. We are all gamblers; even those Victorians who hated the idea were. While discussing a government sale of bonds, British prime minister Harold Wilson once despaired that his country's "strength, freedom and solvency apparently depend on the proceeds of a squalid raffle." That raffle was no more squalid than the raffle we all play every day.

The issues we discussed in this chapter are not, of course, unique to the U.S. All countries must grapple with pressing concerns regarding health care, the environment, and education. These issues cannot be seen solely through a domestic lens. As the Canadians have learned, U.S. acid rain does not respect national borders. In the next chapter we'll look at the international economy, which is more and more the source of investment opportunities, as well as political conflict.

PART THREE

THE INTERNATIONAL SCENE

5 Border Crossings

- *No Man Is an Island: How Interdependent Are We? How Much Does the U.S. Trade?* - *Whom Does the U.S. Trade With?* - *Why Do Countries Trade, Anyway?* - *What Is "Laissez-faire?" What Is Protectionism?* - *Doesn't Protectionism Save Jobs?* - *Do Other Countries Play Fair?* - *What Is Dumping?* - *What Is the Uruguay Round of the GATT?* - *What Is the North American Free-Trade Agreement?* - *What Is the European Union?* - *What Do the World Bank and the IMF Do?* - *Do Economic Sanctions Against Outlaw Countries Work?*

American folklore overflows with stories of rugged individualists: Paul Bunyans who stake out their land and prove their self-sufficiency; wandering gunslingers who cannot commit themselves to jobs or to personal relationships; and Henry David Thoreaus striving to plant, harvest, and feed themselves away from the madding crowd. As Emerson suggested, Americans practically idolize self-reliance.

And that may be too bad. Because our economic successes come from working with people, not shrinking from them. Remember, the United States began as a trading colony—some of our most eminent patriots were smugglers!—and has always prospered by trading and competing, not by retreating behind a moat and a drawbridge. If the Pilgrims had kept just to themselves rather than breaking bread and learning survival skills from the local Indian tribe, they would have been wiped out by disease and famine. Plymouth Rock symbolized how bumpy and unfriendly the soil was in coastal Massachusetts. Behind the myth of rugged individualists lies the true tales of rugged community members. Today outside of Boston, tourists and picnickers overrun Walden Pond, a more accurate symbol of American history than the image of Thoreau gathering his own nuts.

Though Americans have prospered through trade, they continue to suffer occasional relapses into an isolationist mood. Especially during slow economic times, we tend to lash out at foreigners and blame them for our troubles. After all, if they sell goods in the U.S., the thinking goes, they must be taking jobs from domestic firms. In recent years, the Japanese have taken the brunt of our frustration and resentment. Of course, other countries suffer from the same kinds of insecurities. In February 1994, for example, French fishermen began protesting imported fish by hacking at fish that were on sale at outdoor markets. At the same time, French seafood inspectors staged a work slowdown, leaving seventy tons of American fish to rot at Charles de Gaulle Airport. As I will discuss in this chapter, the victims of such action (other than the gashed fish) are usually domestic consumers, in this case the French, who ended up paying more for their meals.

No Man Is an Island: How Interdependent Are We? How Much Does the U.S. Trade?

In almost every year since the *Mayflower* ran aground, the U.S. has expanded its web of economic interdependence. The U.S. grew into a powerhouse in the nineteenth century by greatly increasing trade within its borders as well as beyond. Settlers carved their way across the Appalachians, bringing new sources of foodstuffs and building materials. Meanwhile, entrepreneurs found new markets for U.S. goods in foreign lands. But of course, there were also occasional stumbles into the American self-reliance mode. For example, in 1930 Congress decided to blame foreigners for a recession and therefore passed the Smoot-Hawley Tariff Act, which jacked up tariffs to 60 percent, thereby blocking foreign goods from entering U.S. shipyards. The act hiked tariffs even on goods like cashew nuts (by 1,000 percent!), where the U.S. had no domestic growers to protect from foreign competition. Over a thousand economists petitioned Washington to reject the bill, and thirty-six countries begged Congress to change its mind, to no avail. Our allies in Europe retaliated by striking their own isolationist pose, turning dockyards into barricades. Pretty soon, over sixty countries got into the act. World trade collapsed by two-thirds, and everybody got poorer. The recession of 1930 tumbled into the Great Depression. Crooners tore up happy songs like "The Best Things in Life Are Free" and instead started singing "Brother, Can You Spare a Dime?" In Germany, the waltz gave way to the goose step.

From 1930 until World War II, political pressures continued to squeeze the world economy like a python, and nations nailed NO TRESPASSING signs all around their harbors.

After World War II, European governments looked at their devastated industrial plants and realized that the bombed-out shambles would not permit self-sufficiency. So they dismantled the NO TRESPASSING signs. As the U.S. troops came home, we started sending our products "over there." Since the 1950s, world trade has expanded rapidly, driving incomes higher along the way. While in 1959 the U.S. exported only about 4 percent of what it produced, by 1990 that figure had tripled. More U.S. jobs than ever before now directly depend on selling goods to other countries—about 7.5 million jobs in 1993, up 45 percent since 1986. And the U.S. exports more than any other country, including Japan.

By jumping into the export game, the U.S. has also honed its commercial skills. Hot, intense competition forces our firms to toughen up and wisen up. During the 1970s, American auto firms got lazy, hawking lousy cars that suffered from about twice as many production defects as the Japanese brands. Today, executives of the "Big Three" admit that they had sold cars that fell far short in terms of mechanical design, fit, and finish. And who got caught standing in the rain as gaskets blew and transmissions ground to a halt? The American consumer. A friend told me that he grew up thinking that his family had to spend $500 each year repairing their Pontiac, as if Congress had passed a law requiring it. And American car buyers appeared to have few alternatives. Except for some Volkswagen beetles, few foreign cars were sold in the U.S.

Then, following the OPEC oil embargo of 1973, Americans began to realize that the Japanese auto dealers offered reliable, efficient models. The Japanese won market share from GM, Ford, and Chrysler, sending the Big Three reeling back to their drawing boards. It took them more than a decade to learn their lesson, but today the American auto industry produces far better products because of the bitter challenge from the Japanese. A few years ago, GM spent a fortune on newspaper advertisements that displayed a graph illustrating that while GM cars used to suffer from ten times as many defects as Japanese cars, they now had about the same.

Though the U.S. today sends more goods across its borders than any other country, we also have the largest domestic market. This gives us a tremendous advantage, for firms can perfect products and earn profits at home before trying to adapt and then launch them in the more risky international market. International marketing is an expensive proposition, since tastes differ across national boundaries.

Smaller economies cannot afford to wait, however. Switzerland does not have a big enough population to support a solely domestic pharmaceutical industry. There aren't enough Swiss suffering from the heartbreak of psoriasis to justify the enormous research and development expenses. So Swiss pharmaceutical firms like Roche Holding must export almost immediately to recover their costs. A U.S. firm like Merck can turn a profit just by selling on the West Coast and then look to exports as an afterthought. No surprise, then, that a smaller country like Belgium earns over 60 percent of its income by marketing products abroad—and it's not Belgian waffles that drive up incomes in Brussels! Belgium ranks in the top ten in scientific instruments and medical exports. Germany derives over 30 percent of its income by selling abroad everything from Braun coffee makers to BMW sedans.

Whom Does the U.S. Trade With?

Anyone with the bucks. Naturally, it is easiest to trade with neighbors, which explains why Canada is our biggest trading partner. Next come Europe, Latin America, Japan, and the young tigers of Asia: South Korea, Taiwan, and Singapore.

We have all heard the dreary requiem for America's trade competitiveness. The lyrics of this sorry tune tell us that no one wants our products. Don't believe it. It is an old dirge that struck a chord in the early 1980s when the U.S. dollar rose to record levels against foreign currencies, making our exports appear too expensive (the next chapter will explain this phenomenon). But since the late eighties, U.S. industries have beefed up their quality and their competitiveness. Countries now line up to buy our aircrafts, computers, semiconducting devices, chemicals, and, of course, agricultural goods. Since 1986, our exports to Japan have jumped by almost 100 percent. And European diplomats now fly to Washington to complain that some of our industries are too strong to compete against.

Yogi Berra said that sometimes you can see a lot just by looking around. Well, sometimes you cannot. If you look around your home, you will probably see some Japanese electronic goods: a Sony Walkman, a Toshiba clock radio, a Sharp television. Midwestern plants no longer manufacture many of these wares. But the U.S. leads the world in the sort of goods you won't run across on your nightstand or in your neighborhood: Boeing 747s, Caterpillar earthmovers, fiber-optic cables, and CAT scan devices. The point is, everyday appearances do not necessarily give a clear view of our actual trade flows.

On the other hand, we should not exaggerate our successes, either. Although we do sell more goods abroad than any other country (about $430 billion in 1993), we also buy more goods, leaving us with an overall trade deficit. Each year we import about a half a trillion dollars' worth of OPEC oil, foreign cars, steel, consumer electronics, and clothing. (In the next chapter, we'll discuss trade surpluses and deficits in detail.)

Why Do Countries Trade, Anyway?

For the same reason individuals do. Forget sophisticated economic models, just open up your cupboard. Imagine that the Jolly Green Giant and Sara Lee have dysfunctional families. The Giant's basic problem: his kids can't stand eating only veggies. Though Dad is awfully good at growing green things, the Little Sprouts pine for something sweeter. Meanwhile, contrary to the television jingle, Sara Lee's plump kids don't like her bakery products. They are tired of carbohydrates and freeze-dried doughnuts. "Why can't you make some green beans once in a while?" they ask.

What to do? The Little Sprouts sneak out of the house with some extra veggies. Sara Lee's Plumpsters roll out the back door with some doughnuts. They switch foods. Finally, the Little Sprouts satisfy their sweet tooth, and Sara Lee's plump brood get some fiber.

Of course, the Little Sprouts and the Plumpsters could have kept to themselves. The Little Sprouts could have tried to bake their own doughnuts from scratch, while the Plumpsters could have planted some seeds and waited a year. Instead, in one quick trade, they saved themselves endless frustrating efforts.

In the same way that the Sprouts and the Plumpsters agreed to switch rather than fight for self-sufficiency, Germany decides not to try to grow its own bananas, Costa Rica decides not to build automobiles, and the U.S. decides not to raise silkworms.

How does a country or region know what to produce? This time we can take Yogi Berra's advice and just look around. For instance, fertile land and buckets of rain lead Iowans to plant corn. In addition to natural resource differences, some regions have built up more technical expertise over the years or have built on the cultural affinities of the populace. Thus, New York and London reign as financial capitals and "grow" new financial instruments each year, while Silicon Valley, California, sprouts new computer technologies. South Africa controls the world's diamond mining business, but those diamond are frequently refined and cut in Amsterdam and Tel Aviv.

As regions specialize and expend production, they can lower their average costs. Swiss pharmaceutical companies sell drugs to the entire world. Though they spend billions on research, these costs are shared by customers everywhere. But if a company sells only within, say, Zurich, the few customers in that city must pick up the whole research tab. World trade, then, allows what economists call *economies of scale*. As a result, the customers pay less, and the companies can earn more profits, which creates more jobs and propels incomes higher.

What Is "Laissez-faire"? What Is Protectionism?

The father of modern economics, Adam Smith, brought home the term *laissez-faire* as a souvenir from France, where he studied with Louis XV's friends the Physiocrats. The phrase means "let people do [what they choose]." Combined with Adam Smith's native optimism, the phrase sounds a bit like the

Cajun cry *"laissez les bon temps rouler"* ("let the good times roll"). When economists talk about laissez-faire policies, they mean free trade—let people exchange goods without governments blocking the way.

David Ricardo, the brilliant English stockbroker and member of Parliament who refined Smith's laissez-faire arguments in the early 1800s, taught that whenever merchants sell the same product at different prices in different towns, consumers could do better if merchants were permitted to compete against one another. Ricardo grew frustrated, though, that the British government would not agree to his arguments and tear down the barriers to trade with Europe, particularly the Corn Laws, which prohibited cheap grain imports.

Although Ricardo had climbed higher on the ladder of personal financial success than most anyone else in Parliament, he was not looking after the elite merchants but was truly worried about the common workers. Ricardo despaired that Parliament was protecting wealthy farmers at the expense of the working poor. During his time, workers spent about half their incomes on breads made from grain. Yet the Corn Laws propped up bread prices. Just by letting cheaper grain cross the English channel, Parliament could have raised the real incomes of workers. Not until 1846, twenty-three years after Ricardo's death, did Parliament give in.

While businesses often try to give the impression that they love competition, they are more like the guy who thinks that learning Shakespeare is good for his kids but hopes he never has to sit through *The Tempest* again. Truth is, most firms would prefer a monopoly, and they frequently pressure the government to help them get it.

If Peter Pan flew through the sky and delivered free peanut butter to kids everywhere, how could we keep our peanut butter plants running? Unfortunately for David Ricardo and free-traders everywhere, peanut growers would propose that we catch Peter Pan in our cross hairs, take aim, and blow him out of the sky. For Peter Pan is foreign competition. They would claim that Peter was stealing jobs from them. Never mind that Peter's delivery service gives kids free meals and helps poor families. They would demand "protection" from competition.

And they would probably get it. How do we know? While Peter Pan may not flit around offering free peanut butter, low-cost foreign peanut growers do offer us their crops. And the U.S. government just says no. Congress permits only 1.7 million pounds of imported peanuts into the country. While that may sound like a lot, it's peanuts—*less than one tenth of 1 percent of the U.S. crop.* And who pays for this quota? Besides the lost business to foreign producers, American consumers pay more for peanuts than they otherwise would. Poor families feel it most, since they spend a bigger share of their budgets on peanut butter. Child nutrition programs end up costing taxpayers more and feeding poor people less, because the U.S. government chooses to shoot down Peter Pan.

Naturally, U.S. peanut producers do not want to lose their protection, which makes them rich. Studies show that peanut producers "earn" nearly half a billion dollars in extra income from these import quotas.[1] Jimmy Carter may have started as a humble peanut farmer from Plains, Georgia, but the government made him rich and humble.

Adam Smith would not be surprised. He knew that while businessmen love to rhapsodize about man-to-man competition, deep down they like the comfort of special favors. Ask businessmen—first give them truth serum—to clap their hands if they would like protectionism for their firms, and the applause would release enough energy to turbocharge Tinkerbell and keep her alive forever.

The U.S. likes its peanut quotas so much, it slaps stiff quotas on sugar as well, costing consumers about $1.4 billion each year, with over 40 percent of the benefits going to just 1 percent of the sugar growers.[2] Naturally, the U.S. sugar industry loves it. But they are not alone. The U.S. corn industry would go mad if Congress threatened to erase sugar protection. Why? Go to your refrigerator and take out some jam and a bottle of soda. Read the ingredients. Chances are you will find corn syrup listed as a sweetener. Since when do we put corn in strawberry jam? Ever since Congress decided to jack up the price of sugar. In fact, corn farmers probably have as big a stake in sugar quotas as do sugar growers!

So now we discover that kids who want peanut butter and jelly sandwiches get socked by the government for both the peanut butter and the jam. How about the glass of milk? Don't ask. We have foreign and domestic restraints against competition there. The government props up milk prices through a "support" system. One of Washington's powerful lobbying groups is the Committee for Thorough Political Education of Associated Milk Producers. If George Orwell were alive, he would have to rewrite *Animal Farm* to show how the cast of characters denied receiving price supports, import protection, and direct subsidies. We've already seen that lobbying makes strange bedfellows, but in 1937 milk producers helped lead the effort for Philippine independence. Why? Because as a territory of the U.S., the Philippines could send large amounts of coconut oil into the U.S., threatening the butter market.

While we think how sugar quotas punish American kids, we should also consider how they punish foreign kids by condemning Third World countries to economic stagnation. Many Caribbean and Latin American countries, for example, can grow sugarcane successfully and cheaply. But we tell them to keep it to themselves. Sugar quotas today are tighter than anytime in the twentieth century. No wonder they find coca leaves a more profitable venture, and the Mafia a more hospitable trading partner. How can we blame them for growing illegal drugs, when we forbid them from selling legal crops? Our government's policies would classify Betty Crocker as a hardened criminal if she freely used Jamaican sugar.

One cannot blame Third World nations for calling advanced countries "hypocrites"—after all, we lecture them to give up on socialism and pursue free-market policies. Yet if they get successful, we freeze them out of our wealthy world. "First World" bureaucrats pledge to Third World leaders that we want them to grow, but we have our fingers crossed behind our backs. And although we've crossed our fingers, we manage to tie their hands. For example, eighty percent of Bangladesh's exports face barriers from other countries. Bangladesh, that intimidating export powerhouse, has a GDP per person equal to about six pairs of sneakers. And in 1994, the U.S. Department of Commerce announced quotas on pillowcases from Kenya, a country with per capita income equal to the cost of a set of good-quality bed-sheets and a comforter.

Doesn't Protectionism Save Jobs?

Yes, but at what cost? Free trade is not pain-free trade. When someone develops a better product or a cheaper way to produce, competitors have good reason to get scared. Often they go out of business. The Underwood typewriter company was not happy to hear that IBM was working on a personal computer. Carbon paper executives probably jumped off buildings when they learned about Xerox copiers. Ice deliverers must have threatened Frigidaire executives with cold forceps.

If the government prevents progress, it does save some jobs in the old-fashioned firm. Likewise, preventing trade saves some jobs in the protected company. But the total number of jobs usually falls, and the total costs to the economy usually rise. Often, the government would do better just to pay displaced workers to stay home rather than artificially keep the business afloat. Communist Eastern Europe proved how keeping jobs around destroyed innovation and ensured widespread poverty. The inside joke in Russia was that the workers pretended to produce, and the government pretended to pay them.

During the 1980s, the U.S. blocked steel imports, which drove up the cost of automobiles and everything else made from steel. Studies showed that these restraints cost American consumers almost a billion dollars in 1988. Rather than protecting steel producers and forcing consumers to bear the hidden cost, the government would have done better to retrain and directly compensate displaced workers. Pressure to protect steel intensified during the 1990–91 recession, and various duties and antidumping penalties on foreign suppliers cost steel users over $800,000 for each job "saved"![3] While we protected some steel jobs, we lost jobs in all the manufacturing industries that used steel. Contrasting them with Adam Smith's free-market "invisible hand" that creates jobs and wealth, one congressman called such trade barriers the "invisible foot" that kicks people out of work.

Remember, the government's goal should not be simply to keep the same old jobs alive in the same quantity. Workers should be producing what people want to buy. After all, we could have tried to freeze the workforce in place in 1879 and arrested Thomas Edison for being so disruptive. As Milton Berle once mused, if it weren't for Thomas Edison, we'd all be watching television by candlelight.

During the 1840s, a great French pamphleteer named Frédéric Bastiat penned a number of essays blasting protectionism. In one facetious article he promised to show the government how to double the number of jobs in the railroad industry. How? Cut off everyone's right arm.

Do Other Countries Play Fair?

No. Many countries are worse than the United States. The French even protect their film and television industry from foreign competition! Government ministers are so embarrassed that Frenchmen like reruns of *Dallas* and Arnold Schwarzenegger movies that they have cut back the number of American shows that can appear on television and the proportion of our movies that can be shown in French theaters. Free-traders believe that if the French love Schwarzenegger or Jerry Lewis, viewers should be able to watch *Terminator 2* or *The Nutty Professor* all day long, but the French government doesn't agree.

In addition to quotas, the French government has devised another way to grab profits from U.S. producers: force them to engage in joint ventures with French firms. This kind of shotgun marriage leads to authorized blackmail and front-door payoffs, in which the Americans end up writing fat checks to French companies to get them to play along.

This French resistance goes back many years. Frédéric Bastiat composed a devastating bit of sarcasm disguised as a petition from

> *Manufacturers of Candles, Tapers, Lanterns, Candlesticks, Street Lamps, Snuffers, and Extinguishers, and from the Producers of Oil, Tallow, Resin, Alcohol, and Generally of Everything Connected with Lighting.*
>
> *To the Honorable Members of the Chamber of Deputies.*
> *Gentlemen:*
> *. . . We are suffering from the ruinous competition of a foreign rival who apparently works under conditions so far superior to our own for the production of light, that he is flooding the domestic market with it at an incredibly low price. . . . This rival . . . is none other than the sun. . . .*
> *We ask you to be so good as to pass a law requiring the closing of all windows, dormers, skylights, inside and outside shutters, curtains, casements, bull's-eyes, deadlights and blinds; in short, all openings, holes, chinks, and fissures. . . .*
> *If you shut off as much as possible all access to natural light and thereby create a need for artificial light, what industry in France will not ultimately be encouraged? . . .*
> *If France consumes more tallow, there will have to be more cattle and sheep. . . .*
> *The same holds true for shipping.*[4]

And the same argument holds true for almost any manufacturer who hates competition. If you think the French have gone too far, consider the Japanese, who have claimed that their "unique" Japanese snow requires skis made in Japan, and that U.S. baseball bats are not good enough for Japanese baseball! Though the Japanese have begun to open up their rice market, the bureaucrats force popular California rice to be mixed and sold with inferior grains.

Despite these glaring examples, the U.S., Japan, and the European Union are about equally guilty. Average tariff rates hover between 1.5 and 3 percent, depending on the product. But tariffs on such key goods as steel, agricultural produce, vehicles, and textiles average between 25 and 50 percent.

Since most politicians know that *protectionism* is a dirty word, likely to get them in trouble with enlightened editorial boards, they reach for euphemisms in order to avoid a bad reputation. One handy—and underhanded—euphemism is *voluntary export restriction* (VER). Under a VER, leaders of an importing country corner the leaders of an exporting country and, in Mafia moviespeak, make "an offer you can't refuse. Stop shippin' us so much stuff."

This was the story after Japanese autos started flooding the U.S. market in the 1980s. Cowering before Congress, Japanese automakers "voluntarily" held back on exports. Because the VER choked the supply of cars, their prices rose, and the American firms were able to charge more for their clunkers. Who paid the price? The American consumer, who saw prices climb about $3,000 during the first three years of the VER. The "government handed the American consumer to [the Big Three] on a platter, and they couldn't resist carving them up," observed Brookings Institution economist Robert Crandall.[5]

What Is Dumping?

Domestic producers frequently claim that foreign goods must be stopped at the border, because the foreigners are *dumping* them on the market. This means that a producer is selling abroad at a price below cost, or at a price below what it charges at home. If the government finds that a firm has dumped, it can impose a *countervailing duty* to drive up the sales price. Sometimes countries seem to stretch these criteria. In the 1980s, for instance, the U.S. accused Poland of dumping, of all things, golf carts on the market, even though Poland does not sell any golf carts at home. When was the last time you saw Lech Walesa working on his backswing?

While domestic producers shout "Dumping!" almost everyday, dumping typically takes place temporarily, during recessions, when an exporter has extra goods that it cannot sell at home. However, if an exporter permanently sells at a low price, it is not dumping but just a good deal.

General Motors, Ford, and Chrysler have claimed for several years that the Japanese are dumping minivans and recreational vehicles on the shores of the U.S. No matter that the Big Three absolutely dominate the market and sell their vehicles at lower prices than the Japanese! They continue to ask Congress to classify such vehicles as trucks. Why would a family minivan be called a truck? Because if Congress agrees to define them as trucks, they must slap a 25-percent tariff on the imports. This tariff originated in 1963 as "temporary" retaliation for a European restriction on U.S. poultry!

The Brits are particularly worried about the "truck" tariff, since the U.K. exports Range Rovers to the U.S. The British government has lobbied everyone in Washington who would listen. Their lobbying pitch: "The queen drives a Range Rover around her palace grounds. And the queen would *never* drive a truck."

Dumping sometimes comes out of desperation. For example, in the early 1990s Russia needed cash so badly it began selling all the aluminum it could produce. From 1990 to 1993 its aluminum sales multiplied eightfold. Russian firms were probably not covering all of their costs, but they did not seem to care. Covering costs is something for accountants to worry about in the long run. "Cash now!" is the cry in a crisis.

Governments end up turning away most dumping claims,

since most are specious. Smart governments know that by allowing trade, nations gently coerce their citizens to shift precious resources from low-productivity to high-productivity industries. If
firms shift, households can enjoy more goods with less sacrifice.

What Is the Uruguay Round of the GATT?

Every nation protects some industries. No one comes to the
bargaining table with thoroughly clean hands, but we can be
thankful that they still show up. The table is called the General
Agreement on Tariffs and Trade (GATT). Most nations learned
their lesson during the 1930s, when trade imploded and incomes
plunged. In 1947, the industrialized nations set up the GATT,
which sliced tariffs on 45,000 different goods. The U.S. led the
way by slashing tariffs on about three quarters of its imports,
while foreign countries cut tariffs on about one third of U.S. exports. Though disputes continue to bubble up, world tariffs have
plummeted from an average of 40 percent in 1947 to about 4
percent today. Still, these averages mask a lot of protectionism
for individual sectors.

The ongoing GATT talks are categorized by "rounds," which
makes sense if you imagine the negotiations as boxing matches
among contentious diplomats. Rounds are named after a meeting place—the Tokyo Round, 1974–79—or a world leader—the
Kennedy Round, 1964–67. The participants try to end each
round with a new agreement.

The bell for round eight rang in 1986 in Punta del Este, Uruguay. Delegates from more than a hundred countries jumped off
their stools and invaded the seaside resort. Besides fattening the
wallets of local merchants, the negotiators challenged each other
to solve disputes on agriculture and textiles. In addition, round
eight tried to develop rules to cover service industries that had
become more important to world economic relations since the
Tokyo Round, including financial services and intellectual prop-

erty rights. After seven years, world leaders finally reached an agreement in December 1993, after hundreds of little compromises.

The U.S. International Trade Commission calculates that each year American artists, inventors, and businesses lose about $50 billion to patent, copyright, and trademark theft. Since the world economy now rests more on brains than on brawn, intellectual property protection is crucial to honest trade. Let's say that DrugCo spends millions of research dollars on a risky effort to cure a disease. If other companies can wait for them to shout "eureka!" and then rip off the formula, DrugCo's incentive to perform more research collapses. Having spent hundreds of millions of dollars to build EuroDisney in France, the Walt Disney Company cannot afford to let a Parisian truck stop owner paint Mickey Mouse on his wall and declare his gas pumps the "official nozzles of EuroDisney World."

Economists estimate that over the next 10 years the Uruguay Round agreement could raise U.S. incomes by between $100 and $200 billion dollars. That's about $1,000 to $2,000 for every American family. The negotiating stakes were obviously very high. Had the world's leaders failed to cobble together a Uruguay Round deal in 1993, they could have launched a dangerous worldwide trade war that could have wiped out any hope of higher incomes.

Europe's farmers have placed the biggest stumbling block in front of new agreements. They insist on producing more foodstuffs than Europeans can eat and preventing other countries from sending foodstuffs to their markets. They are tenacious negotiators. In particular, a few thousand French farmers in round eight have shown more muscle than the entire French army did in World War II. A few years ago, then agriculture minister Edith Cresson was chased through a field by farmers wielding pitchforks, in protest of subsidy cutbacks. After watching her run through the stalks like the Scarecrow in *The Wizard of Oz,* other French politicians have learned to stay in Paris.

What Is the North American Free-Trade Agreement?

In 1988, President Ronald Reagan and Prime Minister Brian Mulroney of Canada signed the U.S.-Canada Free-Trade Agreement, which tore down most barriers between the two countries. Jimmy Durante used to complain that "everyone wants to get into the act." Pretty soon, the Mexican government proved the old comedian right and asked to get into the agreement.

The North American Free-Trade Agreement (NAFTA), which the three countries concluded in 1993 after years of negotiation, is meant to turn the whole continent into a duty-free shop. Because Mexican tariffs are generally twice as high as U.S. tariffs, American exporters see enormous opportunities. U.S. exports to Mexico have already shot up over 130 percent since 1986, when Mexico joined the GATT and began cutting its tariffs from even higher levels.

Nonetheless, many Americans fear that they will lose their jobs as a result of the trade pact. Ross Perot has described in twangy Texan tones "a giant sucking sound" as jobs head south. While Perot exaggerates the sound, it's true that some Americans will lose jobs. Some citrus farmers in Florida, for instance, may not be able to compete with the Mexicans. On the other hand, experts expect California peach growers and Iowa corn growers to expand their sales to Mexico. In the first six months of 1994, U.S. apple growers nearly doubled their shipments to Mexico.

The key questions: Will more jobs be created than destroyed? Will the jobs created be better than the jobs destroyed? In a comprehensive study, the Institute for International Economics answered yes to these questions. Still, the U.S. is wisely setting up a multibillion-dollar fund to compensate those Americans who do lose out from the deal. Further, the U.S. has made sure that NAFTA has "surge protectors," that is, if Mexican goods start flooding certain markets, the U.S. can slow down the flow. Despite these safeguards, most American unions bitterly oppose the pact.

Negotiating NAFTA was tricky, especially since the countries had to determine what constitutes a North American good. For instance, what if Toyota assembles cars in Mexico? Do those cars count as North American goods that should enter the U.S. and Canada duty-free? Or should Japan have to shave its tariffs to zero before Toyota can take advantage of NAFTA? The bottom line on the treaty is that Japan cannot use Mexico as a "launching pad" for exports to the U.S. The U.S. and Canadian negotiators insisted on tough "rules of origin."

Now that NAFTA has been approved by the three countries, Chile and a host of other Latin countries are asking for permission to join. As Durante said, when it's a good act, everybody wants to get in. These negotiations to extend NAFTA southward will be difficult. California vineyard owners are already preparing to wine and dine congressmen and lobby them against Chilean competitors.

What Is the European Union?

As I have pointed out, the easiest way to kick-start economic growth is to tear down barriers to trade. Self-sufficiency is a recipe for staleness. Like a good cake, a healthy economy should have some springiness, some resiliency. Since Roman days, European leaders have struggled to avoid letting the Continent break down into the smallest ethnic and familial territories, each with their own currencies and rules. At its worst, Europe has been dotted with an almost infinite number of toll bridges, making it impossibly expensive to send goods to other markets.

Tearing down these trade restraints and pushing for more unity among some thirty-five countries is not easy. After all, each country has its own preferences and prejudices. The British, historically, have preferred sharing tea and crumpets with their former colonies than with their neighbors across the English Channel. They continue to bait the French by calling them "Frogs," and many cannot understand who would be interested in a "chunnel" connecting the two countries. The French, for their part, have enough trouble merely agreeing on policy among themselves. Charles de Gaulle once lamented that he simply could not rule over a country that had 385 different kinds of cheese!

In the years after World War II, though, European leaders realized that by fostering fragmentation on the Continent, they had squandered opportunities for economic gains. If the United States could weave together disparate colonies into the world's most powerful force for creating wealth, perhaps Europe could begin moving toward a "United States of Europe." Amid much dissension, Europe has plodded toward this goal during the past half century.

The first step, taken in 1957 by Belgium, the Netherlands, France, Italy, West Germany, and Luxembourg, was to form the European Coal and Steel Community, later called the European Economic Community, then the European Community, and starting in 1994, the European Union. During the next decades Britain, Spain, Greece, Denmark, Ireland, and Portugal signed up as well. From an economist's point of view, the key decision by the countries was to form a *customs union*. A customs union creates a free-trade zone among the participants but also adopts uniform tariffs on goods and services coming from outside the area. The last point—uniform tariffs on outside goods and services—is crucial. For if each country maintained different tariff levels, an outside country, say China, would merely export to the low-tariff member of the EU, which would then give the goods free access to the high-tariff states.

Of course, a customs union would spur even more growth if it totally removed barriers even to outsiders. Instead, the EU looks at times like Fortress Europe, open to one another but closed to outsiders. You can almost hear the cacophony of a dozen European languages singing the old nursery rhyme "Tick tock, the game is locked, and nobody else can play." In particular, the Union's Common Agricultural Policy (CAP) props up inefficient Euro-farmers at the expense of Euro-consumers and farmers all over the world. These prejudicial policies often incite dissension within the Union. The Germans, for example, are downright disgusted that their supermarket shelves are stocked with puny, soft bananas from France's former African colonies, rather than with the big bananas available from Latin American exporters.

In the 1980s, Western Europe realized that it needed to take further steps on the road to a unified market. What motivated their leaders? Fear. They looked across the Atlantic and saw the U.S. creating millions of new jobs. They surveyed Asia and saw Japan stealing market share in their most advanced industries. With its fragmented labor and capital markets, overregulation, and bulging social welfare states, Europe looked sick. Pundits dubbed the sickness "Eurosclerosis," while government leaders prescribed a rapid program to deregulate and integrate called the Single Market Program.

Over three hundred recommendations for the Single Market Program came out of a 1985 white paper published by the European Commission. (One might conduct a separate inquiry into why governments love to form "blue-ribbon" commissions to produce "white papers.") Now being implemented, this new system wipes out, for example, internal border checks for EU goods, controls on shifting funds within the EU, and work permits for EU residents. Erasing these rules from the books should make Europe more efficient.

Yet adopting uniform rules should not be the ultimate goal. It is easy to imagine a Europe with regulations that are uniform but that discourage innovation and productivity. What if, for example, every country agreed that every employer must provide housing for its employees? We would see perfect uniformity and a perfect disaster. I found it interesting that a recent European Commission publication called *European Union* chose a spiderweb as a symbol of its "sense of organization."[6] Euro-skeptics wonder just who is caught in this web.

Along with a single market, the EU is lurching toward a single currency. Despite adopting basic principles of monetary union spelled out in the Maastricht Treaty, presented in 1991 in the Dutch town of Maastricht, this goal will probably have to wait until the twenty-first century. As we will discuss in the next chapter, few countries are eager to give up control over their monetary policy. This, despite the claims of EU economists that a single currency would save so much on transaction costs that Europe's average GDP would rise by 1 percent.

Europe always seems to be balancing some accommodation between unity and separatism. Even Charlemagne, in trying to master the continent, recognized the need to respect its diversity. About languages, he purportedly said, "I speak Italian to my women; French to my chef, Spanish to God, and German . . . to my horse."

While the wealthy western countries of Europe and North America struggle through internal trade skirmishes, it's easy to forget those poorer nations where people must still worry about simply surviving. To aid these less-developed areas, the West has created the World Bank and the International Monetary Fund.

What Do the World Bank and the IMF Do?

First of all, they host a lot of cocktail parties and receptions. Each fall thousands of bureaucrats and private-sector bankers invade a world capital for the annual World Bank meetings. So many bigwigs showed up for the Washington, D.C., meetings in 1992 and 1993 that limousine services had to bring extra vehicles down from New York to fill the demand. During the evening, banks took over buildings like the National Gallery and decorated them for lavish soirees.

Besides extravagant parties and generous salaries, the World

Bank is known for lending money at low interest rates to developing countries, about $24 billion in 1993. Where does the World Bank get its funds? From wealthy countries, as well as from international investors who are willing to lend the World Bank funds. Although the World Bank does not lend money to Western Europe, that is where the Bank got its start. After World War II, the bank was established in Washington to funnel capital into the devastated European continent. Its first beneficiaries included the Netherlands, France, and Denmark.

The International Monetary Fund (IMF) works in coordination with the World Bank to provide economic advice and emergency funds for struggling economies. While the World Bank finances long-term projects, the IMF provides ongoing counseling to make sure the economy is on the right track. The IMF can be rather stern and insistent with its advice. Like a tough diet doctor, the IMF will generally draw up a rigorous plan to get the struggling country's economy back into shape. Developing countries have a tendency toward growing bloated bureaucracies, giving fat subsidies for friends of the government, and building barriers to new businesses starting up. The IMF will insist that the government leaders stick to a disciplined plan, or else that country will not receive IMF or World Bank funds. Furthermore, a thumbs-down from the IMF will usually disqualify the country for private-sector loans, as well.

Like the World Bank, the IMF has become more market-oriented over the years, due in part to the influence of such top international economists as Harvard's Jeffrey Sachs, Columbia's Jagdish Bhagwati, and MIT's Stanley Fischer and Rudiger Dornbusch. While during the 1960s and 1970s World Bank bureaucrats often encouraged large government spending plans and tax policies that redistributed income, the World Bank and IMF now focus on deregulation and breaking down barriers to trade.

This discussion of the World Bank and IMF assumes that countries want to be helped by the West and drawn into the industrialized world. But in fact, the West frequently faces unfriendly or belligerent nations that we try to isolate, in order to urge political reform or even revolution. In 1994 the U.S., for example, led international trade sanctions against Haiti, Iraq, and North Korea.

Do Economic Sanctions Against Outlaw Countries Work?

Because the United States prides itself on being a moral superpower as well as an economic and military one, politicians perennially jump up and down, shouting that America must use its economic might to right a moral wrong. We have a long history of such jumping and shouting. Even the professorial Woodrow Wilson sometimes loosened his collar and gave a yelp for sanctions against Germany. (His predecessor, William Howard Taft, weighing over three hundred pounds, did not jump and yelp much.) More recently, the U.S. slapped sanctions on Iraq in 1990 to drive army forces out of Kuwait. Since sanctions usually accompany other ways of sending nasty messages to our enemies (bombs in the case of Iraq, cyanide milkshakes in the case of Cuba's Castro), it is often difficult to judge how effective they are.

What are sanctions? Basically, sanctions are a government-led boycott against another government. Sometimes the boycott is on the other country's exports (the U.S.'s refusal to buy Iraqi oil, a policy in place since 1990); other times it involves boycotting the foe as a customer (our refusal to sell arms to South Africa in 1977). Still another option is freezing the target country's foreign assets, as was done to Japan's during World War II. The classic kind of sanction is a naval blockade to choke off another country's food and arms supplies.

Since economic sanctions are a form of punishment, the classic motivations for punishment come into play: the desire for justice and the need to deter and rehabilitate. But just as communities have gone sour on the prospects for rehabilitating hardened criminals, economists are skeptical that sanctions alone can transform "evil empires" into do-gooders, or even deter them from their despised activities. In fact, the motive for sanctions frequently seems to be internal—that is, the U.S. wants to send a message to itself. We do not have high hopes that our sanctions will change our foe's behavior, but we feel that we have validated our national conscience by trying. After the massacre in China's Tienanmen Square, the U.S., Europe, and Japan slapped sanctions on China without seriously expecting that the ruthless regime would repent and invite young protesters to camp out in the square again. But the citizens in the democracies felt better, and it was certainly a lot cheaper than going to war.

During the years prior to its collapse, the Soviet Union must have felt puzzled by the threat of U.S. sanctions. First, the Soviets got great news from President Nixon, who despite his anticommunist reputation, promised to sell them tons of wheat. This drove up bread prices in the U.S., spurring some U.S. consumers to a nasty boycott of bread in supermarkets. Since the shoppers often blamed the supermarkets, ironically, it looked as if teenage Safeway and A&P stockboys were the enemies and target of sanctions!

Then, during the Carter years, the liberal-moderate Carter slapped a grain embargo on the Soviet Union to protest its invasion of Afghanistan. Who got the most bruises? American farmers, who howled and boycotted Jimmy Carter's reelection campaign. To really hurt the Soviets, Carter also blocked the U.S. team from competing in the 1980 Olympics. Again, Carter was censured for putting foreign policy before America's obsession, televised sports.

In the penultimate act of the comedy, Ronald Reagan, the commie-hating hard-liner who would soon call the Soviet Union "the evil empire," promised in his presidential campaign against Carter never to embargo U.S. farm exports again. And in the final act, the Soviet Union collapsed, no thanks to sanctions, but because its rusty, vicious system could not keep up with the expectations for economic improvement.

The biggest problem with sanctions: people are sneaky. And outlaw countries tend to be among the sneakiest. Unless all other countries agree to enforce sanctions, outlaw countries can wiggle or slither out of most strangleholds. Here is a classic case where sanctions backfired in the most embarrassing way: In the mid-1980s, Australia cut off uranium shipments to France to protest France's nuclear weapons testing in the South Pacific. What did France do? It laughed. Uranium prices were dropping on the world market by about 50 percent, so the French just took their business elsewhere, having saved money when Australia broke its contact. And Australia? It wept, because no other country would give it a good price for the uranium it had promised to France. In the end, the Australian government spent millions of taxpayer dollars to bail out its orphaned mining industry.

This tale of the South Seas is repeated frequently when the boycotted product is a commodity, like oil, grain, or metals. Because such goods are not individually marked MADE IN AN OUTLAW STATE, once they get into the streams of trade, one cannot track down their origin. The U.S. might refuse to buy, say, Chinese silk, but since China can sell its silk to Italy, the U.S. might end up buying "Italian" silk that got its start in Beijing.

In 1994 the U.S. tried to embargo Haiti in order to squeeze out the ruthless military junta that overthrew the democratically elected government. Yet since Haiti shares an island with the Dominican Republic, observers immediately reported increased sailing activity into the Dominican Republic, as well as truck passage across the porous border with Haiti. It finally took the threat of the U.S. Air Force, bombs loaded, to push the junta aside.

A comprehensive study of 116 case studies from World War I to the United Nations embargo of Iraq yields the same conclusions. Sanctions are most likely to change behavior when:

1. The goal is modest, like winning the release of a political prisoner
2. The target is economically weak and politically unstable
3. The target usually conducts substantial trade with the sanctioner
4. The sanctions are imposed quickly and decisively
5. The sanctioner does not suffer much from imposing the policy.[7]

I would add one other rule. Sanctions work best where the target's leaders do not have psychological and material strangleholds on their population. That is, in truly evil empires, to borrow Reagan's phrase, the leaders can stay in power a long time, despite the hardship that sanctions may bring to the general populace. Nice guys give in fast.

While this chapter has focused on moving products back and forth across national borders, someone has to pay for them. In the next chapter, we'll look at the international financial system and explain how people come up with the dollars, yen, and pesos to make these deals happen.

6 Money Makes the World Go Round

CURRENCIES AND FINANCE

• *What Is a Trade Balance?* • *How's the U.S. Doing on Trade?* • *What Is a Capital Account? What Is the Balance of Payments?* • *Is It Good or Bad to Have a Current Account Deficit?* • *Is There Too Much Foreign Direct Investment?* • *What Spurs Foreign Investment?* • *Is Foreign Investment Good?* • *What's the Bottom Line on Foreign Investment in the U.S.?* • *Why Isn't There Just One Currency?* • *What Are Floating Exchange Rates?* • *Why Do Currencies Change Value?* • *Did We Always Have Floating Exchange Rates?* • *What Is the European Monetary System (EMS)?* • *Who Are Currency Speculators?* • *What Is Capital Flight?* • *What Is a Safe-Haven Currency?* • *What Is the Gold Standard?*

As we discussed in the last chapter, businesses move truckloads of goods across borders every day. Since most people don't barter anymore, money has to change hands as well. But what kind of money? And how much is another country's money worth? Children in elementary school are often told stories of the Dutch buying Manhattan from the Indians for $24 and some wampum. The implicit lesson: oh, those silly Indians, taken in by the sly Dutch. Maybe not. Have you checked out the price of wampum these days? Nobel Prize–winning economist Paul Samuelson has figured out that $24 invested in the seventeenth century would be worth more than all of Manhattan's real estate (the magic of compound interest!) today. Plus, the Indians did not have to live with the heartbreak of watching the Dodgers leave Brooklyn in 1958.

What Is a Trade Balance?

While entrepreneurs, salesmen, and industrial workers scurry around trying to produce and sell their wares, government accountants basically stand on the docks and at the borders, asking, "Where's this stuff going, and how much is it worth?" These accountants from the Department of Commerce in the U.S. and their counterparts abroad tally up the comings and goings of products to calculate the *merchandise trade balance*. Periodically, a country's government will then report whether that country bought more from abroad than it sold to foreigners.

Once upon a time, when people judged a nation's "competitiveness," they looked only at merchandise trade. Most of what the U.S. sold abroad was tangible, visible stuff: cars, refrigerators, steel. America's GNP was, one might say, literally heavy. But with the computer and information revolutions, our GNP "weighs" less; intangible, invisible services have become valuable "products" that we trade. New York bankers, for example, earn a lot of money giving financial advice to Arab states, but they don't ship that advice, they just talk on the phone. Silicon Valley computer programmers consult with the Japanese, suggesting new codes worth millions of dollars and trillions of yen. Again, the government accountants cannot stand at Norita Airport in Tokyo expecting the advice to land on the runway.

You may think of these precious parts of our economy as "GNP Lite," but do not underestimate their value. The U.S. motion picture industry alone generates billions of dollars in foreign sales. Each pound of celluloid yields millions of dollars for U.S.-based firms, yet none of the ultimate consumers (the theatergoers) ever actually touches the stuff.

Just because a product was not made with rivets does not

mean it is not a valuable export. The merchandise account seems outdated, then. To recognize the importance of "lite" goods and services, countries calculate a *current account balance,* which adds services, investment income, and other transfers to the merchandise account balance. Because it is a broader measure than the merchandise account, the current account balance better illustrates how a country is doing in the race to sell goods abroad.

But since services are invisible, they are tougher to count. Plus the accounting rules are trickier. For example, suppose Mr. Ono, a Japanese tourist, flies to Disney World and buys some linguine at a restaurant at Epcot Center. The government counts Mr. Ono's linguine lunch as an American export to Japan. Even though the linguine never got to Japan, it did get to a Japanese stomach. Though the U.S. does not send out spies to track Mr. Ono's steps, the government estimates tourist spending by gauging the amount of foreign currency exchanged for dollars.

Switzerland "exports" billions of dollars worth of banking services, merely by managing bank accounts for wealthy foreigners in Zurich. Though the funds never leave Zurich, when the Swiss bank collects its fees, those fees show up in Switzerland's current account statistics as a Swiss export. Now, if Swiss banks gave away toasters to foreign customers, the government would tally the appliances as a Swiss export in the country's merchandise trade balance. But of course, Swiss banks attract worldwide funds—some from underworld figures—because of their famed secrecy, not their giveaways. Mafia kingpins get their toasters from other sources.

How's the U.S. Doing on Trade?

In recent years you have probably heard much about the U.S. trade deficit. It is true the U.S. has piled up deficits in merchandise trade, but at the same time, the U.S. has large surpluses in services and foreign investment income. We are buying tank-loads of oil and shiploads of autos (though recently U.S. auto-makers have won back some market share from the Japanese). But we are selling more computer, banking, and insurance services abroad than anyone else. In 1991, for instance, the U.S. bought about $73 billion more in *goods* than it sold. However, if you then subtract the U.S. successes in services, investment income, and other transfers, the *current account balance* (that is, the excess of all imports over all exports) came to a modest $8.3 billion deficit. Not much in a $7 trillion economy.

After 1991, the current account deficit widened, not because the U.S. became less competitive, but because Europe and Japan fell into very deep recessions, which made it more difficult for them to buy more U.S. goods and services.

What Is a Capital Account?
What Is the Balance of Payments?

Accountants hate leftovers and messes. They insist on neat balance sheets where everything comes out even. (Freudians describe this kind of obsessiveness as "anal retentive.") Assets must always equal liabilities, accountants tell corporations. Government accountants, then, do not stop their analysis when they conclude that the U.S. ran an $8.3 billion current account deficit in 1991. They must know where to record those extra $8.3 billion that U.S. citizens sent to foreigners to purchase their goods. The answer: the accountants keep a parallel set of books called the *capital account,* which keeps track of foreigners buying and selling U.S. stocks, bonds, and currency.

The capital account is always the mirror image of the current account. If foreign sales of U.S. goods bring in $8.3 billion less than the U.S. spends abroad, and we have therefore run up a current account deficit, the mirror-image capital account would show the U.S. with an offsetting $8.3 billion surplus. Why? Because foreigners are holding $8.3 billion more U.S. dollars than they started the year with.

Let's look at an example. If the U.S. buys more French goods and services than the French buy U.S. products, the French must end up holding a lot of greenbacks. Those "extra" dollars get tallied up in the capital account. The French, who are willing to hold dollars, will eventually want to trade them in for either more U.S. goods or for French francs. Again, a deficit in the current account (e.g., if sales of U.S. goods abroad bring in less than the U.S. spends on other countries' goods) will be precisely offset by a surplus in the capital account. Countries like Japan, which run up huge export surpluses in goods routinely amass huge capital account deficits, because they end up holding so much foreign currency from other countries. When the accountants finish their calculations, all countries have an overall *balance of payments* equal to zero.

Is It Good or Bad to Have a Current Account Deficit?

It depends. A growing country often needs to buy more than it sells and to borrow money for new projects and investment. During the nineteenth century, the U.S. needed foreign money to pay for bridges, dams, schools, and railroad tracks. U.S. citizens simply did not have enough wealth to pay for these investments up front. Those beams and trestles may have been stamped MADE IN USA, but they could have been marked PAID IN ENGLAND. Though the U.S. racked up current account deficits, it did not matter. The investments paid off by helping the U.S. economy expand and allowed the U.S. to pay back foreign investors without much worry.

During the early 1980s, the U.S. balance sheet seemed to list like the *Titanic*. While in 1981 the U.S. enjoyed a $5 billion current account surplus (by selling more to foreigners than we bought from them), by 1987 the ledgers flip-flopped and the U.S. rang up a $167 billion deficit. Pundits panicked and Congress took dramatic actions—by Washington standards: it held hearings. The Chicken Little chorus clucked on about how the U.S. had lost its competitive edge and was losing jobs daily.

Remember, though, that the $167 billion *current account deficit* was offset by the mirror image $167 billion *capital account surplus*. This meant that foreigners were willing to hold on to dollars, many in the form of U.S. Treasury bonds. In effect, these bonds served as a huge loan from the rest of the world to the U.S. The loan would have ended disastrously if the U.S. had squandered the funds. Instead, we invested enough of these borrowed funds in plant, equipment, and technology so that by the middle 1980s the U.S. displayed far greater productivity growth than its European trading partners, while creating 12 million new jobs. Meanwhile, Europe watched itself ossify. Of course, it would have been better to invest even more and to finance these projects domestically, by getting Americans to save more. But the U.S. would have been in worse shape had it not borrowed from abroad, which, once again, appears on the balance sheet as a current account deficit and a capital account surplus.

During the 1950s, Japan's books were in the red, as the nation sold fewer goods abroad (current account deficit) and furiously borrowed from the U.S. (capital account surplus) in order to build factories. Sure enough, at that time, some analysts worried that Japan was becoming a nation of borrowers and would never recover.

Here is the bottom line: we should not scorn countries that do not earn as much abroad as they spend. This is usually a temporary phenomenon, since no country can keep it up indefinitely. If foreigners lent money to Mexico in the 1990s, the U.S. in the 1980s, or Japan in the 1950s, they must have concluded that investing in these countries was a better bet than keeping their money at home.

Is There Too Much Foreign Direct Investment?

Just as pundits panicked when they saw the U.S. borrowing funds from abroad, they panicked when they saw foreigners buying U.S. assets, from the RCA building in Rockefeller Center to the Pebble Beach Golf Links in California. But it must be bad to sell off "national treasures" like the eighteenth hole overlooking the Pacific, you say? Don't be so sure.

First of all, the Japanese buyers of these landmarks got fleeced; the phrase "buy low, sell high" must not translate well. During the height of the 1980s real estate boom, Japanese banks bought up lots of California real estate. Then the market got soft as sushi, and the banks' balance sheets started bleeding red ink. In fact, whatever the Japanese touched seemed to turn to dust. From California real estate to French Impressionist paintings, almost as soon as the assets changed hands in the late 1980s, their values plunged.

The worriers in Washington again held hearings, decrying the "sell-off" of America. Watching foreigners buy a bond or a few shares of stock in a U.S. firm (indirect investment) was bad enough, but letting them purchase big stakes and even whole properties (direct investment) seemed unconscionable. At times critics talked as if the Japanese were actually planning to dismantle Rockefeller Center one art deco brick at a time and ship it back to Tokyo. (Ironic, since John D. Rockefeller actually did buy a French monastery and ship it to New York, to build the Cloisters on the Hudson.) After Sony purchased Columbia Pictures, the paranoid crowd talked as if the Tokyo owners would rewrite the plot of *Tora! Tora! Tora!*[1]

In 1988, Democratic Presidential contender Michael Dukakis tried to exploit the issue by telling some St. Louis autoworkers that "the Republican ticket wants our children to work for foreign owners . . . but that's not the kind of future Lloyd Bentsen and I and Dick Gephardt and you want for America." Rather than applaud wildly, the audience snickered. Their plant had been owned by Italians for over a decade.[2]

Perhaps a few facts will put the situation in perspective. First of all, the Japanese are not the biggest foreign owners of U.S. assets, the British are. The Brits control about 2 percent of U.S. GDP, while the Japanese control 1.5 percent and the Dutch 1.2 percent. During the 1980s buying spree, the Japanese bought less than a hundred U.S. firms, placing them substantially behind the Brits, Canadians, Germans, and French.[3]

Moreover, the U.S. has done some buying of its own. So while the Brits may own 2 percent of U.S. GDP, the U.S. controls almost 7 percent of the U.K.'s economy, including such veddy British nameplates as Jaguar. The U.S. controls about .7 percent of the Japanese economy and over 8 percent of the Dutch economy.[4]

Foreign direct investment is just one of the topics that pessimists love. No matter which way the money flows, they can conjure up a depressing fable: If foreigners buy U.S. assets, they worry about the U.S. "losing control of its destiny and sovereignty." If foreigners do not buy U.S. assets, they fret that America no longer looks like a promising land in which to invest one's money.

What Spurs Foreign Investment?

Foreigners invest money for the same reason that natives invest money: the prospect of making even more. Foreigners are not dumb. As Damon Runyon paraphrased the Bible, the race is not to the swift nor the battle to the strong—but that's the way to bet. Most developing countries must beg for foreign investment because they cannot demonstrate competitive returns.

Over the last decade, international investors have seen the U.S. economy as one that has grown "mean and lean" while the EU continued to look flabby and hooked on government narcotics called subsidies and protectionism. Thus, the U.S. stock market climbed over 15 percent annually, while European markets dipped well below that mark.

Further, the U.S. has always appeared politically stable. Even in the depths of a bitter presidential race, when George Bush called Bill Clinton a "bozo" who knew less than his dog about foreign policy, foreigners trusted that a change in the U.S. government would not undermine the economy. The U.S. promises both stability and opportunity. Though Switzerland appears as stable, it does not demonstrate the same dynamism and opportunity for extraordinary returns. Where is the Swiss Bill Gates, founder of Microsoft?

I am frequently asked by clients to gauge the political economy of various countries. What are the chances that Ghana will nationalize its gold mines again, if the opposition party takes power? Will Poland continue on the path to privatization, or will the ex–Communist party return to its old ways? Investors don't have to ask such questions about the U.S.

While the U.S. enjoys a stable political system, politicians are almost always threatening to monkey around with the tax system. Such situations can affect foreign investment. In September 1993, the U.S. bond market felt a jolt because investors heard that Congress might slap foreigners with a tax on their holdings of U.S. bonds. Our G7 Group office phones rang with worried American clients who were ready to dump their U.S. bonds. They figured that if the foreign investors tried to avoid the new tax by shedding their U.S. bonds, it would drive down the price of all bonds. I told the clients that the Clinton White House would fight almost any proposal that would hurt the bond market. Then I called the Treasury Department and warned them that this rumor posed a major problem. Several hours later, the Treasury Department (responding to similar unsolicited advice) denounced the idea and stanched the flows out of the market.

Is Foreign Investment Good?

Usually. Of course, some foreign buyers are blowhards who end up destroying companies and themselves. Robert Campeau of Canada gobbled up a bunch of U.S. retail clothing stores, issued junk bonds, and then saw his business thrown into the junk pile itself. Basically, though, by attracting foreign money, firms can expand their plants and buy new equipment, which puts better tools in the hands of workers and allows productivity to rise and wages to climb as well. Since newer facilities tend to be more technologically advanced than older plants, the average foreign multinational in the U.S. actually spends more on wages and equipment per worker than the average U.S. firm.[5] So, for example, Alabama residents are eager to start work at the new Mercedes-Benz plant.

But foreign investment does not help just those working in the plants. When more foreign funds come into the U.S., the country's overall borrowing costs (interest rates) fall. Every borrower benefits when there is more money to spread around. Therefore, even firms that are a hundred percent domestic get an extra lift from lower interest rates.

What about "national security"? Doesn't foreign investment sap our ability to defend ourselves? This is the last refuge of fearmongers. The scare tactic goes like this: If the French buy up all of our video games, our troops won't have Gameboys if we ever have to fight the French. But in fact, we have several defenses in such a crisis. First, the host government can always take over the foreign country's assets in a desperate emergency. Second, most governments, including the U.S., restrict certain investments in, for example, nuclear energy. The Committee on Foreign Investment in the U.S. (CFIUS) investigates proposed foreign investment and can recommend that the president prevent particular acquisitions. But when I served at the White House, most requests for CFIUS intervention came from firms who feared competition, not from the Pentagon.

What's the Bottom Line on Foreign Investment in the U.S.?

Here is the real story on foreign investment. America is finally becoming "normal." By that I mean that the U.S. is integrating itself into the world economy, joining the other industrial countries, which have been integrated for a long time. For European countries, trade and foreign investment were always crucial. British residents would not blink if a French firm opened a plant near their town. Because the U.S. domestic market was so huge, America didn't need other countries quite so much. While we were willing to occasionally build plants in Asia, we certainly did not expect the Japanese to turn around and buy up some of our companies.

But now the legal and psychological barriers that used to restrict capital from migrating toward the places that give the highest return have been lowered. All around the world, investments flow more freely, and the U.S. now gets the benefit not only of building and selling abroad, but of attracting foreign attention as well. No surprise, then, that the U.S. foreign investment profile is now looking a little more like the rest of the world's.

Of course, even if a project in a foreign country looks like a golden investment opportunity, you have to be able to pay for it. And that brings us to a discussion of currencies and finance.

Why Isn't There Just One Currency?

Some frustrated American tourists who try to communicate in foreign lands by screaming English words at a hundred decibels may wish that everyone just spoke English and used the dollar. Wouldn't that make it easier for international trade? No more standing in line at the bank window waiting for the teller to exchange currencies and take a cut off the top.

That might work well—except for three things. First, most people like their national currency. The depictions on paper money and coins reinforce national icons and symbols. Why would the Brits want to trade in Queen Elizabeth's noble chin for George Washington's wooden-toothed grimace? Second, national currencies allow countries to manage their own banking system (though they cannot insulate themselves from the policies of trading partners).

Third, most countries are reluctant to surrender control of their macroeconomic policy to foreigners. Suppose Spain's 20-percent unemployment rate demands urgent attention in the form of lower interest rates, yet Portugal's higher inflation rate makes the authorities nervous about easier money. If Spain and Portugal shared a currency, they would have to share policy prescriptions. That would be like two patients in a doctor's waiting room agreeing to take the same medication, even though they suffered from different ailments. (We will discuss this further in "What is the European Monetary System (EMS)?" p. 219)

Etymologists tell us interesting stories about the linguistic origins of today's currencies. Many, including the Mexican peso, Spanish peseta, British pound, and Italian lira derive from words meaning "weight," because in olden days merchants would weigh coins made from precious metals to determine their value. The French, Swiss, and Belgian franc are descendants of coins minted by the Francs, the Germanic tribe that conquered the region in the third century. The German mark, or deutsche mark (D-mark), was named for the signs on currencies showing their precious metal content. The names of the Chinese and Japanese monetary units, *yuan* and *yen,* derive from a Chinese word for "round." Finally, *dollar* derives from a region of Bohemia called Joachimsthal, which issued coins called "thalers." So you can see that if the U.S. ever tried to drop the dollar, the Bohemian Anti-Defamation League would protest.

What Are Floating Exchange Rates?

As tourists discover, the value of a currency changes almost every day. (In fact, over the course of a day, currency traders send the values up and down millions of times. More on this when we discuss speculators.) Many of us have received postcards bemoaning the cost of everything, including postcards themselves, from friends traveling abroad. These notes are postmarked from countries where the dollar has just gotten weaker, or *depreciated*.

Let's take an example. You are visiting London and your hotel sells you British pounds for $1.50 each. You walk to Trafalgar Square, where you can have your photograph taken with Sarah Ferguson, the former dutchess of York. The price of a photograph: one pound (the equivalent of $1.50). Now, suppose the dollar depreciates, so your hotel now sells British pounds for $2.00. Even though Fergie will continue to charge the same one pound, an American will have to cough up an extra 50¢ to get the snapshot: when the dollar gets weak, it takes more dollars to buy the same amount of foreign goods.

Of course, the dollar may *appreciate,* as well. During the early 1980s, tourists and eager shoppers flocked to London shops for Burberry coats and other British luxury items because, with the U.S. dollar so strong against the British pound, the savings on their purchases paid for the airfare. From September 1992 until September 1993, the dollar catapulted into another power phase, rising 45 percent against the Swedish krona, 40 percent against the Spanish peseta, and 20 percent against the British pound. Suddenly, foreign travel looked cheap, and millions of Americans took advantage of the deals. In fact, so many Americans jammed into Paris that the Louvre began to look like Filene's Basement.

The dollar did not skyrocket everywhere, though; in Japan it plunged 20 percent against the yen. Merely opening up the door of a Tokyo taxi cab today costs an American the equivalent of

$6. At that price, Americans aren't so impressed that Japanese drivers wear white gloves.

Why Do Currencies Change Value?

Supply and demand, what else? More specifically, here are four different forces that could send the dollar upward by increasing demand for greenbacks:

> *Trade.* Let's say that the Japanese go cuckoo for Cocoa Puffs cereal. To buy it from General Mills, they must trade in their yen for dollars. Thus, dollars become more valuable.
>
> *Real Investment.* This time, the Japanese want to build a cereal plant in Battle Creek, Michigan. To pay for the land and steel, they need more dollars.
>
> *Financial Investment.* Suppose that rather than building a plant, the Japanese decide to buy stock in General Mills. Here again, they must trade their yen for dollars.
>
> *Currency Speculation.* If Japanese money managers think the dollar is going to rise as a result, perhaps, of the scenarios above, they will trade yen for dollars now, so they can take advantage of the expected appreciation.

Each of these factors places powerful pressures on the foreign exchange market. If you turn these factors upside down, you can see why people might turn in their dollars for foreign currencies, leading to a dip in the value of the greenback: First, if U.S. households buy more from abroad than we sell in foreign markets. Second, if Americans build plants abroad. Third, if Americans buy foreign stocks or bonds. Fourth, if speculators bet that the above factors will come into play.

Inflation is another strong force. Who, after all, wants to hold a currency if it will be worth less because of high inflation? Check currency rates in your newspaper the day after the U.S. government releases a distressing inflation report. Usually, the dollar will fall in response.

Interest rates matter too. If a U.S. Treasury bond, for example, pays a higher real rate than a German bond, international investors will flock to the U.S. offering. But they must pay for the bond in dollars, so the dollar gets pushed up higher. This scenario took place in the early 1980s, when ballooning federal budget deficits, which required the U.S. to borrow more and issue more bonds, along with tight monetary policy shoved both real interest rates and the dollar upward.

Did We Always Have Floating Exchange Rates?

The world has had floating exchange rates only since 1973. From 1946 until 1973, countries tried to set in stone their currency values under the Bretton Woods system, named for a New Hampshire town that hosted international negotiations in 1944. What went wrong with the "fixed" system? Under the Bretton Woods Agreement, each central bank was obliged to buy or sell its currency in order to keep the value in line with others. For instance, if Germany ran a trade surplus (meaning it earned more for goods sold abroad than it spent abroad), that would tend to boost the deutsche mark upward, since foreigners buying more Braun coffee makers needed to pay for them in deutsche marks. To keep the deutsche mark from rising, though, the Bundesbank would have to dump its stash of deutsche marks on the market and instead buy foreign currencies.

Germany did not like this game, for ever since the 1920s, the German central bankers have had nightmares about dumping D-marks that recall the German hyperinflation of the 1920s (nightmares in which they see Weimaraner dogs pushing wheelbarrows full of useless bills). In 1970 and 1971 Germany's rising trade surplus with the U.S. put pressure on the Bundesbank to print more D-marks. But the old central bankers faced a tough dilemma: while increasing the supply of D-marks would pump up Germany's domestic economy and encourage more buying from abroad, it would also pump up price pressures and bring back those haunting Weimar memories. After boosting the D-mark supply by about a billion dollars on May 5, 1971, in a failed defense of the fixed exchange rate, the Bundesbank called it quits and simply let the D-mark rise ("revalue").

In fact, though finance ministers claimed that we had "fixed" exchange rates in the 1950s and 1960s, so much cheating went on that the system was better described as "adjustable pegs," currency goals that were fudged every so often. In 1973, the industrialized world just got a little more honest and allowed rates to float.

Even now, though, central banks intervene in the market and sometimes coordinate to push currencies one way or the other. In 1985, for example, finance ministers from the U.S., Japan, the U.K., Germany, and France met at the Plaza Hotel in New York and agreed to work together to bash the U.S. dollar downward, because they believed that the U.S. trade deficit was growing too fast. Generally, such multigovernment schemes flounder, unless private players in the financial markets are pushing in the same direction. In the case of the Plaza Accord, U.S. interest rates were falling anyway, which would have sapped the dollar's strength even without intervention.

Central bank governors have blown fortunes trying to fight against momentum in the international currency market. During August of 1993, the Bank of France spent 300 billion French francs (about $55 billion) trying to keep the franc from falling against the D-mark. This fight was a matter of pride, since French politicians and civil servants had struggled to make the franc as strong as the D-mark—their so-called Franc Fort policy. But French taxpayers ultimately lost out, because the bank could not stop the momentum against the franc. The French had to swallow their pride and stomach a weaker franc.

As the French example shows, Europe has turned exchange-rate intervention into a kind of traveling show, a tragicomedy in which central banks frequently lose in their attempt to fight the economic fundamentals that naturally push currencies up or down.

What Is the European Monetary System (EMS)?

It is a mess. The EMS is the system by which European governments try to keep their currencies from floating outside of narrow "bands." The EU hopes that the EMS will pave the way for a single European currency by 1999, but EU leaders, like Nellie in *South Pacific,* are probably "cockeyed optimists."

Why is the EMS a mess? Fixed exchange rates, or agreements to limit fluctuations to a very narrow band, work only when countries have the same economic conditions. Suppose Italy and Spain have "fixed" their exchange rates between each other. Now, if both countries suffer from depressed economies and low inflation, they both could use a jolt of monetary stimulus, such as printing more money, which would generally reduce the value of the lira and the peseta against other currencies (printing more lira makes the existing lira less valuable). No problem, since the lira and peseta would keep their fixed levels against each other.

But what if Italy did not suffer from the same conditions as Spain? Pumping up only Spain would depress the peseta against the lira. If Spain has promised to keep the peseta even with the lira, it must either buy up pesetas, thus reversing the stimulus, or raise its interest rates, also reversing the stimulus. So, fixed exchange rates or narrow bands simply do not allow countries the flexibility to solve their internal economic troubles.

The EMS broke down in 1992 and 1993 when a reunified Germany faced inflation problems, while its neighbors all faced deepening recessions. To fight inflation at home, the Bundesbank jacked up interest rates, thus pressuring the D-mark higher. This move proved disastrous and embarrassing to Germany's neighbors. To keep their currencies from slipping below the promised narrow, 2.5-percent band, other EMS countries were forced to prop up their rates as well. The problem: *their economies actually needed lower rates.*

Finally in 1992, Italian and U.K. leaders threw up their hands after speculators bet that the officials would not continue hurting their economies for the sake of EU cooperation. When in the summer of 1993 the French, among others, could not keep up the franc after the Germans refused to dramatically chop interest rates, the EMS countries gave up the narrow bands in response to the crisis and instead agreed to a wider, 15-percent floating range.

Nearly everyone blamed the Bundesbank for the fiasco. The French were furious, complaining that if those Bundesbankers had not been so selfish, the old EMS bands could have been preserved. I think the Bundesbank was adopting rocket scientist Wernher von Braun's attitude, when he allegedly said, "I'm responsible for sending the missiles up; where they land is somebody else's problem." The Bundesbankers felt they were just not responsible for the shock waves their actions sent across the border.

The real lesson is not that German bankers are self-centered. It's that currency rates can stay aligned only if the underlying economies warrant it.[6]

Who Are Currency Speculators?

They are financial swashbucklers, ready to throw down fortunes betting that a certain currency may rise or fall. Among the most successful swashbucklers are George Soros and Julian Robertson, who each control multibillion-dollar portfolios. Soros is known in London as "the man who broke the Bank of England," for on September 16, 1992, Black Wednesday, Soros bet that Britain would give up trying to maintain the value of the pound against the D-mark. Soros kept his bet on a cheaper pound even after the chancellor of the exchequer promised that Britain would not flee, and even after the Bank of England sharply boosted interest rates and spent $30 billion to defend the pound. During this period, Sweden actually cranked interest rates up to 500 percent to deter a speculative attack on the krona! Soros's fund apparently earned a billion dollars from the British bet.

Not all risky bets turn out so well. In early 1994, Soros admitted that his fund lost about $600 million by betting incorrectly that the dollar would strengthen against the yen, along with watching some other investments turn sour.

I have been advising such investors since leaving the White House in 1992. While some pundits denounce them, I believe they play a useful role, keeping politicians and central bankers honest. After all, Soros made his billion dollars off of Britain because the politicians were trying to maintain a currency arrangement that imperiled the feeble British economy by propping rates up too high.

For all the glamour, players in the currency markets get by on hard work and tough analysis. Before speculators place their bets, they try to figure out the answers to key questions like, Is the central bank acting responsibly on monetary policy? Is the government allowing social spending to spin out of control beyond the means of the taxpayers? Are the politicians honestly portraying the country's ability to meet its debts? If the answer to any of these questions is no, the currency traders will swoop down and dump the nation's currency until leaders deliver honest answers.

Ultimately, the currency is a symbol of a country's credibility and integrity, and of its commitment to paying its debts. The international financial markets stand ready to discipline and expose fraudulent governments.

What Is Capital Flight?

Sometimes government leaders really screw up, scaring away investors and their money. No one wants to hold a currency that they expect to plummet in value. During the 1970s, Mexican president Jose Lopez Portillo presided over an implosion in the oil market, a ragtag private sector, a booming debt to foreigners, and a nationalized banking sector. Not even Mexicans wanted to keep their savings at home. About forty to fifty billion dollars in Mexican capital fled to foreign banks. I know a number of wealthy Mexicans who flew regularly across the border to Houston to deposit funds in American banks. With this financial debacle, Mexico certainly could not attract much foreign investment.

Portillo's successors, Miguel de la Madrid Hurtado and Carlos Salinas de Gartori, turned the crisis around, by privatizing companies, cutting tariffs, joining the GATT, and selling shares of Mexican firms to foreigners. Most important, they announced that they would reverse the disastrous 1982 policy of nationalizing banks. The result: funds moved back into Mexico, and Mexico began an economic revival.

There is only one good solution to capital flight: shaky governments must restore confidence by adopting sensible policies. Passing laws that prevent citizens from taking out their savings only intensifies the confidence crisis. Plus it discourages funds that have already flown the coop from changing course and heading home again. Even the threat of death in 1931 could not keep Germans from sneaking their savings across the border during the Weimar crisis. And if you cannot get those orderly Germans to follow orders, you can give up on the rest of the world.

As markets become more fluid and global, leaders must be more careful about alienating investors. Since money can now be transferred electronically, leaders cannot hold savings hostage as they used to. This too is healthy and keeps politicians from acting too recklessly.

What Is a Safe-Haven Currency?

I recall seeing a bumper sticker that said WHEN THE GOING GETS TOUGH, THE TOUGH GO SHOPPING. In currency markets, when the going gets tough, the investors go to safer places. Since the U.S. government appears so stable and insulated from threat of foreign invasion, nervous investors will often flee to the greenback when they hear the drums of war. During September 1993, as soon as Boris Yeltsin dissolved the parliament, risking a civil war, investors dumped D-marks and bought dollars. The reason? While Germany is geographically vulnerable to a Russian bloodbath, the U.S. appears to be at a safe distance. Even Japan looks a bit more exposed to Russian tumult than the U.S.; as a result, the dollar jumped against the yen as well.

Of course, if the U.S. experienced severe domestic turmoil, such as a presidential assassination, even the greenback could get shot down in the currency markets, until traders could figure out how risky the U.S. political situation had become.

The constant volatility in the currency markets makes many people nervous (exporters must worry that fluctuations will severely distort their profits earned from abroad). In an effort to calm things down, that old favorite, the gold standard, gets tossed into the air for economists to bat around.

What Is the Gold Standard?

A magic bullet for inflation, claim some writers. Some of my friends rhapsodize about gold with eyes so glazed I wonder whether it's some old, totemic symbol hiding deep in their Jungian subconsciouses. I'm skeptical and feel like Moses looking down at the golden calf and wondering why the Israelites are worshipping something so tacky.

First some history. The gold standard was adopted in eighteenth-century England after the master of the mint, Sir Isaac Newton, overvalued silver. In short, the gold standard obligated the central bank to exchange currency for gold at a fixed price. It was a control on monetary hanky-panky, otherwise known as inflation.

The U.S. moved to a de facto gold standard in the 1830s and adopted it formally in 1900. Tourists who visited Washington could walk up to the Treasury Department building on Fifteenth Street and swap their bills for gold. Every bill was inscribed with the following promise: "The United States of America Will Pay to the Bearer on Demand One Dollar in Gold."

(In the 1930s the U.S. dropped this pledge and replaced the inscription with a promise to "Pay to the Bearer on Demand One Dollar in Lawful Money." A puckish man from Cleveland who decided to test the government then mailed a ten-dollar bill to Washington asking to swap it for "lawful money." The wits at the Treasury Department mailed him back two fives!)

By guaranteeing a fixed exchange price for gold, the central bank basically promised not to print or coin more money (since more money would bid up the price of gold). With a relatively fixed money supply, inflation could not ignite.

So far so good. From 1880 to 1914, the classic gold standard also applied internationally to offset trade surpluses and deficits. For example, if Britain had a trade deficit with the U.S., the extra British pounds that the U.S. had amassed by selling so many American goods would be exchanged for British gold. Thus, Britain would settle its trade deficit by shipping gold to the U.S. Now, watch how this repairs the trade imbalance: by collecting more gold, the U.S. would be permitted to print more money, bidding overall prices higher. Higher U.S. prices would drive down exports to Britain. Meanwhile in Britain, less gold and a smaller money supply would hurt overall demand for goods, sending prices down and making sales to the U.S. more attract- ive. Presto, the gold standard controlled prices and alleviated trade imbalances.

But here's the problem. First, countries like France and Bel- gium did not always play fair and sometimes refused to adjust their money supply as gold moved in and out. Since gold does have a mesmerizing power, it seems, people and institutions don't like to give it up. Second, gold is found in mines. We do not know where all the veins are or when they will be found. Why subject the world's monetary system to the vagaries of the mining industry? The California gold rush of 1849 boosted the U.S. money supply, raised domestic spending, and ballooned the trade deficit. All because of prospectors holding out pans. And before South Africa dropped its apartheid system and the Soviet Union collapsed, the world's gold supply was vulnerable to two virtually pariah nations.

Furthermore, close studies show that while gold prices did not change much in the long run between 1880 and 1914, short- run blips confused and destabilized the monetary system.

All this skepticism does not mean that gold prices are useless pieces of information. When investors get nervous about infla- tion, they often buy gold. Fed chairman Alan Greenspan says that he keeps an eye on gold as a signal of whether interest rates are too high or low. The lesson of history is that one eye is okay, but no more.

In sum, a myopic gold standard could make us more vulner- able to, not safer from, market fluctuations. If all these risks are not convincing enough, rent the James Bond movie *Goldfinger.* Remember, if Sean Connery had not stopped the villain who was holding Fort Knox hostage, we would all be in a terrible depression.

Though I have advised on corporate and U.S. domestic fi- nance, I have found international finance and currencies the most intellectually challenging. Practitioners must simultaneously weigh in their minds interest-rate policy, inflation concerns, and political dynamics, as well as the resolve of both speculators and central bankers. The dramatic challenge that speculators pose to government officials creates a discipline that ultimately improves policy for even the most risk-averse investors. Economics teaches us that there is no easy way out of uncertainty, whether through strict old standards or fixed exchange rates. We must live with the drama, even if we can take some steps to hedge against it.

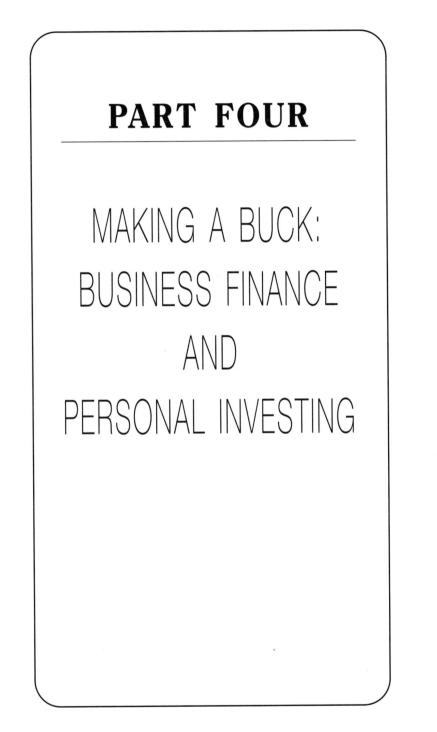

PART FOUR

MAKING A BUCK: BUSINESS FINANCE AND PERSONAL INVESTING

7 Going for Broke

How Businesses Finance Themselves

• What Is the Difference Between a Proprietorship, a Partnership, and a Corporation? • How Can a Corporation Limit Liability for Owners? • What Is the Difference Between a Public Company and a Closely Held Corporation? • How Do Firms Pay for Their Growth and Expansion? • What Is Equity? • What Are Corporate Bonds? • Who Determines How Risky a Bond Is? • What Is an Asset-Backed Security? • Does It Matter Whether the Corporation Finances Itself Through Bonds or Equity? • Can Investors Beat the Stock Market? • Are There Exceptions to the Efficient-Market Hypothesis?

Winston Churchill, who spent much of his political career arguing with socialists, could not understand their priorities, especially the idea that making profits is a vice. "I consider the real vice is making losses," he quipped. If socialists are right to perceive losses as a virtue, there are a lot of holy people in the capitalist world.

Most of the great economists were not particularly gifted investors. Only David Ricardo and John Maynard Keynes excelled. Poor Thomas Malthus had to rely on Ricardo, his rival, for advice. And according to Ricardo, Malthus usually chickened out just before investments became really profitable.

Most economics textbooks skip over the subjects of investing and financial markets. There are two explanations: first, the professors know their weak spots after all; second, the more economists study, for example, the stock market, the more skeptical they are that anyone, including themselves, can beat the market. But how is it that the individuals most knowledgeable about markets can resign themselves to sitting on the sidelines? That's like race car driver Richard Petty driving a four-cylinder Chevy and crawling along in the slow lane with his hazard lights blinking. This bizarre behavior is explained by the *efficient-market hypothesis,* which we will discuss at the end of this chapter. But before we can look at complex and frustrating issues like winning in the stock market, we must understand how businesses are set up and how they finance themselves. In the next chapter, we'll take a look at personal investing and see how economic principles can help individuals with their stock and bond portfolios.

What Is the Difference Between a Proprietorship, a Partnership, and a Corporation?

Most businesses start out as sole *proprietorships*—emphasis on the "start out." The dream of many owners is to "grow" the business into a corporation, sell shares to the public, and then hang out with the other *Forbes* coverboys. American history is filled with success stories about some guy who began by pushing a cart of apples and ends up never doing his own shopping again.

Take Tom Carvel, founder of the 750-store Carvel ice cream chain. Carvel not only invented a new process for making ice cream, he also pioneered the idea of proprietors acting as their own radio and television spokesmen. According to the authors of *The Encyclopedia of Bad Taste,*[1] Tom Carvel's awful diction and gravelly voice inspired a common reaction among Carvel store owners: "Get that senile old goat off the air!" But despite the owners' doubts, ice cream consumers liked the homespun approach to advertising.

In 1934, Carvel borrowed fifteen dollars, bought some ice cream, and started selling it from the back of a truck. He decided on the location for his first shop in an odd way: his truck blew a tire near a vacant lot, and so Carvel, a resourceful man, parked the truck, plugged his refrigerator into the electrical outlet of a nearby pottery shop, and started serving ice cream cones.

Carvel continued to show his resourcefulness throughout his career. He was a master at economizing on his investments. After he developed his decorative Fudgy the Whale ice cream cake mold (appropriate for what holiday?), he discovered that he could flip it sideways and use the mold to form a Santa Claus cake—Fudgy's fins resembled Santa's cap—or a leprechaun for Saint Patrick's Day.

With his broken-down truck and borrowed electricity, Carvel was the prototypical sole proprietor. He was responsible for his debts and entitled to any profits. From a legal perspective, he was liable for any damage he did. If his blown-out tire had flown off and smacked, say, chicken maven Frank Purdue in the beak, Tom Carvel would have been personally responsible.

Let's imagine that the pottery store owner next door decided to join forces with Carvel. They could shake hands and form a *partnership*. As partners, they would share profits, losses, and legal liability. Now if Tom Carvel's tire were to smack Frank Perdue in the beak, Carvel's partner would be just as liable for the damages as Carvel himself. Likewise, if Tom Carvel died or went bankrupt, his pottery partner would be personally responsible for all of the partnership's debts. Since partners put their own wealth on the line, they should trust each other. Most law firms and medical practices are partnerships. Thus, if one cosmetic surgeon in a medical partnership messes up a nose job, every other partner's nose will be out of joint, for their personal assets are in jeopardy if the rhinoplastered patient files a lawsuit.

The partnership arrangement makes many businesspeople nervous—who wants to lose his home in a courtroom battle, just because of some teenager's bulging shnoz? Further, a partnership is a very specific organization. If another person joins up, or if a partner dies or wants to get out, a whole new partnership must be set up. Partnerships are legendary for squabbling. I once worked at a partnership where management meetings were so annoying that the administrator had to bribe partners into attending. In this case, a fifty-dollar bill was placed in front of each chair at the table.

A classic story about partnership ethics concerns a shopkeeper whose customer accidentally leaves a $20 bill near the cash register and then walks out of the store. The shopkeeper explains the dilemma to his stockboy. "Now, boy, the ethical issue is this: Do I tell my partner?"

Another way of organizing a business is to form a *corporation,* giving the owners of the firm two key advantages: they limit their liability for losses or from lawsuits, and they make it easier to raise money in order to build up the business. While partners and sole proprietors generally rely on their own money or funds borrowed from friends and banks, corporations can sell shares, thus opening the business to a wider range of financing opportunities.

How Can a Corporation Limit Liability for Owners?

According to the law, a corporation is an organism. It is a legal entity that lives separately from its owners. It is born, it grows, it can be adopted (a takeover), it can get married (a merger), and it can die (bankruptcy). Even better than human beings, it can come back to life (rehabilitation from bankruptcy). An airline named Braniff came back to life three times to haunt passengers with lost luggage.

Since the corporation has a life of its own, it also has its own assets and liabilities. The shareholders, the owners of a corporation, are liable only up to the amount of money they contribute to the firm, basically equal to their shares of stock. In contrast, partners are legally liable for all debts and unpaid bills of the partnership. Because investors in a corporation do not risk their personal assets if the firm goes belly-up, the corporate system encourages people to invest.

Countries around the world limit the liability of investors and signal this special favor with certain abbreviations and designations. In Great Britain and Canada, corporate names may be followed by *Ltd.,* meaning "limited," or *PLC,* meaning "public limited company." French- and Spanish-speaking countries place the abbreviation *SA* after the corporate name, which translates to "anonymous society," to suggest that the shareholders cannot be tracked down for personal liability purposes.

What Is the Difference Between a Public Company and a Closely Held Corporation?

Once upon a time, the American corporate dream, like Henry Ford's, started as a sole proprietorship, grew into a partnership, filed with the state to become a corporation, and then sold shares to the general public. Floating shares on the stock exchange, called an *initial public offering* (IPO), marked true success for an entrepreneur and often brought riches. In November 1993, a company called Boston Chicken completed an IPO, where in one day the price of the newly issued stock jumped from $20 per share at the opening bell to $48 at the close of trading.

By offering shares in Boston Chicken on the public stock exchange, the owners "took their company public." The key difference, then, between a public and a closely held corporation is that shares of a public corporation are widely held, while shares in a closely held corporation are concentrated in the hands of a few owners. Typically, the owners of a closely held corporation actively participate in running the company and have agreements not to transfer their share to anyone else. Family-owned firms frequently are closely held. They want to avoid outsiders butting in on their decision making—they have enough trouble controlling old Aunt Bertha, who inherited some shares.

While "going public" used to seem the peak of entrepreneurial success, the snobbery of public ownership has worn off. Many leading companies have rejected the option of issuing shares to the public. Compare Boston Chicken to Mars, maker of the candy bars. The Mars family lives in seclusion in Virginia, sits on a fortune, and wields complete control over every ounce of chocolate. Mr. Mars does not have to attend public meetings and fight off angry shareholders who think he has been chintzy with the almonds in his M&M's. By contrast, the Boston Chicken clan, by selling shares to the public, must now confront shareholder "owners" who will, no doubt, complain about flabby thighs and scrawny wings.

If going public invites such headaches, why bother? The answer brings to mind the Vaudeville joke about the guy who goes to a psychiatrist because his brother thinks he's a chicken. "Tell him he's not a chicken," the shrink advises. "I can't," says the brother. "We need the eggs." Well, closely held companies often need the money available on the public stock exchanges. Firms can take the money they raise on Wall Street and use it to expand factories, open marketing offices abroad, or bring on more staff.

Sometimes public corporations will do an about-face and "go private." During the 1980s, the phrases *leveraged buyout* and *management buyout* echoed all over Wall Street. These terms usually refer to a public company whose shares were bought up by a small group. Firms like RJR Nabisco, Duracell, and Safeway moved from being public corporations to being closely held firms. In some cases, after spending a few years in the closely held category, the owners issued public stock and moved back again into the publicly held realm. During the private period, the owners would try to slash excess costs and revamp the company so that the stock market would applaud its reentry into public trading.

How Do Firms Pay for Their Growth and Expansion?

Tom Carvel got his start with $15 and a truck. That $15 must have run out pretty soon, even in the 1930s. How do businesses pay for new trucks, new ice cream freezers, and those new uniforms that make high school soda jerks feel silly? As we pointed out, many new firms take in partners to share the costs and the potential profits. But even if an entrepreneur finds partners with similar business philosophies, the cost of new equipment might be beyond their shared wealth. Even the wealthiest moguls do not rely solely on their own assets to fund their companies.

Here are the most popular ways for entrepreneurs to finance their expansions:

> *Internally Generated Funds.* A thrifty business can save up its profits and reinvest them in the company.
>
> *Bank Lines of Credit.* A firm may sign a deal with a bank that establishes a maximum amount the firm can borrow as needed. The firm pays interest only on the money it actually borrows, and it borrows the money simply by writing checks. Businesses usually use lines of credit to pay for day-to-day costs, rather than new projects.
>
> *Venture Capital Funds. Venture capital* is investment money pooled together and poured into firms with the potential for rapid, explosive growth. The investors who put up venture capital know that the risks are high and that most new companies last as long as an ice cube in the sun. Still, they reckon that they

might get in on the ground floor of a high flyer, which could deliver a return on their investments many times the market average. We have all squirmed with envy while some uncle or neighbor bragged about buying stock in Microsoft or Apple back when the founders were tinkering in their garages. A venture capital fund usually lends money but also demands the right to buy a big slice of the firm. While the term *venture capitalist* used to conjure up images of swashbuckling affluent individuals, more and more venture capital is put up by pension funds and insurance companies. Even small-time investors can place their money in venture capital funds traded on Wall Street.

Private Placements of Debt. Though banks lend huge sums to firms, banks are not the only source of lending. Institutional investors like insurance companies and pension funds now control billions of dollars. The managers are constantly seeking a good return on their investments, sometimes in stocks, sometimes in real estate, sometimes in commodities like pork bellies. For protection just in case the business flops, the investor secures a *lien* on the firm's equipment or real estate, which allows the investor to seize that property. Before the investor hands over the money, it usually ties the hands of the borrower so that it cannot borrow more money or further jeopardize its financial soundness. Private placements can cover the costs of everything from paying off old debt to paying for a new factory. A number of years ago, I worked on a private placement to fund a new plant that would make wrappers for wieners. This wienie wrapper deal saved the manufacturer from borrowing at higher rates from a bank.

Public Offering of Bonds. As we will discuss later in more depth, bonds are IOUs that pay a specific rate of interest. Like stocks, they are traded daily in New York and in other financial centers.

Public Offering of Stock. To sell stock to the general public, a firm must disclose all important details of its finances and business practices to the public through the federal government's Securities and Exchange Commission. Since the costs of complying with the federal regulations are so great, an "unseasoned" firm (one that has not gone public yet) will generally not try it unless it seeks to raise at least ten million dollars. If a firm decides to go all the way and issue stock to the general public, the drama begins, for no one knows whether the public will embrace the stock and pay as high a price as the original owners want. They may end up with a fabulously successful Boston Chicken, or a sad case like Donna Karan, a women's clothing firm that had to withdraw its public offering just days before the November 1993 sale, when the company realized that Wall Street was about to laugh at the requested price.

What Is Equity?

Although we have discussed selling stock, we have not explained what the stock buyer gets out of the deal. What does it mean to "own" a company? Does owning "a piece of the Rock" mean that you can walk into Prudential headquarters and pick up a stapler, or even better, an insurance policy for yourself? Of course not. *Equity* is the business school term used interchangeably with *ownership.* But there are many kinds of equity. You have probably heard of common stock, but what about *preferred shares* or *convertible shares*?

Why do we have different kinds of equity? Each represents a different degree of ownership. Though owning shares in a company means that you are entitled to some profits, you may not be first in line when the money starts rolling in. The usual pecking order provides that lenders (bank and private placement lenders) get the first crack at the bucks. In fact, most private placement agreements forbid the firm from paying anything to stockholders, until it has paid its regular installment to the lender.

Before common stockholders get a dime, "preferred" stockholders must get their piece of the action. Preferred stock usually pays owners a fixed return, almost like a bond. Common stockholders do not get their share of the profits (dividends), until after the preferred holders receive their fixed payment. If there are not enough profits to go around, the common shareholders go home empty-handed. Further, if the firm goes belly-up, and the owners end up holding a going-out-of-business sale to liquidate their inventory, the preferred shareholders get to cut in front of the common stockholders, who are standing in line hoping to get some money to compensate them for worthless stock.

So far, common stock may not sound like a great deal. Everyone seems to stand in front of you; meanwhile, you take the risk that your shares will be as worthless as a condom concession at the Vatican. So is common stock for suckers? No, not unless you consider billionaire investor Warren Buffet a sucker. Common stockholders take more risks than preferred stockholders or lenders, but they have the chance for much bigger returns. The market works to compensate stockholders for the chances they take. While the common stockholder will usually receive a big chunk of the winnings when a firm hits the big time, the preferred stockholder generally get their cut, either in the form of dividends or in the form of somewhat higher share prices. One dollar invested in a typical common stock in 1802 would be worth over $100,000 today, after adjusting for inflation. If invested instead in bonds or preferred stock, that same dollar would be worth less than $1,000.

Common stockholders also enjoy the advantage of voting

rights, meaning that they elect the firm's directors. Finally, the common stockholders may occasionally get extra bonuses; for instance, Disney gives its shareholders discounts on visits to Disneyland.

For those who want a hybrid that combines some features of common and some features of preferred shares, there is the *convertible preferred share.* The owner of a convertible preferred stock can convert it into a common share at some specified price. The investor basically trades in his preferred shares, which are torn up, and receives instead the common shares.

What Are Corporate Bonds?

When you buy stock in a company, you are volunteering to ride the roller coaster of risk and rewards. Sure, you can jump off if the ride gets too bumpy, but you may lose all or some of your money by giving up on the stock. Not everyone is prepared for such trauma, even though studies show that stocks outperform other investments, *in the long run.* Corporations can raise money, even from risk-averse investors, by selling bonds. In fact, bonds make up a bigger part of the average investor's portfolio than stocks.

A bond is merely a promise to pay a specific amount of money at a certain time in the future. That is why bonds are often referred to as "fixed-income securities." The word *bond* comes from the same root as *bind,* for the corporation binds itself to make the specified payments. On the appropriate dates, the bondholder receives from the corporation the original amount borrowed, known as the *principal,* as well as interest, the bondholder's reward for lending to the firm.

So far, this probably sounds almost too simple. What is the catch? It's that even though bonds pay set amounts of money on specific dates (the *coupon payment*), the value of a bond can fluctuate from day to day. "Hey, didn't you say that they were fixed-income assets? How can something that is fixed move every day?" Let me count the ways.

First, even though the payment schedule for a particular bond is fixed—let us say that a $1,000 bond pays $100 interest per year for ten years—other bonds may pay a different return. To judge the value of the bond, you must compare it with competing bonds in the marketplace. If other $1,000 bonds pay, say, $200 each year, the $100-a-year bond is not such a good deal. The point is that if market interest rates go up, the value of bonds goes down. If interest rates fall, the value of bonds goes up.

How does the value actually go up or down? Bond traders will not be willing to pay full price for a bond that has a low interest rate. They will push down the traded price of that bond until it becomes competitive. Imagine that right after the firm sells the $1,000 bond, interest rates double from 10 percent to 20 percent. Since the $1,000 bond pays only $100 each year, while other bonds pay $200, traders will be willing to pay only $500 for that bond. By paying just $500 for the bond, they have effectively changed the yield from 10 percent to the competitive market level of 20 percent. Again, the bondholder still gets the same fixed $100 per year, but she receives it after paying just $500 for the bond itself.

Second, bonds, despite their fixed income status, lose value if inflation is expected to rise. Since its future payments will be worth less, the bond is worth less now. Bond buyers will demand higher interest payments to offset the fear of rising inflation. Whenever the government releases a particularly bad inflation report, the bond market takes a dip. Likewise, a good inflation report usually lifts the bond market. Some countries, for instance Israel, "index" their bonds for inflation, so that the coupon payment climbs by the same margin as overall prices. By doing this, the government keeps the bond market from swinging widely with every inflation report.

Third, bondholders must worry about whether the corporation will pay them back. Bondholders dread the word *default*.

Obviously, some firms compete in riskier industries than others. In fact, some firms do not even compete—they may borrow money through bonds even before they are ready to sell their product in the marketplace, but the bond helps to raise the money needed to get started. Bonds issued by riskier firms will pay a higher return than bonds issued by safe, stable firms.

Who Determines How Risky a Bond Is?

Can you imagine poring through all the financial papers of a company before buying its bonds, assessing its expected profits, market share, labor costs, lawsuits, as well as the amount of money the firm already owes to others? You probably cannot. Good news, then, that the independent rating companies like Moody's and Standard & Poor's (S&P) examine firms that issue bonds and make judgments based on such factors. Like stern teachers, they give out grades ranging from AAA (meaning you can sleep soundly) to DDD (meaning, "Run like hell!"). *Junk bonds,* known to bond salesmen as "high-yield securities," receive grades of Ba3 or lower from Standard & Poor's. Despite the disparaging name, over 95 percent of U.S. firms issue bonds that fall into the "junk" category. If a firm's business becomes less risky, its bonds can receive a rating upgrade. By stepping up a grade, the bond will be more valuable in the market.

When a borrower starts missing interest payments, the rating firms will slap it with a C, or even lower. Bankruptcy usually brings a D.

Naturally, firms worry that their bonds will be downgraded, and they hope that their bonds will qualify for an upgrade. Because riskier firms must pay higher rates to borrow, each letter in the grading system can cost a firm millions of dollars. Like a student afraid of a bad grade, firms will meet with rating agency auditors and vigorously argue that they can easily pay off their debts. Several years ago, casino king Donald Trump almost lost his fiefdom when the ratings companies downgraded his bonds. Nervous creditors threatened to take back the huge stone lions that Trump had purchased for the beachfront entrance of his Taj Mahal casino in Atlantic City. Ultimately, Trump regained his financial standing, saw his bonds upgraded, and was able to keep his tacky lions. To this day, tourists from India actually visit the casino and snap photographs of themselves in front of the Taj Mahal sign.

The grading process is certainly not perfect. Auditors sometimes miss big potential problems that blow up in the face of bondholders. Perhaps the most famous blowup hit holders of the A-rated Washington Public Power Supply System bonds in 1983. The utility defaulted on over $2 billion in borrowing, used to pay for nuclear power plants. Though a blowup in bonds is certainly preferable to a blowup in nuclear plants, the holders were badly burned and Wall Street wags nicknamed the bonds "WHOOPS bonds," based loosely on an acronym for Washington Power.

Sometimes the bond rating firms are "behind the curve" and adjust their ratings after the millions of players in the global securities market have already concluded that a borrower's creditworthiness has climbed or slid back. Investors should be very suspicious, then, of a high grade from Moody's or S&P, if the price of the bonds has started sinking. Remember, when the debt goes whoops! Moody's does not lose any money. It's the sucker holding the fancy piece of paper covered in flowery penmanship who takes the hit.

What Is an Asset-Backed Security?

The 1980s brought numerous innovations, from low-tech wonders like the kitchen gadget called the Salad Shooter to high-tech goods like desktop computers that packed the same power as ten-year-old computers the size of mobile homes. Wall

Street also developed its own new products, among them asset-backed securities, which allow firms to issue bonds that are backed by what other people (or firms) owe them!

This is best understood by example. Let's take Sears, which loans consumers money by letting them charge their shopping goods on the Sears Discover card. Sears fully expects those consumers to pay them back. Based on its long experience in retailing and lending, Sears has a good idea when those funds will show up in the mail. Sears can, therefore, issue bonds on which they pledge to pay interest to the bondholder based on their customers paying back the department store. In recent years, Sears has sold billions of asset-backed securities. What is the asset? The money that customers owe Sears.

Once Wall Street figured out how to package such securities, imaginations went wild. If credit card receivables can back securities, why not loans for autos, or for boats? Like Sears, General Motors Acceptance Corporation (GMAC) has "securitized" billions of dollars' worth of loans, in this case for cars. The market has judged such securities as pretty safe. How do we know the market feels this way? Because credit card–backed and auto loan–backed bonds pay only about half a point to a point more than extremely safe U.S. Treasury bills. By wrapping these credit card payments and auto loan payments together as securities, then, Sears and GMAC have discovered a low-cost way of raising money for new investment.

Does It Matter Whether the Corporation Finances Itself Through Bonds or Equity?

This question is the great white whale of graduate school finance courses. We could spend a few hundred pages on the topic, for financial economists have spent decades debating the point, ever since a seminal 1958 paper by Nobel laureates

Franco Modigliani and Merton Miller.[2] Instead, we will harpoon it fast. Modigliani and Miller, also known as M&M, showed that *a firm is worth the same amount regardless of whether it is financed largely by stock or by debt.* In other words, a rose is a rose, or as Mr. Ed said, "A horse is a horse, of course, of course."

Prior to M&M's brilliant paper, textbooks assumed that firms could lift their value by borrowing, since more borrowing allowed owners to control more potential profits without putting up more money of their own. But M&M argued that if a firm started borrowing a lot, it would look riskier and therefore have to pay higher interest rates on the money it borrowed. The higher rate would offset the benefit of leverage (borrowing). The upshot: a firm's value depends on its productivity and cash flow. How the inputs are paid for does not ultimately matter.

So why all the fuss? And why do firms debate whether they are correctly leveraged? Well, M&M missed a few real-world points in their original theoretical argument. Most important, they ignored Uncle Sam. Big mistake. Since Uncle Sam lets firms deduct interest payments to bondholders, he tilts the field toward bonds. On the other hand, Uncle Sam forces individual bondholders to pay taxes when they receive interest payments on a bond, yet he does not force them to pay taxes when a stock's price goes up (investors pay capital gains taxes only after they actually sell the appreciated stock). This deferral could tilt the field the other way.

After considering all the factors, we can only say that it does matter whether a firm uses debt or equity. Yet we cannot say which is better without looking at the specific company, its profitability, riskiness, and the tax status of its shareholders and bondholders. Just looking around the corporate world, you can see that firms in stable, lower-risk industries like utilities tend to depend more on debt, while the young turks in high-growth areas like technology tend to rely on selling stock to fund their futures. That is because utilities—at least, those that are still insulated from competition—enjoy a fairly dependable stream of earnings that they can turn over to bondholders, while new high-tech firms can sell only their dreams of future earnings.

Now that we've seen how a company raises cash for its business endeavors, we can look at the individual investor and discuss why he might be willing to buy the stock offered by the firm.

Can Investors Beat the Stock Market?

Sure, once in a while. But can they beat it consistently? This is the old *efficient-market hypothesis (EMH),* which takes up all the time in graduate finance courses that is not spent on M&M. In short, the EMH says that the stock market moves so lightning fast that all public information is instantaneously reflected in share prices. Therefore, an ignorant person, or even a chimp, will do just as well playing the market as will a studious professional. The chimp does not have to research a firm's prospects, since, for example, expectations about a good sales period will already have sent the price up. If you read in today's newspaper that Boston Chicken has found a new way to cut off beaks that will save millions in butcher bills, forget it. You are too late, because the share price has already moved up.

Even if the profit-making event is months away, you can be too late. Suppose at a New Year's Eve party you cleverly point out to a friend that millions of college students will invade Daytona Beach, Florida, during spring break. You then describe a certain hotel chain whose rooms overflow with eight frat boys or sorority sisters to a unit during spring break. Is this a good stock tip that should send your friend scurrying to the telephone to wake up his broker? After all, he would be buying the hotel's stock three months before the college kids invade.

No way. The stock price already reflects the expected profits that come rolling in when the college kids invade. Even the tenants at Florida's Monkey Jungle theme park know that spring break is a boom time for Daytona hotels. And prices are based on expected future profits and dividends, not just today's financial data.

If the EMH is right, you cannot beat the average return on stocks by religiously studying companies, perusing financial reports, or tracing past price movements. The market already efficiently estimates the future returns. According to the EMH, there is no such thing as an "overvalued" or "undervalued" stock unless just about everyone misunderstands the characteristics of the company, or there is important undisclosed information. The next time a broker tells you he has discovered an "undervalued" firm, ask him what he knows that the rest of the world does not. Using the EMH, the market price, then, becomes an infallible icon, until new information justifies a new price.

You would probably do just as well choosing a stock by throwing a stockbroker at a dartboard as listening to his advice—and you would save money. In fact, since 1990 *The Wall Street Journal* has conducted a test of the EMH by comparing the investment record of professional stock pickers to the performance of their "dartboard portfolio," chosen by tossing darts at their pages listing the New York Stock Exchange companies. This kind of test can be very embarrassing for high-paid professionals, whose fancy services could be replaced with chimps or dartboards. At first glance, the pros look pretty good, having won twenty-four of forty-one contests, as of November 1993.[3] (Of course, if you subtract their fees, the returns are less impressive.) But a closer look shows two flaws in the pros' winning performance. First, the pros are picking riskier, more volatile stocks than the darts. Since the market compensates risk with higher returns, the pros give themselves an edge that many investors would not want: after all, volatility means that stocks will swing lower as well as higher.

Second, the pros benefit from the strong "announcement effect" that sends stocks surging when the pros publicly tout their favorite contenders in newsletters and magazines. Likewise, stocks recommended on television programs like CNN's *Moneyline* will boost stock shares. Stocks chosen by darts or chimps do not have the same following among television viewers.

Despite truckloads of academic studies testing the EMH,[4] brokers and their publicists continue to rave about their predictions. Sunday newspapers bulge with advertisements from self-proclaimed geniuses and stock-picking swamis. Some of the claims look like leftover press releases for promoters who claimed to be able to discover underground springs using divining rods. Today's divining rod is a personal computer and a secret algorithm that no one else has.

Lots of people win in the stock market. In fact, most win. Investors in the market, whether on the advice of darts, chimps, or pros, have averaged about 12 percent per year since World War II. The test for the EMH is whether people can consistently outdo that average. Sure, some may enjoy lucky streaks, just as Atlantic City bettors sometimes beat the odds and beat the pants off Donald Trump. Even when some superstar analyst discovers a winning way to interpret data, others follow, and the method becomes obsolete. So why pay extra money in commissions for financial advice to get only an average return? You might as well build a well-diversified portfolio that balances various risks, or invest in a broad market index that moves with the market average. We will discuss personal investing further in the next chapter.

Are There Exceptions to the Efficient-Market Hypothesis?

Sure. First of all, the EMH does not hold if someone has *inside information,* the secret knowledge of future profits or losses that high company officials may have. In a famous insider trading case from the 1960s, Charles Fogarty bought up shares in Texas Gulf Sulphur. An executive vice president, Fogarty knew that his company had discovered a valuable mineral lode that it had not yet announced to the public. Easy money in the stock market—and an easy conviction in the courtroom. Fogarty went to the pokey because Congress and the Securities and Exchange Commission (SEC) have decided that the poor slob without a seat on the board of directors should have a fair shot at getting rich in the stock market. The SEC provides for stiff penalties, including prison and the "disgorging" of illegal profits, if an insider gets caught. Of course, not everyone gets caught, nor do the laws cover everyone with inside information. Should they?

Suppose Superman, Inc., surreptitiously schemes to take over the Spiderman Corporation by buying up its stock. Superman executives think they can run Spiderman more efficiently, thus boosting the value of Spiderman's assets. For this reason, Superman is willing to pay more than the current price to get Spiderman stock. The takeover plan is a secret that only insiders or superheroes with X-ray vision can figure out. In fact, only the presidents and vice presidents of Superman (along with their attorneys) know.

Naturally, if these executives personally buy up stock before they publicize the takeover attempt, they can be indicted for insider trading. But what if the employee of a printing press that prints the forthcoming publicity documents buys Superman stock before the public announcement? Should he be considered an insider and punished? According to a real Supreme Court case, no. In the 1970s, printer Vincent Chiarella, who netted about $30,000 for his deed, was acquitted by the Supreme Court.

Ironically, when Chiarella was asked whether Ivan Boesky, who was convicted of insider trading a few years later, should be punished, he said, "Throw the book at him."[5]

Since insiders can beat the average market performance, most proponents of the EMH leave them out of the picture. They do stick to their contention that Joe Six-pack cannot outpick the market average. But consider the following ironic hitch in the hypothesis: Stock picking is ineffective *precisely because so many people engage in research and stock analysis.* The current prices "correctly" reflect expectations *because* so many people buy and sell on the basis of available information. You have little chance of consistently interpreting information in a superior way. However, if no one but you researched, you could outpredict a random approach. Therefore, the advice of the efficient-market believers to select randomly becomes itself obsolete if everyone takes the advice!

Efficient-market believers could strike it rich if they could persuade people to give up. Is this their ulterior motive? I doubt it. Most economists are not that ambitious. Sure, they like to talk about money. But they are like the piano player at a bordello, always playing around the action, but never getting very close.

While firms look to the stock and bond markets to pay for their business expansions, individuals look to the market to pay for retirement costs, among other expenses. The choices for individuals are just as great and confusing as the choices for businesses. In the next chapter, I'll try to clear things up.

8 Taking Stock of Personal Investments

- *What Do Most People Invest In?* • *What's the First Question to Ask When Considering an Investment?* • *What Kinds of Risks Must Investors Worry About?* • *What Are the Safest Investments? the Riskiest?* • *What Is a Mutual Fund?* • *How Can You Compare the Riskiness of Stocks?* • *What Does the P/E Ratio Measure?* • *How Can You Reduce the Risks of Investing?* • *What Makes Stocks Go Up or Down?* • *How Do You Read the Stock Tables in the Newspaper?* • *What Is the Difference Between the New York Stock Exchange, the American Stock Exchange, and the NASDAQ?* • *How Can Investors Bet on Foreign Companies?* • *What Are the Added Risks of International Investing?* • *What Are Futures and Options?*

Now that you've read this far and presumably achieved economic literacy, we can try to put this knowledge to work on behalf of your own personal finances, not the nation's macroeconomic goals.

"How do you get a million dollars in the stock market?" the comedian asks. "Start with two million." Like any other pursuit, whether shooting basketballs, playing the oboe, or going shopping, people have varying experiences and levels of success playing the financial markets. Somehow, though, we hear more about the extremes: the woman who stumbles onto a "flyer" and earns a fortune; the man who jumps out a window when his stocks collapse.

Economists call these people "tails." It has nothing to do

with their bodies but simply means that they represent only a tiny portion of the population. The fact is, stock results look like any other bell curve: just as most people earn Bs and Cs in school, assuming grade inflation is under control, most people get unremarkable returns from their personal investments. If there is any validity at all to the efficient-market hypothesis discussed in the prior chapter, your goal in life should not be some near impossible quest to become the tail end of the investment community. Let the Donald Trumps of the world have that glory.

You do not have to set the world afire to make money in the stock market or the bond market. What should you look for? A competitive return. What's that? Enough so that your nest egg grows significantly faster than inflation, without your taking the sort of risks that keep you from sleeping at night or frighten you away from opening up the business pages in the morning to see how your investments have done.

What Do Most People Invest In?

Over 60 percent of American families have invested in their homes. These residential investments make up about one third of their wealth. Only about 20 percent of Americans directly own individual stocks (rather than through pension funds, for example), while 11 percent had mutual funds, and about 8 percent own bonds. Though banks have lost some influence to mutual funds and other financial institutions, about 60 percent of American households still have savings accounts, and 20 percent have certificates of deposit.[1]

How did Americans decide where to put their money? They may have depended on savvy brothers-in-law, or smarmy stockbrokers, or advice columns like "Dear Abby," or business news networks on television. Most people feel that they're deluged by investment information. Trying to sort out all the options is like trying to drink from a fire hydrant. In both cases you can lose your shirt.

And the options keep growing. Just in the past few years, Americans have been pouring money into mutual funds that invest in countries they know nothing about. Studies show that most Americans cannot even find Kansas on a map of the United States, and yet families have poured billions of their investment dollars into places like Singapore and Hong Kong. Why have they done this? They hear that there is a bull market to ride, and they do not care which direction the bull is headed. Investors searching for high returns have also plopped their money on gambles called gold funds, precious metals funds, commodity swaps, and zero coupon bonds.

What's the First Question to Ask When Considering an Investment?

Who am I? This may sound like a question found on a freshman philosophy exam, but Socrates was not just running off at the mouth when he told his students, "Know thyself." You would be foolish to buy a cow if you lived in a studio apartment in New York City. You would be equally foolish to sink your investment funds in a piece of real estate if you needed constant access to your money. Just as a cow owner needs space—and good ventilation—a real estate investor needs time, for houses cannot be bought or sold overnight. Economists call this the issue of *liquidity*.

The first place an investor should look, then, is in the mirror. Do you see wrinkles? Maybe you are heading toward retirement and therefore need investments that can provide you with a steady income. Do you see the gleaming eyes of a young parent, who needs to save an impossibly large sum for her daughter's college education? Then maybe you need an "aggressive" stock portfolio that pays no dividends for a while but builds up value.

After looking in the mirror and figuring out what you see, you should ask several more questions before considering an investment. First, *What is the trade-off between risk and return?* This is the crux of economic life, and it shows up in countless clichés, song lyrics, and book titles, from "There's no such thing as a free lunch," to "Sometimes you have to crack a few eggs to make an omelet."

President Kennedy said, "Life is not fair." Nor is it perfectly safe. The free-market system is not a risk-free system. Happily, though, most investments offer a trade-off between risk and return. Riskier stocks will usually pay higher returns, while super-safe stocks will generally pay low returns. It is hard to get rich by buying stable investments. Of course, it is hard to get poor that way as well. Think of a baseball game, where the coach has a choice between a home run hitter who strikes out a lot, and a scrappy hitter who often gets on base but seldom hits it out of the park. Whom should the coach choose? Depends, of course, on the state of play. Does he need a home run so bad that he should risk the high probability of a strikeout? Can he afford an infield grounder from the scrappy player, which could lead to a double play? Most coaches would consider themselves lucky to have such a choice.

The market provides plenty of opportunities, and trade-offs. A glimpse at financial history should make the point. Compare the annual return of U.S. stocks to U.S. bonds over the last sixty-five years. U.S. Treasury bonds are backed by the federal government, which despite its checkered reputation for balancing budgets, is an extremely safe bet. Stocks, though, swing much wider from day to day and year to year. After all, they are backed by corporations that sometimes hit home runs and sometimes strike out. Suppose the Ruth family puts all its money into the stock market, while the Berras depend on long-term U.S. bonds. Who does better? Sure enough, over time, stocks pay a higher return, to compensate for the higher risk. The Ruths average a one-percent yearly return, while the Berras have earned a yearly return of less than 4.5 percent. The Berras did not get gypped by the market, though. In fact, they had fewer reasons to bite their nails over the course of the century. The Berras did not, for example, have to suffer through a 43-percent drop in 1931. Their worst year was 1967, when the return on U.S. bonds fell about 9 percent.

What if they had invested in a baseball team, instead? That would have been even riskier. The original owner of the New York Mets, a very wealthy woman named Joan Payson, was traveling in Europe during the team's record-breaking 1962 season. What record did they break? Most losses in a season, when they threw away 120 games. Each day the Mets office in New York would wire the score to Payson's hotel room in Europe. Finally she sent back a note asking them to save her some money by only wiring her when they won!

What Kinds of Risks Must Investors Worry About?

Not getting paid back comes to mind first. Companies that issue stocks and bonds can go bankrupt. They may find no buyers for the hamburgers they plan to sell. They might drill for oil and come up dry. Every business has its own inherent risks, no matter how good the managers are. And every investment bet can be ravaged by acts of God, or in the case of OPEC embargoes, acts of sheiks. Tokyo banks continue to fear a massive earthquake that would wipe out the value of the real estate assets underpinning the Japanese stock market. Putting deities and demigods aside, investors must also worry about *interest-rate risk*. If interest rates shoot up, stocks and bonds usually fall in price. Why? Remember, a bond pays some regular, fixed sum. If interest rates climb, new bonds will be paying a higher rate.

That makes old bonds less valuable. A similar process makes stocks seem less valuable. After all, the regular dividend that a stock is expected to pay seems smaller if new bonds are paying higher returns.

Inflation, which depletes the value of stocks and bonds, also keeps investors on their toes. During the 1970s, inflation roared ahead, with overall prices doubling, while the New York Stock Exchange went nowhere. Not only was it a bear market (meaning lousy returns on investment), the bear was in hibernation. At the end of the decade, stock prices were no higher than when the decade began. Bondholders frowned as well. Individuals who during the 1960s bought long-term bonds that promised to pay 3 to 4 percent annual interest realized what a miserable deal they got roped into when consumer prices galloped into double digits.

Individuals were not the only suckers in this depressing game. Savings and loan institutions (S&Ls) had issued thirty-year mortgages in the 1960s at 6 percent, yet by the late 1970s they had to pay savers almost 20 percent to keep their money in the bank. This financial debacle, along with corruption, ultimately led to the half-trillion-dollar government bailout of S&Ls in the 1980s.

The risk of inflation teaches us another lesson: *Do not play it too safe.* As medical researchers discover synthetic fountains of youth, stretching the human life expectancy to near Methusalean range, retirees must worry about outliving their savings. A favorite sport of Florida's senior citizens is searching for early bird specials at restaurants. If these seniors placed their money on only the safest bets—for example, U.S. bonds or bank CDs—they could come up short when they have to pay the cashier. The historic trade-off between risk and reward shows that investing only in U.S. bonds would leave investors a return of only about 1.5 percent annually after inflation. And that meager return is, of course, before Uncle Sam snatches his share through taxes.

The lesson here is contrary to conventional wisdom: *Only the*

rich can afford to invest largely in risk-free assets like bonds.
They can afford not to keep up with inflation. Less wealthy people must take risks, or else the thief inflation and the greedy IRS
commissioner will leave them with little but spare change in
their purses.

What Are the Safest Investments?
the Riskiest?

Before I answer these questions, remember, the "safest" investments run the risk of providing too low a return. But they
are safe in the sense that they do not act too capriciously. They
are, economists say, less volatile. "Safe" or "low-risk" investments often benefit from the U.S. government's pledge to guarantee at least the principal, if not the interest. They include bank
savings accounts and CDs (certificates of deposit, which pay savers a fixed interest rate for a fixed period of time) insured by the
federal government up to $100,000, as well as U.S. Treasury
bonds, notes, and bills.

The key difference among these U.S. Treasury investments is
the duration, or *maturity*. *T-bonds* are the thirty-year variety,
T-notes the second- and ten-year type, and *T-bills* the kind that
mature in three, six, or twelve months. Naturally, the longer-
term bonds are somewhat riskier, since over the course of thirty
years a lot of things can happen. Interest rates and inflation
can jump around much more, governments can rise and fall,
and so on.

Longer-term instruments usually pay a higher interest rate to
make up for this risk. When economists refer to the *yield curve,*
they are referring to a graph that compares the interest rate paid
by longer-term bonds to the rate paid by shorter-term bills. Generally, this curve slopes upward, reflecting the added long-term

risk. On June 3, 1994, to pick a day, the thirty-year T-bond paid 7.27 percent, while the three-month T-bill paid just 4.12 percent.

Occasionally some corporations feel so confident about their longevity that they try to sell super-long-term bonds. In the summer of 1993, for example, Disney successfully auctioned hundred-year bonds. Clearly, enough investors think that Donald Duck will quack on into the twenty-second century! These bonds paid a 7.50-percent interest rate, just one point higher than the safer thirty-year U.S. Treasury bonds yielded at that time. This reflects Donald and Mickey's stability, and a great deal of confidence in Mickey's corporate managers of the future. Certainly Disney's current management team is known for their tight grip and no-nonsense approach. Can the firm extend a winning streak for a hundred years, without losing its high credit rating? No one knows. I would be skeptical, though. After all, just fifteen years ago, most analysts thought Disney was a tired, wheezing firm. It could happen again, and Disney bonds could look riskier and their value could slip.

In fact, shortly after Disney began selling those 100-year bonds, market interest rates shot up, leaving buyers of the 7.50-percent bonds feeling rather like Goofy.

Because corporate bonds are not backed by the federal government, they fall into the *limited* risk category, along with blue-chip stocks and high-rated municipal bonds (remember the discussion of bond ratings in chapter 7). *Blue chip* refers to firms with long track records for turning profits and paying dividends. Of course, the track could turn bumpy, but firms with household names like GM and K mart receive so much attention, investors can usually expect that there'll be plenty of notice before they skid into a crash.

In contrast to solid blue-chip stocks, *growth* companies are moderately risky. Growth companies have not reached the regal blue-chip stage and are trying to expand their business by reinvesting most of their profits. Thus, they do not usually pay dividends. Investing in growth stocks makes a lot of sense for people who do not need regular payments but would like to take a little more risk in exchange for the promise of substantial profits in the future.

Rental real estate usually falls into the moderately risky category. Of course, you must consider the particular property in question. As real estate lore says, the three best guides to real estate investment are "location, location, location." Even during the real estate depression of the early 1990s, rental prices in Washington, D.C., held firm, since the federal government kept hiring more and more bureaucrats. But the regional issue does not alone answer the question. What is the location and condition of the particular rental unit? Buying a rickety old rental house with a flooded basement sunk into mushy clay would be highly risky and stupid, even in an otherwise booming market.

The riskiest investments include junk bonds (discussed in chapter 7) and speculative stocks, as well as commodities, futures, and options (to be discussed later). While growth stocks are shares in companies that have successfully cracked open a market niche, *speculative* firms have not yet broken through. Their futures may depend on a new invention, patent, or on government approval of a drug, for example. The thumbs-up of the Federal Drug Administration (FDA) can turn a speculative stock into a growth stock within seconds. That is why dull, technical FDA hearings may be standing-room-only, as drug stock analysts crowd the aisles.

Rather than choosing particular stocks or bonds to invest in, many people prefer to entrust their money to an investment manager who pools the funds together in a *mutual fund.*

What Is a Mutual Fund?

A *mutual fund* is a portfolio of stocks or bonds that is jointly owned by a large number of investors. If you invest in a mutual fund, you are not buying the actual stocks that make up the portfolio, but rather a share of the total value of the group assets. Mutual funds may be risky or safe, depending on what kind of investments their managers make. A mutual fund that purchases high-rated government bonds is fairly safe, but a mutual fund that buys stock in new, untested companies is very risky. The word *mutual* certainly does not by itself mean that the fund is especially safe. Think of the *Titanic* as a mutual vacation.

How Can You Compare the Riskiness of Stocks?

There's no foolproof way. And it's not just fools who can be deceived by the market. Assuming you are comparing stocks that trade on the public exchanges, economists often look at a statistic called the *beta,* which tells you whether the stock moves in sync with other stocks. If a stock has a beta equal to 1, that means that the stock mirrors the stock exchange itself. If the stock exchange climbs 10 percent, for example, this particular stock will climb 10 percent as well. Higher betas mean more volatility: a stock with a beta of 1.5 will rise 15 percent if the market rises 10 percent or fall 15 percent if the rest of the market slips by 10 percent.

Analysts calculate beta by comparing historical changes in a stock's price to historical changes in the stock exchange as a whole. You can obtain the beta statistic from major stock brokerage houses or from information services like Value Line. Betas lower than 1 show that a company's shares are less volatile than the rest of the market. By adding to your portfolio share with low betas, you can lower the combined risk of your holdings. Low volatility is not necessarily good, however. Remember, low-beta stocks will not reap the gains of a bull market, when other stocks may be riding high. If you are feeling bullish about the market, you should consider buying more high-beta stocks.

So which firms score high on the beta test, and which score low? Technology stocks move around a lot, so their betas can exceed 1.5. Meanwhile, solid utility stocks can plant themselves firmly with betas of less than .5 percent. Some stocks even earn negative scores. How is that possible? They tend to move in the opposite direction of the market. Some gold stocks will earn negative betas because when the rest of the market looks sour, people sometimes rush to place their money in precious metals.

In sum, while the beta test can help investors judge how volatile a stock is, it does not explain how volatile the overall market is, or whether the individual stock is a good bet. A high-beta stock, after all, can leave the rest of the market in the dust and take its investors laughing all the way to the bank.

What Does the P/E Ratio Measure?

The *price-earning ratio* (P/E ratio) offers another way to judge a stock's risk. Investing professionals toss around P/E ratios the way twelve-year-olds toss around baseball batting averages. Like the sports pages, each day the business pages of the newspaper list such averages. While beta can help you figure out whether the stock jumps around more than the market, the P/E ratio can warn you whether the other investors may be overly optimistic about a particular company.

Basically, the P/E ratio compares the stock's current trading price to the firm's earnings for the past year. A high P/E ratio means that the stock price is far above the earnings per share. Imagine that a firm pours all its earnings into a pot and then divides it among the shareholders. A higher P/E ratio means that the shareholders would get a smaller portion. Nonetheless, they hold on because they expect much bigger earnings in the future to eventually fuel dividend payments. In other words, they are willing to pay a premium for a chance to own shares. It is generally riskier to own a stock with a high P/E ratio, since the current earnings do not seem to support the high price.

Why do P/E ratios vary? Because investors are more optimistic about some stocks than others. A higher P/E ratio, then, shows more risk, but also shows greater confidence that earnings will eventually grow. If Bozo, Inc., has a P/E ratio of 35, then investors are willing to pay thirty-five times the current earnings per share to own one share.

The average P/E ratio for U.S. stocks is around 21. Japanese stocks enjoy a P/E ratio of around 100! Investing in Japanese stocks, then, makes sense only if you can confidently count on those Japanese companies to rapidly expand their output and profits. Many so-called "value" investors deliberately seek out low P/E stocks (ones with P/E ratios in the single digits). They figure that the market may be wrongly underestimating their potential. Market professionals call them "value investors" but think of them as cheap bargain hunters.

While the P/E ratio remains a favorite piece of evidence in judging stocks, it does not always tell the whole truth and nothing but the truth. For instance, what if Bozo, Inc., suffers through a recession and earns just one penny? In this case, the P/E ratio would look huge. What if the firm took a lot of tax deductions to cut its reported earnings? In this case, the P/E ratio would also look huge compared to firms that did not take many deductions. Since corporate accountants can massage earnings numbers for tax purposes, investors must look behind the P/E ratio to really figure out whether a company "justifies" its stock price.

How Can You Reduce the Risks of Investing?

Diversify. Variety is not just the spice of life, it is the way to run your personal affairs, at least your personal financial affairs. In managing your finances, you should look at your assets the way a football coach looks at his team. Each member has a specific role and a specific characteristic. Although your five-foot-two-inch field-goal kicker might be the best in the league, you would not want his skinny little feet filling the shoes of a defensive tackle. Nor would you want all of your team to be hulking giants, who work best only on the line of scrimmage. Some of your team should be spry, others should be massive. It would be downright risky to form a team where all members looked alike. By diversifying your team, you lower the risk of being beaten on the playing field.

Almost like a law of nature, diversity cuts risks. Just as human inbreeding can lead to receding chins and mental retardation, an "in-bred" portfolio can lead to receding asset values.

In finance the old saying "Don't put all your eggs in one basket" gets translated into sophisticated mathematical models. In fact, two Nobel laureates, economists Franco Modigliani of MIT and James Tobin of Yale, earned their prizes partly on research that vindicated this Mother Goose–like philosophy.

What are the different baskets that financial eggs should go into? A balanced portfolio usually contains some stocks, some bonds, some cash (or money market deposits or CDs), and perhaps some real estate or commodities (like wheat, lumber, pork bellies) or precious metals (such as gold and silver). Of course, as we discussed, within these broad categories there are riskier and less risky investments—for instance, the speculative technology stock versus the stable utility. Therefore, investors need to balance within these categories: if you own shares in a new DNA research firm that will either skyrocket or flame out into that black hole called corporate bankruptcy, you should also own a household-name stock as well.

There is no "correct" balance. Though many professional advisers recommend a portfolio comprised of a third each stocks, bonds, and cash, I would generally suggest a higher concentration on stocks, since over time they outperform the others. The answer, though, depends on the investor's situation. Again, Socrates's "Know thyself" applies here. If a stock-oriented portfolio makes you nervous and more likely to die young from a heart attack, forget it.

Employees should also be careful not to stake too much of their personal wealth on the company they work for. Your firm may be a great place to toil during the day, but by working there, you have already pinned your current income on it. If the firm turns downward, you could lose your job or see your pay check sliced. At that depressing time, you would not want your investment income to fall as well. In fact, you should structure your investments to move in the opposite direction of your current income.

How can you do this? Let's say you are an airline pilot. Airline stocks generally move up and down as the rest of the economy does. During boom times, businesspeople and tourists crowd the skies. During bust times, the planes sit empty in a desert location out west. Economists describe such stocks as *cyclical*. Since your current income fluctuates with the business cycle, you should be looking for *defensive* stocks that do not follow the economy. Health care and food stocks would do, since in recessions, unhappy people eat themselves sick. Actually, no matter what happens to the business cycle, people will continue to eat and to get sick.

Does this mean that you should run away from employee stock-ownership plans? No, but be careful. Make sure you have kept enough aside to offset the risks.

One last caveat. If by working in a certain industry you have developed an in-depth knowledge that helps you pick out the future winners and losers, you should certainly give it a try. Just do not put all of your eggs on the line.

How many eggs should you own? In stocks, you have over 30,000 to choose from. You do not need all of them. Stock in just a half dozen or so diverse companies would cut your risk significantly. If you were tempted to buy all of them, you could instead purchase shares in an *index fund,* a kind of mutual fund that tries to replicate the performance of the stock exchange as a whole. In other words, index fund managers strive to buy shares that give the fund a portfolio with a beta equal to 1. Depending on the fund, it could mirror the New York Stock Exchange, Italy's Borsa, or any other.

I am a fan of index funds, especially because their management fees tend to be very low. Instead of trying to scheme around the market and waste money on overhead, the managers take a very direct and inexpensive approach. The idea is almost like buying one of everything, rather than making tough choices among all the stocks. The efficient-market hypothesis strongly supports index funds over more active mutual funds. In fact, most actively managed mutual funds, because they cost much more, fail to perform as well as simple index funds. This is terribly embarrassing to the hotshot stock pickers in the mutual funds.

What Makes Stocks Go Up or Down?

Supply and demand, of course. Like most goods, stocks are a kind of popularity contest. Popular stocks go up, ugly ones go down. How do you play this kind of contest? That wizard John Maynard Keynes developed a brilliant approach, recommending that you choose *not the stocks that you find most attractive, but the ones that you think other people will embrace.*

Keynes deployed a marvelous analogy, comparing stock picking to "those newspaper competitions in which the competitors have to pick out the six prettiest faces from a hundred photographs, the prize being awarded to the competitor whose choice most nearly corresponds to the average preferences of the competitors as a whole; so each competitor has to pick not those faces which he himself finds prettiest, but those which he thinks likeliest to catch the fancy of the other competitors, all of whom are looking at the problem from the same point of view."[2]

Keynes's description always reminded me of Woody Allen's line about cheating on his metaphysics exam by looking into the soul of the student sitting next to him.

Most news reports on the stock market's performance are almost comical in their descriptions of why the market has moved. The S&P 500 index, which is a blend of the prices of five hundred different stocks, is currently about 450 points. A move of ten points, then, represents about a .2 shift, in a market that sees millions of trades every day. Nonetheless, on the evening television news, some blow-dried dunce who started as a weatherman in Tuscaloosa will proclaim that "the S&P Five Hundred fell ten points today because of new concerns about" blah, blah, blah. This effort to ascribe blame makes no sense, because the dip was too small to matter. A more realistic description would be simply to say that out of millions of people playing in the market today, 50.001 percent thought the market would fall, while 49.999 percent were more optimistic.

If you can figure out in advance whether the market will embrace a particular stock, you can then follow the timeless but often useless tautology and "buy low, sell high." But most people should not plan on beating everyone else to the prettiest firm and should instead rely on good old-fashioned fundamentals, that is, buy stocks in well-managed firms that are selling goods and services that people want.

Aside from popularity, a number of forces can push a particular stock up or force it down. First, the state of the market or of the industry: as we discussed above, a stock with a high beta will move in the same direction as the rest of the market, but at a faster pace. Cyclical stocks will move with the rest of the economy.

Shifts in the interest rate can hurt or help a stock. If interest rates plummet, stock dividends look more attractive to investors, and firms become more profitable, since their borrowing costs fall. Certain stocks, like housing company shares, are acutely sensitive to interest rates, since lower rates mean more mortgages and more home buying.

A stock price may shift if the firm issues additional shares. More shares means that each share represents a smaller piece of the same pie. In a *stock split,* a firm may double the number of shares but give each shareholder twice as many shares in order to compensate for the share prices being cut in half. Why would a firm bother? Sometimes a company's directors believe that the share price looks too high to attract investors. The split does not affect the value, though it does make the purchase price appear cheaper. Splits do not have to be 2-1; they can be just about any ratio. Occasionally, a firm will perform a *reverse split;* shareholders turn in, say, two shares and in return get one share that is worth twice as much. Reverse splits make a stock appear more expensive and can attract buyers who will not purchase shares that sell for a pittance.

Stock prices also move when the financial outlook of the firm shifts, due to changes in its earning power, assets, and liabilities. Many other factors can push the stock around, including the death of the chief executive officer. One study showed, embarrassingly enough, that stocks usually climb when the CEO unexpectedly drops dead. An odd finding, given the stratospheric salaries firms pay to their leaders.

How Do You Read the Stock Tables in the Newspaper?

By squinting or using a big magnifying glass. You also need to understand some abbreviations, starting with the name of the firm, which is listed alphabetically. Firms with shorter names like Boeing do not get chopped off; Minnesota Mining and Manufacturing, better known as 3M, shows up as the less familiar MMM. Sometimes you will need to know something about the corporate structure; American Airlines, for example, trades under its corporate parent's name, AMR.

Let's locate MMM in the stock tables, where we'll also see a string of numbers and headings like the following:

52wk										
Hi	Lo	Sym	Div	Yld%	P/E	Vol 100s	Hi	Lo	Close	Net Chg
58½	46⅛	MMM	1.76	3.4	18	20357	52	50	51¾	+½

Moving from left to right, the first two columns tell us where the stock has been for the past year, its high and low points. A big spread would suggest volatility. The next column, of course, give us the firm's symbol, or abbreviation. The abbreviation *pf* would indicate that the stock is a preferred stock. *Div* stands for *dividend* and is an estimate of the amount that the firm pays out for each share annually. In this case, if you owned a share of MMM, you would receive $1.76 per year. Typically, the highest dividends are paid by stable, long-lived companies. Growth stocks and speculative stocks tend to reinvest their profits rather than pay them out to shareholders. The shareholders are betting on future dividends and would rather forego them today.

The next column, headed *Yld%*, which stands for *percent yield*, shows how big the dividend is compared with the stock price. By looking at the percent yield, you can compare the dividends to other financial assets, like bonds. Remember, though, dividends are not the whole story. Stocks can rise in price as well. When someone happily sells a stock for more than he paid, that profit is called a *capital gain*. If the stock does not pay out any dividends, this space will be left blank in the newspaper table.

Following the dividend yield is the P/E ratio discussed earlier. *Vol 100s* gives volume—that is, how many times the stock has been bought and sold during the day. Since newspapers do not have room to print large numbers like 100,000, they divide the actual number of transactions by 100. The columns headed *Hi, Lo,* and *Close* give the highest price, the lowest price, and closing price for the stock that day. *Net Chg,* the net change, is calculated each day and given in the last column, preceded by either a plus or minus sign, indicating whether the stock has moved up or down that day.

What Is the Difference Between the New York Stock Exchange, the American Stock Exchange, and the NASDAQ?

The biggest difference is in the size of the companies traded. Generally, the New York Stock Exchange (NYSE) has the biggest tigers, while the American Stock Exchange (AMEX) has the medium-size companies, and the NASDAQ the feistier ones hoping to go through a growth spurt. The NYSE, for example, demands that its firms have a market value of about $20 million, while firms with only a million dollars can make it onto the NASDAQ, which is the computer-based trading system set up by the National Association of Security Dealers. As NASDAQ firms expand, they sometimes switch exchanges. Why? Some investors perceive NYSE firms as less risky. Further, the bigger the tigers, the more volume; that is, the more the stock is traded. More trades means more liquidity to get in and out of stocks. While this rule generally holds, NASDAQ fans point out that in the 1987 stock market crash, many panicked NYSE investors could not get their sales through the system, while the NASDAQ continued to operate smoothly.

How Can Investors Bet on Foreign Companies?

During the last few years, a new rage has swept through the American investment scene: going international. People have plunked down their savings on countries like India and China, even though they may not have been able to name their currencies (the rupee and the yuan). Two factors have spurred this move. First, Americans grew dissatisfied with the meager yields they received on domestic stocks and bonds. Second, they saw foreign stock markets galloping along, delivering returns in the high double digits. What self-respecting amateur investor could stomach buying CDs paying 3.5 percent interest when his neighbor bought the Hong Kong index and almost doubled his money in one year? As we discussed earlier, you have to be rich to afford a CD's recent, paltry yield.

Naturally, most firms around the world want your money. More money makes corporate life easier. Some countries, though, prohibit certain firms from selling shares to foreigners. Despite its thirst for foreign technical expertise, the Mexican oil company, Pemex, remains thoroughly Mexican, out of some ancient fear perhaps that the Aztec gods will punish any government that gives away the power to pump petroleum out of the ground.

Pemex aside, there are three common ways to ride the international wave. First, find a broker in the foreign country you want to invest in and ask her to buy shares on your behalf. Considering that most Americans have enough trouble speaking English, this sounds awfully tough. But even if you speak many foreign languages, such transactions become difficult for currency reasons. After all, the firm will pay dividends in a foreign currency, and its share value will swing as that currency fluctuates.

There is an easier way—in fact, two easier ways. Investors can, for instance, buy stock in a *single-country fund* that trades on the NYSE. Such funds can be bought with U.S. dollars through U.S. brokers. Dividends are paid in dollars as well. The Mexican Fund, for example, is a stock that itself owns stock in leading Mexican firms. Likewise, the Korea Fund owns stock in South Korean corporations.

Investors who insist on owning shares in a single foreign company, rather than a set of companies, can purchase an *American depository receipt* (ADR). ADRs for leading firms like Volvo and Telmex, Mexico's leading telephone company, trade on U.S. stock exchanges and represent the rights to foreign shares. ADRs offer the convenience of buying and selling foreign stock in U.S. dollars.

What Are the Added Risks of International Investing?

U.S. investors have it easy. They live under a stable political system. Their central bank does not fool around with the currency to avoid debtors, and their country's firms know how to compete for business. So why would Americans look across their borders for investment opportunities? Because they want high yields, and as I have pointed out many times, a higher return generally entails more risk. Safety is not only boring, it is foolish, if you need extra dough.

Two risks cannot be ignored, though. First, currencies can tumble. If Lufthansa Airlines boosts its profits by 20 percent, but the deutsche mark falls against the dollar by 40 percent, you can expect to lose a lot of money on your Lufthansa stock. Of course, the deutsche mark could just as easily rise against the dollar, reinforcing the new Lufthansa profits.

Since the currencies of developing countries can swing so broadly, banks will denominate loans to poorer countries in more stable currencies like the dollar, rather than in the borrower's currency. This also removes the incentive such countries might have to quickly depreciate their currencies in order to pay loans back with worthless notes. Prior to the 1994 Mexican presidential election, a very risky time for investors, the Mexican government sold billions of dollars worth of bonds denominated in dollars rather than pesos. These "tesobonos" bonds appeared much less risky to foreign investors than peso bonds.

Second, investors cannot ignore the political risks. The Korean Fund might look very attractive from a financial point of view, but what if North Korea threatens to detonate a nuclear device, or if the South Korean government encounters widespread worker protests? Your stock could lose favor with Wall Street and take a big slide. Also consider changes in government policy. Demagogic governments sometimes paint foreigners as scapegoats, leading to nationalization or laws restricting foreign investment. Certainly investors in pre-Castro Cuba learned a lesson in political-risk analysis when their properties went up in smoke like a Havana cigar.

International investing has a place in most portfolios. However, unsophisticated people should not let peer pressure push them into a fad. Your local broker who is pushing the SuperDuper Moldavian Mutual Fund quite possibly did not do well in geography class in fourth grade and has not learned much since. Ask him, What is the local currency? What does it trade at? When did the government last change hands? If he cannot answer these questions, he has not done his homework, and you should not jeopardize your savings with a failing grade.

Those who can place their money in the hands of foreign executives and workers without losing sleep might even consider riskier ventures, such as futures and options, which we will now discuss. These financial instruments are too volatile for most people, though they made the front pages in 1994 with reports that Hillary Rodham Clinton had "earned" $100,000 in cattle futures by investing just about $1,000. In the following section, we'll see how these markets operate, but don't expect a lesson in how to replicate Clinton's unusual, to say the least, gain.

What Are Futures and Options?

Among movie mogul Sam Goldwyn's legendary malapropisms was "Never make any predictions, especially about the future." Despite Goldwyn, many Wall Street moguls have gotten rich betting on the future. Futures and options give them the tools to try. By signing a *futures contract,* a would-be mogul promises to buy—or sell—a particular stock, bond, currency, or commodity in the future at a fixed price. Where's the money to be made? Let's say Hillary wakes up in February believing that the price of pork bellies will skyrocket next August from fifty-five cents to seventy-five cents per pound. A futures contract can let her bet on the August price months in advance. If pig prices plummet instead, Hillary will lose money on her bet. There are two winners from Hillary's disastrous bet: the investor who sold Hillary the futures contract and who correctly bet that prices would fall, and young pigs, since lower prices will mean fewer will be turned into bacon.

Another way to bet on the future of the bacon business is by buying an *option*. Options give investors the right to decide, at some later point, whether they want to buy or sell something. For example, many corporations reward executives with stock options in addition to salary. The stock option might state that Mr. Too-Big-For-His-Britches can buy a thousand shares of FatPants Co. for $50 per share, between 1997 and 1999. Though FatPants stock may now trade at only $45, this option to buy at a *strike price* of $50 could become very valuable if FatPants shares jump to, say, $70.

Because options are potentially valuable, they are not free! While Mr. Too-Big received his options as partial compensation for his work as a FatPants Co. bigwig, most of us have to pay a fee for an option. Remember, option holders do not have to use the option and will not use the option, unless the market price of the asset makes it worthwhile.

So far we have seen that optimists can buy futures contracts or options to buy at higher prices (technically a *call* option). What do pessimists do? Collect canned meats and store them in basements, of course. More daring pessimists can buy options that are referred to as *puts*. A put gives the option holder the right to sell the asset, if it falls in price. Suppose Too-Skinny-For-His-Skivvies thinks that stock in BigPants Co. will shrink in price, since sales of exercise equipment are on the rise. He can buy a put, which would let him sell the shares at a fixed price at a later date. If BigPants Co. stock actually falls, Too-Skinny can buy those shares at the lower market price and exercise his option to sell them at the higher price.

How did all this betting get started? While on the surface

these transactions seem to add tumult to the world, in fact, they smooth out the world's natural rhythms of feast and famine, boom and bust, rainy and dry. Futures and options markets began when farmers tried to hedge against the great uncertainty of weather and agricultural markets. A New Zealand shepherd would have trouble gauging next year's international wool and lamb chop output. But by entering into futures contracts, he can guarantee that his fuzz and chops will not go without buyers.

Banks got into the act when they realized that they too could cut back their exposure to a dangerous and cyclical world. A bank that lends mostly at fixed rates but borrows at floating rates can use options to make sure it doesn't get caught in a destabilizing gulf.

Of course, futures do not take away all risks, but they help investors and producers follow the advice of Tennessee Williams's eccentric Amanda Wingfield: "The present becomes the past, the past becomes the present, and the future becomes something you regret all your life unless you plan for it."[3]

So now that you've learned how to make money, or at least, lose less of it, we can ask the question, where did all these economic ideas come from? Who's responsible here? The final chapter is a rapid tour through the history of economic thought and a primer on the schools of thought that will shape the future of the discipline.

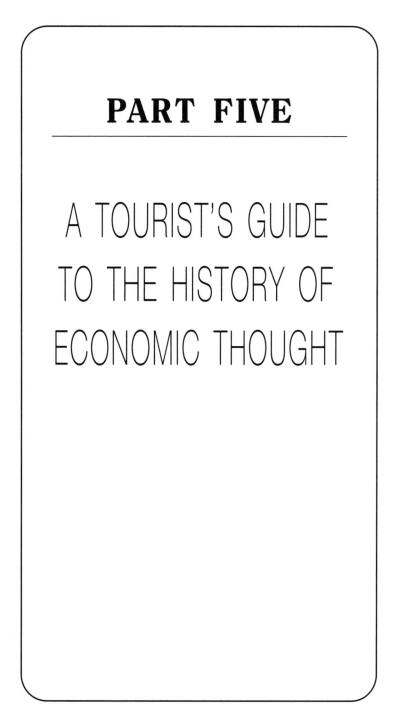

PART FIVE

A TOURIST'S GUIDE TO THE HISTORY OF ECONOMIC THOUGHT

9 They Shoot Economists, Don't They?

GREAT ECONOMISTS AND SCHOOLS OF THOUGHT

• *Where Did Economics Start?* • *Who Were the Mercantilists?* • *How Did Adam Smith Attack the Mercantilists?* • *Was Adam Smith a Dismal Scientist?* • *How Does* The Wealth of Nations *Portray People?* • *What Is Adam Smith's Invisible Hand?* • *Why Did Smith Praise Division of Labor?* • *Who Was David Ricardo and How Did He Improve Adam Smith's Trade Theory?* • *Why Was Thomas Malthus So Depressing?* • *What Was Jeremy Bentham's Felicific Calculus?* • *Why Did John Stuart Mill Oppose Welfare?* • *Why Was Alfred Marshall the Darwin of Economics?* • *Rebels with a Cause: Schools of Thought That Break from the Mainstream* — *What was the Austrian school about?* — *Who has rational expectations?* — *Why do "new Keynesians" disagree with the RE School?* — *What is supply-side economics?* — *Why do public choice scholars distrust government?*

Now that we've sprinted through the basic ideas behind modern economics, it's time to take a step back and ask, Who is responsible for all this? Economics did not just bubble up, like a natural spring. It took some curious and diligent minds, and sometimes even some courage. Let's take a look at the great economists who built the science, as well as the modern schools of thought that are now pushing the discipline to new frontiers.

"The first thing we do, let's kill all the lawyers." The American Bar Association cringes at the oft-repeated line from Shakespeare's *Henry VI,* yet if economists existed in Elizabethan times, there is a good chance they too would have been running for their lives, on stage, if not in the streets. Economists suffer from a confused image: they appear indecisive, they frequently bring bad news, and yet they seem utterly incapable of improving the situation.

George Bernard Shaw most effectively mocked their indecisiveness by proclaiming that if all the economists in the world were laid end to end, they wouldn't reach a conclusion. (Ironic, since most economists were convinced that Shaw's embrace of Stalin showed economic naiveté. Stalin in return saw Shaw as a clown.[1]) Their image is often further diminished by a general dronishness. Another antieconomist slam asserts that most economists do not have the personalities to become accountants. In fact, actor-writer Ben Stein has staked his Hollywood career (most notably in the movie *Ferris Bueller's Day Off*) on parodying his nerdy father, Herbert Stein, former chief economist for Presidents Nixon and Ford.

I won't try to rebut these lethal charges. Obviously, there have been some fascinating, even beguiling economists. Joseph Schumpeter was downright eccentric, showing up for classes dressed in jodhpurs and carrying a riding crop. There have even been scandalous economists like Thorstein Veblen, who slept around. By and large, though, the top-ranking economists have been hardworking, academic sorts like the Victorian scholar Alfred Marshall, who as a boy snuck his mathematical papers into his bedroom, the way more "normal" boys today will sneak a copy of *Playboy.*

In fact, it is ironic that economists suffer the slings and arrows of outrageous jokes and general disdain, for as Keynes noted, many started out as do-gooders, searching for ways to improve the world. Marshall saw economics as a profession that should blend shrewd science with a devotion to people. While the medieval world saw three grand professions—medicine (concerned with physical health), law (concerned with political health), and theology (concerned with spiritual health)—Marshall hoped to make economics the fourth noble vocation, with the aim of promoting better material health, not just for the rich but for all. While Marshall succeeded in launching a new discipline at Cambridge University, his disciples have not been able to preserve it as a "grand profession." Do-gooding is often tough, thankless work. Economists who must put up with taunting at cocktail parties should remember that the road to good intentions is paved with hell.

Where Did Economics Start?

The temper of our times tells us to answer such questions by going as far back in history as possible and announce that some cave dweller actually understood complex ideas like Keynes's multiplier a million years before Keynes, a privileged white man, stumbled onto it. It will come as no surprise that I am not a fan of this historical method. Surely, premodern men and women worked, sheltered, and fed themselves. They implicitly calculated the costs and benefits of hunting, gathering, and eating each other. That is not economics. Economics is the study of such choices, and the developing of testable models to explain such behavior. Running away from a hairy man wielding a saber-toothed tiger tusk may be an economic decision, but it does not contribute to our understanding of households, businesses, and the creation of wealth.

We could start with the Bible, which contains many statements on land, labor, and capital. But the Bible presents more commandments than careful analyses.[2] Although Adam Smith may have gotten his name and his moral posture from the Bible, it provided little inspiration for his economic theorizing.

We could also explore Aristotle's articulate remarks praising private property and denouncing the accumulation of wealth for wealth's sake. But Aristotle knew just enough about economics to know that time was a scarce resource. Therefore, he devoted more of his time to philosophy and to educating Alexander the Great than he did to economic theory. It shows. He left few marks in the annals of economic discipline. Economics was all Greek to him, and still he did not understand it.

The Middle Ages could have used some Merlins to turn poverty and starvation into Camelot. Instead, they got theologians mired in debates over questions of justice and morality in the marketplace. The Catholic Schoolmen devised the doctrine of the "just price" and refined the Church view of usury. Whereas the Old Testament specifically forbade lending at interest to members of the same community, medieval theologians tried to separate the different components of interest such as risk, inflation, inconvenience, and reward for deferred spending in order to rip holes in the solid prohibition against lending and to permit loopholes.

The Schoolmen were stuck in a dilemma: if they continued to deliver orthodox interpretations of the Bible that condemned commercial activities, they would lose their relevance, because most people had already decided to take their chances with divine retribution. On the other hand, if they simply smiled and condoned commercialism, they would lose their credibility and their biggest weapon: guilt. They cobbled together their economic theories, then, while straddling the secular and the sacred. This is a terribly uncomfortable position, unless you have either very long legs or a big rear end. They spoke on economics because it was a duty to their flock. But the duty was to guide the flock to heaven, not to a higher standard of living and a credit-based economy. Moses said, "Let my people go," not "Let my people charge it." When Protestants split the flock, the task grew even more unwieldy.

The first economists, then, did not arrive on the scene until the Enlightenment, in sixteenth-century Europe. We call them the *mercantilists*.

Who Were the Mercantilists?

They were the writers and courtly advisers who hung around the European monarchs from the sixteenth through the eighteenth centuries. They did not share a common "good book," nor did they create a coherent school of thought that systematically spawned disciples. They did not even share common interests. But as royal families of England, France, Spain, Portugal, and Holland consolidated their boundaries and battled for colonies across the seas, lawyers and merchants began advising kings and queens on how to manage their economies.

Despite their inconsistent approaches, the mercantilists did share several tenets: A nation should keep its house in order by awarding monopolies, patents, subsidies, and privileges to loyal subjects of the crown; merchants and nobles with that "lean and hungry look" should be squashed, lest they support insurrection. A nation should chase after colonies for the purpose of extracting precious metals and raw materials, which were considered good measures of national wealth, for they could pay for further wars of conquest. A nation should restrict its foreign trade so that it exported more finished goods than it imported. A consistently positive balance of trade would bring in gold (wealth) from debtor nations.

Under mercantilism, we see nations stretching their borders. At the same time, however, we see a tightened control over the internal economy, as guilds, monopolies, and tariffs give economic power to political favorites. In some nations the control extended ridiculously far. French finance minister Jean-Baptiste Colbert thoroughly regulated the manufacture of many goods during the reign of Louis XIV and endowed the guilds with great authority. In a stunning display of imperial power, he once announced that fabric from Dijon would contain 1,408 threads! Imagine what Colbert would do today to Dijon mustard. Contemporary French politicians sometimes invoke Colbert's name when fighting for protectionist policies. During 1993's rancorous trade debates in the Uruguay Round of GATT, some French forces defended farm subsidies and high tariffs by shouting, "We are the country of Colbert, not Adam Smith!" This erudite yet effective battle cry helped French prime minister Balladur squeeze extra concessions out of the U.S. and other European negotiators.

How Did Adam Smith Attack the Mercantilists?

The mercantilists provided the perfect target for the eighteenth-century Scotsman Adam Smith, who is widely credited as the father of modern economics. He excoriated their theories on several levels. They measured wealth on the basis of coins and precious metals, while Smith believed that real wealth should be gauged by the standard of living of common households. In his view, bags of gold did not necessarily translate into bags of food. To paraphrase Moss Hart and George Kaufman's famous comments about money, you can't take it with you and you can't eat it.

Adam Smith said that the economic health of its consumers is the measure of a nation's wealth. Tactics that shunted money into the hands of prime ministers or sycophantic merchants did not generally help the citizens of a nation. Smith also knew that individual motivation, invention, and innovation inspire an economy to greater prosperity. By bestowing gifts of monopoly and protection, mercantilist policies paralyzed the body politic. Smith's denunciations spawned modern economics.

Was Adam Smith a Dismal Scientist?

Belying the cliché of a tormented genius, Adam Smith led a relatively contented personal life. Born in 1723, Smith grew up with his mother in Kirkcaldy, a small port located across the

Firth of Forth from Edinburgh. His father, a comptroller of customs, had died months before his birth.

More important than Smith's birthplace, though, is his birth era. He was born into the Enlightenment, that fiery period of European intellectual history when brilliant men like Newton and Galileo began questioning religious doctrine and searching for their own rational explanations for natural phenomena. Like these scientists, Smith sought out cause-and-effect relationships. But instead of focusing on physical forces and planets, he focused on people.

When he focused on his image in the mirror, Smith saw an odd-looking fellow with a large nose, bulging eyes, a protruding lower lip, and a nervous twitch. He also had a speech impediment. None of these flaws showed up in the Adam Smith neckties that were ubiquitous in the Reagan administration. Smith once acknowledged his less than classic features, saying, "I am a beau in nothing but my books."

Smith attended Oxford, where he complained about poor teaching and academic censorship. Like most college men of the day, he was studying for the clergy. But when Smith caught the Enlightenment fever through the books of philosopher David Hume, he could not continue on the path to the pulpit. Instead of becoming a disciple of the Church, he became a protégé of his former teacher Francis Hutcheson, who taught that it is possible to know good and evil without knowing God.

Note that Smith's ideas, which are today associated with conservative politics, started out as radical notions that challenged the political and moral structure.

Smith began to teach logic and moral philosophy at the University of Glasgow. Far from following the sleepy style of the Oxford dons he had assailed, Smith quickly gained a reputation for lucid lectures and concern for his students. Though he lectured, tutored, and held informal discussions, Smith also found time to serve as dean of faculty.

Smith never taught a course in economics; in fact, Smith never even took a course in economics. Nobody did. Until the nineteenth century, academics considered economics a branch of philosophy. Not until 1903 did Cambridge University establish an economics program separate from the "moral sciences."

Freud observed that people tend to puff up the status of their forefathers. He called this the "family romance." Budding economists might be disappointed to discover that their forefather was not as intelligent as Newton, not as witty as Voltaire, and not as scandalous as Byron. In fact, Smith was a bumbler.

Though professional economists are weary of the stories of Smith's absentmindedness, they can still amuse the uninitiated. For example, one day while the Rt. Honorable Charles Townshend was in Glasgow, Smith took him on a tour of a tanning factory. While rhapsodizing on the merits of free trade, Smith tripped into a huge nauseous pool of goop. After workers dragged him out, stripped him, and threw a blanket over him, the father of modern economics admitted that he could never keep his life in order.

How Does *The Wealth of Nations* Portray People?

Adam Smith's lectures and tutoring took him to France in the 1760s; he sent a letter back to Hume, reporting, "I have begun to write a book in order to pass away the time."[3] In 1776 he finally completed the book, called *The Wealth of Nations*. Following the sycophantic works of the mercantilists, Smith's book is a declaration of independence for economists. The book starts by teaching us about people. Like Thomas Hobbes, who spoke of the heart as a "spring," Smith—again in the tradition of the Enlightenment—tried to figure out what made people tick.

Smith discovers natural drives or "propensities" that form the foundation for economics. First of all, all human beings want to live better than they do. Smith finds a "desire of bettering our condition, a desire which, though generally calm and dispassionate, comes with us from the womb, and never leaves us till we go to the grave." Second, Smith points to a "certain propensity in human nature . . . to truck, barter, and exchange one thing for another. . . . It is common to all men."[4]

Smith's advice to government follows from these insights, namely, harness these natural drives. While Moses told Pharaoh, "Let my people go," Adam Smith told kings and queens, let your people go about their business. Governments should not repress self-interested people, he said, for self-interest is a rich natural resource. While charity and altruism are great, they do not show up often enough to sustain a society. Smith admits that man almost constantly needs help from others, but it is foolish to "expect it from their benevolence only. He will be more likely to prevail if he can shew them that it is for their own advantage."

In the most cited passage in the history of economic thought, Smith proclaims: "It is not from the benevolence of the butcher, the brewer, or the baker, that we expect our dinner, but from their regard to their own interest."[5] Even those who actually enjoy slaughtering cattle, brewing beer, or baking bread would not want to do it all day if they were not compensated. Smith never suggests that workers are motivated only by self-interest; he simply states that self-interest motivates more powerfully and consistently than kindness, altruism, or martyrdom.

What Is Adam Smith's Invisible Hand?

If everyone charges ahead in his own direction, why does society not devolve into anarchy? Imagine an intersection of ten-lane highways, with broken traffic lights. Shouldn't we hear a frightening crash when self-interests clash? If roads cannot be safe without a traffic authority designating who can move when, can a community survive without a central planning agency to decide who produces and what is produced?

Yes, Adam Smith said. Not only will it survive, but the community will thrive far more than any community with central planners. Smith had studied astronomy and embraced the idea of a natural harmony in the planets, even as each planet moved in its own orbit. People, he thought, could move in different paths yet harmonize and help each other, but not intentionally. In his classic statement, Smith announces that if all seek to promote their self-interest, the whole society prospers: "He . . . neither intends to promote the publick interest, nor knows how much he is promoting it. . . . He intends only his own gain, and he is in this, as in many other cases, led by an invisible hand to promote an end which was no part of his intention."[6] This "invisible hand" becomes the transparent symbol of Adam Smith's economics.

Smith starts his career by doubting God and then ends up with his own supernatural force, the invisible hand. Why should we believe him? In fact, Smith did not rest his argument on hocus-pocus. *The invisible hand merely symbolizes the true orchestrator of social harmony, the free market.* For market competition leads a self-interested person to wake up in the morning, look outside at the earth, and produce from its raw materials not what he wants, but what others want. Not in the quantities he prefers, but in the quantities his neighbors prefer. Not at the price he dreams of charging, but at a price that reflects how much his neighbors value what he has done.

Smith's invisible hand works through the price system to harmonize supply and demand. Recall the earlier example of the surfboards and skateboards. Smith did not know anything about either implement, but his principles apply nonetheless.

Why Did Smith Praise Division of Labor?

Pins. That one word says it all, just as the line "Plastic" does in the movie classic *The Graduate*. Smith's visit to a pin factory showed him that by dividing labor tasks, output could skyrocket by a startling 400,000 percent: while one worker "could scarce, perhaps, with his utmost industry, make one pin in a day, and certainly could not make twenty," Smith found that by dividing the process into eighteen distinct operations, each person averaged "four thousand eight hundred pins a day."[7] More hocus-pocus? Smith studied the situation and came up with three ways in which specializing and dividing labor lifts output: each worker develops more skill and dexterity in her particular task; workers waste less time changing from one task to another; specialized workers will more likely invent machinery to help with the particular task they focus on daily.

Smith never promised that division of labor alone brings wealth to a nation, of course. Free trade among manufacturers, suppliers, towns, and cities is also necessary. What good are 10,000 pins if they cannot be traded because of restrictions or high transportation costs? The manufacturer might as well make twenty or perhaps none. Further, division of labor should take place among towns, not just among workers in factories. Particular towns can specialize, just as particular individuals can. Boise may produce wheat, while Boston produces computers. The point is, the wealth of a nation grows if markets expand, that is, if more and more markets are hooked up to trade routes.

Consider the United States in 1750, when trade routes along the eastern seaboard delivered goods relatively smoothly from Baltimore to Boston, yet settlements west of Pennsylvania had to fend for themselves. A self-sufficient settlement is analogous to a pin worker who must cut, bend, attach, and deliver by himself. In the United States, as transportation routes over rivers and land developed and distribution costs shrank, more and more towns could be brought into the common market, boosting overall wealth. In fact, as the maritime industry built safer ships and developed better navigational skills, it drove down the cost of shipping across the Atlantic, which invigorated the Colonies and Britain throughout the eighteenth century. Even the defeat of pirates contributed to the wealth of nations.

Emersonian self-reliance may be part of the American psyche, but the American pocketbook fattened in spite of it.

Smith liked to use simple examples. He looked at his overcoat and imagined all the varied and geographically divided laborers who together made it possible for him to stay warm through the chilly Scottish winters: shepherds, wool sorters and combers, dyers, spinners, weavers, wool merchants, and sailors. Most striking, none of these laborers had to know each other, and certainly they didn't know Smith. One of Smith's most eminent contemporary disciples, Milton Friedman, chose the pencil as a symbol of Smith's economics. Friedman argued that no single person, even a Nobel laureate, could make a pencil. With graphite from Sri Lanka, an eraser made from Indonesian rapeseed oil and sulfur chloride, wood from Oregon, and assembly in Wilkes-Barre, Pennsylvania, the pencil that costs just a few cents is a miracle of the international marketplace.

Who Was David Ricardo and How Did He Improve Adam Smith's Trade Theory?

The old saying "Those who can't do, teach, and those who can't teach, teach gym" certainly doesn't apply to David Ricardo. Ricardo did quite well as an economic actor before he ever considered being an economic scholar. In a testament to on-the-job-training, Ricardo amassed a fortune in stocks and bonds without ever attending college or formally studying finance. In retrospect, formal training during the period around 1800 would have made Ricardo less effective in the markets than he was when left to his own hunches and insights. The son of Jewish immigrant stockbrokers in London, David Ricardo mastered the financial markets by dint of his brilliant mind and boundless energy.

Although wealth surrounded him, Ricardo did not read *The Wealth of Nations* until he was twenty-seven, and then only "by accident." During a boring vacation in Bath, the future leader of classical economics happened upon Smith's masterpiece. It was a good thing that in those days hotels couldn't offer television in guest rooms, or Ricardo might have skipped the lengthy tome. At the urging of James Mill, a political economist and father of John Stuart Mill, Ricardo jumped into London's intellectual and political community to share his clever insights on the British economy. A splendid raconteur, Ricardo soon found himself writing pamphlets and treatises, as well as winning a seat in the House of Commons. So this son of an immigrant, with a wide span of knowledge and of intellectual interests, soon became the very model of a major English generalist.

We do not know how many members of Parliament actually understood Ricardo, especially his views on trade. This was not because his views were cloudy but because he tried to argue perhaps the most complex and counterintuitive principle of economics. In today's world, where politicians' messages fit on bumper stickers and display the linguistic complexity of a Mother Goose story (Grimm's tales are too tough), one cannot imagine a president explaining Ricardo's law of comparative advantage.

Ricardo's law of comparative advantage actually eclipsed Adam Smith's law of absolute advantage. Smith merely pointed out that other countries and regions might be better at making or growing certain products, and if so, Britain should trade with them. If, for example, the dreary Danes baked better danish at a lower cost, the Brits should buy them and not try to make their own.

Ricardo proved, though, that Brits should trade with other countries, even if those countries were inferior in all their goods. Let's take a few examples. Suppose a skillful liposuction surgeon who sucks out fat tissues from thunderous thighs also excels at typing up medical forms. Meanwhile, his receptionist cannot vacuum fat, nor can she type as fast. According to Ricardo, the surgeon should not act as both vacuumer of fat and typist. Rather than putting down the vacuum hose, he should continue to let his receptionist do the typing. Sucking out fat is, after all, a more valuable use of the surgeon's time.

For those who like numerical examples, consider the old television show *Gilligan's Island*. Hapless, hopelessly clumsy Gilligan is washed ashore along with the competent, self-assured skipper. Two tasks must be done—fishing and building shelter. Assume that the skipper can catch a fish dinner in 10 hours and build a thatched hut in 20. But Gilligan takes 15 hours to catch fish and in the process usually hooks himself, and he takes 45 hours to build a hut. By Adam Smith's logic, the skipper should move away to the other side of the island, building and fishing on his own, since he outperforms Gilligan in everything. But economists still shudder with reverence for Ricardo, when he shows that the skipper should actually split the chores with his feckless friend!

Let's first calculate how many fish dinners and huts they can build on their own, spending half their time fishing, the other half building. Assume that during a year, the skipper will work a total of 2,000 hours, and his first mate Gilligan is ordered to work 3,600. If the skipper spends 1,000 hours fishing, he will catch 100 fish dinners, and in 1,000 hours of hut building produces 50 huts. Gilligan's 1,800 hours of fishing will bring 120 dinners and his 1,800 hours of hut building will make 40 huts. So the total number of dinners on the island is 200, eaten in the comfort of 90 huts.

What happens if they specialize? If the skipper spends all of his time on huts, he will construct 100; if Gilligan concentrates on fish, he will return with 240 fish dinners. Thus, the island has increased output dramatically just by specializing, even though Gilligan was far less competent at both tasks!

The next key question is, How do we know what to specialize in? Let's go back to the island. Since it takes the skipper twice as long to erect a hut as it does to catch dinner, he gives up two dinners every time he nails those trees together. But Gilligan, who takes three times longer to build a hut than to catch a fish, gives up three dinners every time he builds a hut. Since building a hut is a smaller sacrifice for the skipper, he should build huts. Ricardo showed that people and countries should specialize in whatever leads them to sacrifice less. This is their *comparative advantage*. And the sacrifice they make by not producing a good is their *opportunity cost*. Thus, specialization is determined by whoever has the lower opportunity cost.

The point of Ricardo's analysis: free trade makes it possible for households to consume more goods *regardless* of whether trading partners are more or less economically advanced. What works for liposuction surgeons works for countries, and that's what makes David Ricardo the most brilliant economist prior to the twentieth century.

While Ricardo could have pointed to a rosy future if governments followed his advice, he often ran into pathological pessimists who sang the Chicken Little chorus, telling the world that the economy must tumble. Thomas Malthus was such a man.

Why Was Thomas Malthus So Depressing?

Thomas Malthus, a tall, witty Cambridge graduate who only briefly practiced as a minister in the late 1700s, is usually depicted as a dour, Bible-thumping preacher. The image is all wrong. In fact, he was fun-loving and not a fundamentalist. His economic theories, however, made him a party pooper.

What party did he poop on? Around the time of the French Revolution, writers like William Godwin and Marquis de Condorcet began glorifying human progress and painting utopian visions of the future. Visions of sugarplums danced in their heads, as Godwin wrote that "Man is perfectible. . . . Every man will seek, with affable ardour, the good for all."[8] (Godwin found many followers, though his daughter Mary Shelley, author of *Frankenstein,* did not seem so enthusiastic!) Malthus's "fairy godmother," Jean-Jacques Rousseau, a good friend of Thomas's father, Daniel Malthus, seemed to buy into this naive hope for universal comity.

But Thomas would have none of it. He especially rejected Godwin and William Paley's claims that an increasing population meant more total happiness. Malthus thought their more-the-merrier theory was hopelessly loony and downright dangerous. More mouths to feed, Malthus contended, meant less food in each mouth. After an argument with his father, who also sympathized with Godwin, Thomas in a fury dashed off "An Essay on the Principle of Population as It Affects the Future Improvement of Society, with Remarks on the Speculations of M. Godwin, M. Condorcet, and Other Writers."

Few essays have ever been more shocking. Imagine that every twenty-five years the earth splits in half, one half remaining in orbit, the other spinning toward the sun, igniting and exploding. People must scramble and trample toward the half that will survive, carrying with them children, grandparents, and whatever sacred possessions they can hold on to. Even worse, they do not know which half of the earth to run to.

Malthus's prophecy is slightly different but only a bit less frightening. Instead of the globe cleaving and exploding, Malthus describes the population swelling and spreading at an explosive pace, while food supplies only inch along. Using data from the United States supplied by Benjamin Franklin, Malthus asserted that population tends to double every twenty-five years. Of course, it could double even faster. Actually, Malthus chose relatively conservative examples. Franklin reported that some villages double in only fifteen years! Though armed with no reliable data from Franklin on the food supply, Malthus concluded that output could never keep pace with population. Unchecked population grows at a geometric ratio, Malthus posited, while food increases at merely an arithmetic ratio.

What does this mean? Trouble. A geometric ratio (or exponential rate) means that a number continually multiplies itself by a constant, for example, a perpetual doubling. An arithmetic ratio simply adds a constant. Malthus provides a good example: if the present population is one billion, with doubling every twenty-five years, humans would increase from 1 to 2, 4, 8, 16, 32, 64, 128, 256 billions, while food would grow arithmetically by 1, 2, 3, 4, 5, 6, 7, 8, 9. Whereas each person had 1 basket of food at the beginning, two hundred years later, 256 people would have to share 9 baskets. Only one hundred years after that, 4,096 people would have to share 13 baskets.

If the earth halved and halved again, we would see a frenzied rush. But what exactly happens when mouths exceed spoonfuls? Long before geometric growth soars off the graphs, two kinds of obstacles block the advance: *positive checks* and *preventative checks*. By "positive" Malthus clearly did not mean optimistic ones. He meant checks that raise the death rate, like war, famine, and plagues. Preventative checks instead lower the birth rate, though Malthus had little confidence in birth control, especially among the lower classes.

In a wonderful understatement, Malthus admits that his scenario has a "melancholy hue." It seems strange to speak of such a black vision of the future as a hue. Critics quickly painted a black hat on Malthus's head. The poet Robert Southey compared him to "menstrual pollution" and wrote that he would "be very glad to lend a hand in some regular attack upon this mischievous booby. . . . We may in a few evenings effectually demolish him."[9] Critics loved to jeer at the multiplication of Malthus's own offspring, and although the Malthuses had only three, somehow the 1958 and 1967 Everyman Library editions of "An Essay" awarded him eight more—all girls!

Malthus also spawned thousands of disciples, who themselves kept reproducing, especially in the 1960s and 1970s, when the so-called "population explosion" seemed a much bigger threat than Russia's atomic bombs or Castro's poisonous cigars. But how accurate were Malthus's predictions? Actually, not very. He missed some of the most important trends in the history of the world, as well as some obvious statistical blips. On the trivial side, he forgot to ask Ben Franklin whether the rising population figures distinguished natural-born Americans from immigrants. In other words, by lumping them together, Malthus in effect assumed that mothers of English descent in remote American villages were giving birth to Dutch children arriving in New York by boat. He saw rising numbers, so he essentially declared the American mothers extremely fertile—certainly a painless method of childbirth, even if a flawed statistical method. More crucial, Malthus missed major advances in medicine, an agricultural revolution, and the start of the industrial revolution, all of which would twist his projections like taffy into novel shapes rather than support steady geometric trends.

Let's take a look at agriculture. At the beginning of the eighteenth century, European agricultural productivity was no higher than it had been twenty centuries earlier. But from 1700 to 1800, output per worker doubled in England. Crop rotation, seed selection, better tools, and the replacement of oxen with horses reduced plowing time by 50 percent. While 75 percent of Englishmen had to work on farms in 1690, only 25 percent did by 1840, and those 25 percent produced enough for England to feed her citizens and to export as well.

Okay, so Malthus forgot about productivity. How did he bungle the call on population growth? Economists point to four stages in the "demographic transition." In preindustrial societies, high death rates balanced high birth rates; lots of people died, but lots of people were born. In the second stage, early industrial development, better health lowered death rates, so birth rates appeared excessive, and population spurted ahead. It was in this era that Malthus lived and collected his data. He did not and probably could not have seen what would come next. In the third stage, urbanization and education persuaded many to have fewer children. Thus, the death rate continued to fall, but so did the birth rate. Fourth and finally, in our modern society, with successful birth control and often both spouses working, couples seem to desire between one and three children, and the population stabilizes.

Karl Marx once said that whenever the train of history goes around the bend, all the intellectuals fall off. Malthus did not foresee stages three and four. When the figures fell off his plotted chart, Malthus fell off the train.

Just as Malthus tried (but failed) to add precision to population forecasts, the British philosopher Jeremy Bentham tried to make individual economic choices more precise, even creating a new way to calculate costs and benefits.

What Was Jeremy Bentham's Felicific Calculus?

Unlike the Marquis de Sade, Jeremy Bentham took the sensible view that pleasure was good and pain was bad. A clever English social thinker who lived at the turn of the nineteenth century, Bentham thought whips and shackles were for prisoners, not for sex play. He devised a whole social philosophy around the idea that society should foster pleasure and cut back the total amount of pain. While at first this sounds like the Greek hedonism propagated by Aristippus, Bentham added an ethical caveat: individuals should not merely pursue what gives them the most pleasure, but they should pursue activities that produce the most pleasure for society. The battle cry, then, is "Maximize happiness for the greatest number." Bentham argued that government legislators should engrave this idea on their desks and in their minds.

While such balancing of pleasure-pain and cost-benefit might sound callous, in the context of the era, it was very progressive. In words that make democrats misty-eyed, Bentham contended that everyone is created equal when it comes to counting up their pleasures and pains. If the king goes hungry for a day, this counts half as much as his serving wench Janet going hungry for two. If giving Janet the next meal helps her more than it would help the king, she gets the food, and he has to wait. Obviously, Bentham was not popular with aristocrats.

Bentham was not content with the fuzzy character of his pleasure-pain principle. He wanted more precision. In fact, just as Newton mathematically diagnosed physical properties, Bentham wanted to depict social properties. He wanted his gravestone to be engraved HERE LIES JEREMY BENTHAM, THE NEWTON OF THE MORAL UNIVERSE. To reach his goal, Bentham devised a method to quantify the amount of pleasure and pain that any activity brought. The method is called the *felicific calculus*.[10] As we all know, some experiences are more pleasurable than others. Why? Any single experience can be measured by four factors: intensity, duration, certainty, and propinquity. People prefer long, certain vacations with close friends to the mere possibility of a weekend off. Hilarious comedians bring more pleasure than mildly amusing ones.

Bentham apparently gave himself so much pleasure devising this calculus that he prolonged it by adding three more factors: fecundity, impurity, and the effect on others. Some pleasures lead to more pleasures. If by going bowling, Dean increases the chances of making new friends, bowling demonstrates the fifth factor, fecundity. If going bowling might bring pain, because Dean makes a pass at the spouse of a big, nasty bar bouncer, going bowling exhibits the sixth factor, impurity (the chance it will produce opposite sensations). Finally, if many people laugh when the bouncer rearranges Dean's face, we must consider their pleasure.

With these tools, Bentham provided complex directions for adding and subtracting pleasures and pains. Now what does this have to do with economics? Bentham's idea that social scientists should try to gauge the overall, net benefits of decisions, taking into account all the winners and losers, underpins microeconomics and the process that economists use when they try to advise policymakers on such issues as whether the government should require automakers to raise their average fuel economy, and how much oil the U.S. government should keep in the Strategic Petroleum Reserve.

Bentham's ideas also spawned a political force in early nineteenth-century Britain, the philosophical radicals, who included some prominent Parliament members as well as writers.

These radicals battled for government to implement sound economic principles instead of yielding to old-fashioned, aristocratic politics. They also battled bravely for democracy and free speech. They fought the Stamp Act, which taxed periodicals, and attacked the Corn Laws, which kept foreign grains out of Britain at the high cost of hurting common workers and consumers. During the 1820s and 1830s, the radicals won many political wars and skirmishes, far beyond expectations. This, of course, brought them a lot of pleasure.

As for Bentham, he must have taken his third factor, long-term pleasure, very seriously. He bequeathed his body to the University of London to be wheeled out for major administrative meetings, and his body, post-taxidermy, still resides there. Unfortunately, some sporting, pleasure-seeking students stole his head, which just shows how difficult it is to measure fecundity and purity.

Why Did John Stuart Mill Oppose Welfare?

John Stuart Mill started his career as a rabid Jeremy Bentham fan, but then turned on his mentor in a blistering attack.[11] Essentially, Mill thought Bentham's method dehumanized human beings, since there were different levels of pleasure. Bentham had suggested that poker was as good as poetry, if the pleasure given was equal. Mill disagreed. Switching metaphors, he countered that he would rather be a discontented Socrates than a satisfied pig. Mill enhanced Bentham's utilitarianism by introducing Platonic virtues like honor, dignity, and self-development.

Mill then took his version of utilitarianism and applied it to economics in his 1848 masterpiece, *Principles of Political Economy*. On welfare, Mill worried that government aid sapped the work ethic. Mill distinguished the able-bodied from the disabled, elderly, and very young, saying that certainly, these groups should receive support, and society should not worry that they will be hooked on what Franklin Roosevelt later called a "narcotic." But Mill felt less sympathy toward the physically fit. He proposed that recipients work for their welfare money. After ignoring Mill's calls for decades, the U.S. Congress finally took the idea seriously, passing a mild version of so-called workfare legislation in 1988.

During the 1992 presidential campaign Bill Clinton promised to end welfare and replace it with a Millsian ultimatum: get off welfare and get a job within two years. Unfortunately, by 1994 President Clinton had discovered that providing government jobs for welfare recipients would actually cost taxpayers an even bigger sum of money than the welfare payments. Thus, he dramatically cut back his original proposal.

Mill's plan was more severe, though, than Clinton's or the alternatives in the Republican party. He thought that the jobs should be as arduous as those held by the least fortunate independent workers. Modern versions correctly find no reason to prevent recipients from training for more worthwhile jobs. Nonetheless, Mill showed remarkable prescience.

Mill also wanted to link welfare payments to education. But not just education in basic skills like reading, writing, and arithmetic; Mill saw nothing wrong in inculcating a taste for capitalist values. In his view, capitalist societies have a duty to teach all of their citizens how to succeed in a commercial community. What Max Weber later called the "Protestant work ethic" is not a biological trait. To assume that it is deprives poor people of their only hope for rising out of the poorhouse. Mill wanted to combine moral education with economic incentives.

Economists today are frequently attacked for ignoring ethical issues, for focusing too closely on numbers, instead of on people. They are, it is said, "moral dwarfs." While this is sometimes true, the great classical economists like John Stuart Mill and Adam Smith, whose *Theory of Moral Sentiments* anticipated certain aspects of Freud, stood very tall.

Why Was Alfred Marshall the Darwin of Economics?

While the great classical economists like Smith, Ricardo, Bentham, and Mill each aspired to be the Newton of economics, discovering the natural laws that work like gravity to bring supply and demand together, Alfred Marshall of Cambridge University looked instead to Charles Darwin. Marshall's motto, which he inscribed in his 1890 text *Principles of Economics,* was *natura non facit saltum,* nature makes no sudden leaps. While the leap from monkey to man took millions of years, Marshall explained why economic science must study both the long run and the short run.

The businessman and the consumer make no great leaps but try to improve their situations step by step. Individuals, companies, and governments all adapt to changing prices. The fittest firms survive; low profits drive out the weakest. Competitive pressures force firms to cut costs. Although the final results do resemble Adam Smith's Newtonian economics, Marshall teaches us how to closely inspect individual decisions along the way. "The mecca of the economist lies in economic biology," he declared.[12]

Marshall lived his professorial life by the gradualist creed: he dared to be cautious. Sometimes he may have been too slow. While he developed many of his ideas in the early 1870s, he finished his *Principles* so many years later that critics disparaged his claims of originality. Marshall also had some personality quirks, among them hypochondria. He designed his own house in Cambridge to be taller than the others, because he thought the fens made him sick.

Marshall's many accomplishments included developing the marginalist approach, the concept of elasticity, and the idea of long-run and short-run changes, which we will focus on here. Rome was not built in a day, and man did not evolve from monkeys in a week. Darwin taught that paradoxically, whereas a thousand years may be biologically insignificant, the brief lifetime of a mutant could determine the future of a species; Marshall realized that like biological time, "economic time" was not synchronized with Big Ben in London. Ten years does not permit a firm to do ten times what it could do in just one year. For some transactions, one year is a long time, while for other moves, one year barely allows preparation.

During every step of economic analysis, clocks are ticking. During the first OPEC embargo of 1973, politicians grabbed economists by the necks, shaking them to and fro until they answered crucial questions: When will consumers respond to higher prices by conserving? When will General Motors, Ford, and Chrysler respond by producing smaller cars? When will oil companies respond by drilling elsewhere? Eventually, consumers drove less, the Big Three built subcompacts, and drilling firms put more rigs in the North Sea, in Mexico, and in Alaska— but these developments did not take place at the same time.

In August 1990, when Iraq invaded Kuwait, oil prices soared, as the Iraqi army detonated Kuwaiti drilling and refinery stations, sending plumes of dark clouds circulating around the globe. The U.S. organized a world embargo of Iraqi oil exports. At the time, I served on a White House committee to estimate the economic effects of the oil price "spike." Surely, higher oil prices would drive up general prices and work to shrink industrial output. But we could not answer the big question: How long would the crisis last? What we did know was that eventually, the economy would adjust to less output from Iraq and Kuwait; more drilling rigs would come on line, and, once again, manufacturers would conserve more. These responses would temper the long-term impact. But firms cannot move so quickly in the short term. So the economy would slow down in the short term, and Americans would lose jobs.

Let's use a hypothetical example to understand Marshall's approach to economic timing. Suppose clever Debbie develops a new kind of coffee drink called Capu-Latte-Lite, which is so frothy, it makes people look like they are foaming at the mouth. Though at first Capu-Latte-Lite worries the health department's rabies watchdog, soon the drink catches on. The slogan, "Foam at Home or at Work for Capu-Latte-Lite" turns office typing pools into pools of suds. On any particular day, the supply of Capu-Latte-Lite is fixed. If the typing pool loses its electricity and more than the usual number of typists take breaks, some will go thirsty and frothless. By the time Debbie's factory hears about excess demand, pumps out more Capu-Latte-Lite, and ships it to the offices, the working day is over. *In the time frame of one day, therefore, only demand can fluctuate.*

With advance notice, producers can ratchet up their factories and boost supply. The second time period, which Marshall called the "short run," lasts long enough for producers to change the amount they supply. To supply more, they can hire more labor and buy more raw materials. But they cannot expand too much. Marshall's short run does not last long enough to build new manufacturing plants. What if Capu-Latte-Lite advertises on television, which sends demand soaring? In the short run, Debbie can buy more coffee beans and hire more workers to grind them and milk the cows. If demand falls, she can fire the workers and cut back on udders.

In the third period, the "long run," Debbie has enough time to build new plants, plant new coffee trees in Colombia, as well as vary labor and materials. In the long run, then, supply becomes most prominent. New competitors can enter the field, trying to capture some of Debbie's fantastic profits. If she cannot keep up the quality of her product and keep the frenzy for foam going, competition can force her from the market. The survivors in this competitive struggle would earn only normal profits, since excessive profits would induce yet more entrants into the market.

How long are the long and short runs? It depends on the particular industry; the periods are defined by how long it takes to alter capital and capacity. Obviously, Marshall did not discuss Capu-Latte-Lite, though his bushy white mustache would have looked amusing in it; instead, he discussed fish. In the fishing industry, Marshall supposed that it would take a year or two to deploy new ships. As technology improves, however, the long run—the reaction time to new events—may shrink.

Marshall died at the age of eighty-two, the grand old economist of Britain having himself lived the long run. His most eminent pupil, Keynes, compared him to the ideal master economist, who must be "mathematician, historian, statesman, philosopher. . . . He must study the present in light of the past for the purposes of the future."[13] Marshall's lasting contributions to economics have proved Keynes right.

Rebels with a Cause: Schools of Thought That Break from the Mainstream

What was the Austrian school about?

While Marshall and his brilliant pupil Maynard Keynes were refining mainstream, neoclassical economics in Cambridge, Vienna was also bubbling with intellectual excitement but taking economics in the opposite direction. The Viennese approached economics using a different method and derived different conclusions. As Anglo-American professors started developing mathematical models, Austrian scholars launched a philosophical attack on graphs, curves, and calculus. Starting with Carl Menger's *Principles of Economics* (1871), the Austrians declared that humans do not act as predictably as mathematical models would permit. In fact, this insistence on studying human beings, not abstract institutions or statistical data, explains why Ludwig von Mises, the hero of modern-day Austrians, called his masterpiece on economics *Human Action,* rather than, say, *My Theory of Markets.* (While readers who fear mathematics might want to cheer the Austrians and learn more, the fact is that their philosophical discussions can be tougher going than calculus.)

The Austrians used their method to develop some unique theories. First, they devised their own idea of why economies go belly-up, leading to unemployment and depression. Building on Menger's work, Friedrich von Hayek argued in the early 1930s that people are constantly balancing their desire for immediate consumption with their wish to save and consume more at some later date. When governments intervene in the economy, they almost always destroy this balance between today, tomorrow, and the day after tomorrow. In particular, by toying with interest rates, governments throw this balance off kilter. Suppose the central bank tries to speed up the economy by pushing down interest rates. According to Hayek, people would be artificially pushed into more business investment than the "natural" balance would have provided. Eventually, this imbalance tumbles the country into a boom-and-bust cycle, because the economy is not producing the right match of consumer and business goods.[14]

Even more important than their business cycle theory, the Austrians devised the most focused attack on socialism. Under the socialist model, government planners would tell industrial plant managers how much they could produce and how it would be allocated. Mises and Hayek "double-teamed" central-planning enthusiasts and showed that central planners could never collect all the information that spontaneously arises in a market system and guides production decisions. Savvy socialists like Poland's Oskar Lange tried to answer this charge by contending that factory managers could judge how much to produce by simply watching the buildup or build-down of inventories. Lines of customers meant they should produce more. Empty stores meant to produce less.[15] In practice this, of course, never worked. Socialist countries like the Soviet Union had plenty of long lines, but either shelves of goods that no one wanted or not enough of what they did want.

The problem was not just information, as Mises and Hayek stressed, but also the lack of incentives. Socialism, in practice, may have given everyone a bed—but no one a good reason to get out of it and get to work. I have heard the following story attributed to Stalin:

> Our factories did not produce enough nails. So I told the factory manager to make more. He did. But the nails were lousy and crumpled when struck with a hammer. Why? He couldn't get any more steel from the steel plant, so he just put less steel in each nail. So, we told him to make stronger nails, and forget about raising the number produced. What did we get? One big, strong nail.

Though the Austrians led the economic attack on socialism, like socialism itself, they had trouble sustaining themselves. First of all, the Nazi era forced many to flee, creating a geographic diaspora. Second, the two most promising disciples, Hayek and Joseph Schumpeter, eventually broke with the school, angering the old guard and leaving the Austrians rather directionless and homeless for a good part of the twentieth century. Since the 1970s, though, they have reenergized a bit, particularly at New York University and George Mason University in Virginia. Still, they feel they've been frozen out of mainstream economics and seldom get even a footnote in standard textbooks.

While Austrian economists have fought a hundred-year war for recognition, rational expectations economists burst on the scene in the 1960s and almost immediately wrote their way into the textbooks.

Who has rational expectations?

Einstein once commented that he never thought about the future, since it came soon enough. Well, if that rumpled genius didn't bother, why would we expect normal people to have "rational expectations" about the future? According to the rational expectations school (RE school), Einstein *did* subconsciously think about the future, even if he was too lost in the time-space continuum to realize it. The RE crowd (also known as new classical economists), which began to form after a 1961 pathbreaking paper by University of Indiana professor John Muth, argues that people make decisions with certain expectations in mind. Just as I expect the mailman to deliver my letters, I expect him to run away if I sic my nasty Doberman pinscher on him just as he gets to my front porch. So far this thesis sounds fairly simple, if mean-spirited. But here is where the RE school adds their zest: they insist that *people continuously update their forecasts so that they will not be systematically fooled.* When my mauled mailman returns to the neighborhood tomorrow, he will not so blithely step up to my front porch. In fact, he will probably sidestep my house altogether.

RE should take its motto from both P. T. Barnum and Abraham Lincoln: there may be a sucker born every minute, but you cannot fool all of the people all of the time. Individuals may make forecasting errors, but they will not continue making the same mistake. Cartoon characters are often funny simply because they do make fools of themselves in the very same way time and time again. Every autumn in Charles Schulz's world of *Peanuts,* for instance, Charlie Brown tries to kick a football that Lucy inevitably jerks away at the last moment, sending Charlie flying onto his rear end. According to the RE school, most economic models portray consumers and producers as moronic Charlie Browns. As a result, RE scholars think mainstream models are not worth peanuts.

Let's leave the metaphors now and go to some actual economic examples where RE research has enhanced mainstream thought. First, the RE school explains why households usually save their gains from temporary tax cuts. Traditional Keynesian theory suggested that if the government cut taxes, people would spend most of the newfound dough. Why? More income leads people to do more shopping. Yet the RE school, following seminal research by Milton Friedman, is skeptical. After all, people subconsciously ask themselves, Will this temporary boon change my long-run income expectations? Will the government merely raise taxes at some later date to make up for it? Apparently, the government cannot fool people into going on spending sprees.

The RE school has similar doubts about the investment tax credit (ITC), Congress's favorite investment nostrum. The ITC, with which the government helps pay for new private business equipment, has come and gone from the tax code at least half a dozen times since 1960. By now firms know the game. Whenever the economy dips into recession, Congress considers an ITC to stimulate spending. But firms are not stupid. They actually slow down their buying of equipment, waiting for Congress to pass the ITC again, so that their purchases will qualify for the credit. This waiting game tends to slow the economy just when it needs some thrust, and then it jerks the economy forward just when the recovery would have begun anyway.

The RE premise yields some rather kooky-sounding implications, including the idea that allowing a chimp to choose your stock portfolio is better than hiring a broker. The most important result, though, is known as the Lucas critique, named for economist Robert Lucas of the University of Chicago.[16] If people continually update their understanding of the economy, the forecasting models are obsolete. Why? Because the models must be based on old data.

Suppose the Treasury Department discovers a startling correlation between a stronger stock market and NFC teams winning the Super Bowl. If it then tries to prop up the stock market by passing laws that favor NFC teams, economic actors will see this policy as new information and refine their models. Thus, *old behavior is a poor basis for creating new policy*. The Lucas critique suggests that government efforts do not work unless they surprise people; reaching into the old, tattered bag of tricks—public spending, ITCs, for example—to combat recessions merely leads to cynicism from households and businesses that have learned from the past.

Why do "new Keynesians" disagree with the RE school?

Though most economists think RE scholars go too far in assuming that people process information lightning fast, there is little doubt that the Lucas critique and the RE school's work on financial markets have sent mainstream economists back to the drawing board. The RE rebels drum up the most trouble when they insist that all markets "clear," meaning that prices always adjust simultaneously to get rid of any surplus or shortage. They say that no gluts can exist. If fish produce too much caviar, the price must fall. If demand for labor falls, wages must plunge.

Now, most economists agree that markets eventually clear, but what's the rush? Traditional Keynesians and monetarists have always talked about "transition periods" before the economy reacts to government spending or money supply changes. New Keynesians especially stress "sticky wages" and "menu costs." Union contracts generally last three years, making quick wage adjustment nearly impossible. Likewise, many firms cannot easily change their prices once they have been announced. The prices printed in the L.L. Bean clothing catalogue for the spring season cannot be changed so swiftly by the company after the catalogue has already been mailed to millions of potential buyers—even if demand leaps and a particular preppie sweater becomes a best-seller. Certainly, those buyers would resent telephoning the toll-free order line only to hear that the catalogue prices have been jacked up.

While these attacks on RE have some weight, computer technology seems to be pushing us closer to an RE world. Led by airlines, more and more industries are using flexible pricing systems to quickly adapt their prices to tiny shifts in demand. "Suggested retail prices" seem to count for less and less, as more sellers are willing to deal in order to clear the market.

New Keynesians sometimes find the RE folks exasperating because they always seem to have an airtight, logical answer, even if it does not seem realistic.[17] The RE school suggests that unemployment during the Great Depression was largely voluntary, for example. Why? Workers could have gotten jobs if they had only agreed to work for reduced wages. Despite the RE school's logical allure, most economists find it pretty hard to explain away record unemployment during the Great Depression as twelve years of surprising information that fooled workers into not renegotiating their wages.

The RE self-confidence reminds me of a story Stephen Hawking tells in his book *A Brief History of Time*. Hawking describes a famous scientist delivering a lecture on astronomy, describing how the earth circles the sun, and the sun orbits the galaxy. Finally, a little old lady stands up in the back of the room. "What you have told us is rubbish," she says. "The world is really a flat plate supported on the back of a giant tortoise." The scientist gives a superior smile, and asks, "What is the tortoise standing on?" "You're very clever, young man, very clever," says the old lady. "But it's turtles all the way down!" Since it's so difficult to prove such things, Hawking rather facetiously admits that she may be right. And so may the extremists among the RE buffs.

Around the same time that RE scholars began challenging conventional economics, supply-side economists launched their attack on the mainstream as well. While the RE folks had more luck in the academic arena, the supply-side advocates won more battles on the political stage.

What is supply-side economics?

Few topics disrupt economic conferences and political debates as much as *supply-side economics* (SSE). If you listen to the foaming critics, you would think they were describing some evil plan hatched by Goebbels. Words like *fraud, swindle,* and *hoax* are tossed around. On the other hand, if you listen to the most enthusiastic fans, you would think they had discovered a new inscription on Moses' tablets. In fact, SSE can be discussed without calling for a squad of cardiologists. SSE asks two simple questions: Can we get individuals and firms to produce more if we cut their tax rates? Is it worth it?

Since these questions sound rather harmless, we may have to look elsewhere to explain the rhetorical fisticuffs. Perhaps the deep resentment to SSE stems from the unorthodox crowd who promoted the idea in the late 1970s. An entertaining history of this movement comes from one of the key proponents, *Wall Street Journal* editor Robert L. Bartley. He describes SSE's best publicist, Jude Wanniski, as wearing "dark shirts and light ties [that] were a holdover from his days as a newshound in Las Vegas."[18] This kind of attire did not go over well at the Brookings Institution, which consistently attacked SSE as a kind of snake oil that would fuel inflation and drive up interest rates. Nor did the hyperbole that occasionally came out of the supply-side camp go over well, with its suggestions that tax cuts could not only bring in more tax revenue but could even cut government spending.[19]

Perhaps the debate might have been more gentlemanly had it occurred at an easier time in history, but by the mid 1970s, the U.S. seemed, well, pathologically sick. Still reeling from Vietnam and Jimmy Carter's malaise-struck presidency, the political system was not delivering the goods. Nor was the economy, which had drifted back into stagflation, following OPEC oil embargoes and confused macroeconomic policies. The Keynesian paradigm appeared ill-equipped to handle simultaneous inflation and recession, since Keynes had devised his policy prescriptions during the Great Depression, when prices were falling, not rising. In sum, frustration reigned, and policymakers felt, rightly, impotent.

The supply-siders pointed out that during this bleak period, tax rates had been climbing upward, while productivity had slipped downward. Even without overtly raising taxes, Congress had permitted families to move into higher tax brackets as inflation bumped up their nominal incomes. While in 1965 the average family of four found themselves in the 19-percent tax bracket, by 1980 they had moved up to nearly 30 percent. A family earning about twice the median income, which was about $30,000 in 1980, found their tax bracket had more than doubled, from 22 percent to 49 percent.[20] At the same time that taxes skyrocketed, the share of GNP that the U.S. devoted to business investment plummeted by about 40 percent. Looking at this mess, the supply-siders came up with the prescription to cut taxes.

How exactly did they explain that cutting taxes would make the situation better? Remember that people and firms are always making choices between working or not working, consuming or saving, reinvesting profits or paying dividends, etc. Taxes affect these choices, by changing the actual prices we pay. Ronald Reagan's stories always seemed to capture the dilemma. He described his discovery of supply-side effects, long before the 1970s:

> At Eureka College, my major was economics, but I think my own experience with our tax laws in Hollywood probably taught me more about practical economic theory than I ever learned in the classroom. . . . At the peak of my career at Warner Bros., I was in the ninety-four-percent tax bracket; that meant that after a certain point, I received only six cents of each dollar I earned and that the government got the rest. The IRS took such a big chunk of my earnings that after a while I began asking myself whether it was worth it to keep on taking work. . . . If I decided to do one less picture, that meant other people at the studio in lower tax brackets wouldn't work as much either; the effect filtered down, and there were fewer jobs available.[21]

In economists' terms, Reagan "substituted leisure for work," because the IRS made the rewards of working too small. (In movie critics' terms, the IRS may have done the world a favor.) Likewise, higher taxes on business can make investment less attractive. Such taxes may therefore reduce the supply of resources and shrink output.

High taxes twist the economy in other ways as well. They send people fleeing into the arms of creative accountants who concoct tax shelters rather than searching for legitimate businesses to invest in. And they can send people "underground" to do business. The Canadian government recently slashed its tobacco taxes after too many reports of smuggling and other tax-avoidance schemes. High taxes can also send people away from home. German tennis great Boris Becker technically lives in Monaco to escape taxes. To avoid high tax rates, professionals will accept more of their compensation in the form of nontaxable fringe benefits, like fancy offices and autos, rather than in taxable income. They will invest in more nontaxable municipal bonds, rather than taxable bonds. Moreover, high taxes foster tax-deductible hobbies like collecting antiques, rather than more productive activities.[22]

Nothing in the above paragraph is particularly controversial among economists. The controversy surrounds the question, Is this a big deal? That is, does cutting taxes create enough energy to make a big difference? Naturally, supply-siders say yes, while critics—mostly Keynesians—shake their heads. Critics point out that aside from wealthy movie actors, most people do not have much choice over how many hours or weeks to work during a year. Not too many mortals enjoy the freedom Reagan had to "just say no" to another Warner Bros. film. Reasonable supply-siders acknowledge this but reply that female spouses do seem to be sensitive to tax rates. Cutting income taxes for spouses would unleash more labor.

Critics warn that supply-side effects tend to come around rather slowly. If firms decide to beef up investment and build more plants, the new supply will not come on line for years. In fact, the investment will first show up as new demand for bricks and mortar. Again, responsible supply-siders will agree, but they never promised instant nirvana.

The critics also contend that tax cuts will lead to higher, not lower, budget deficits, since the government will "lose" money on the deal. Once again, supply-siders agree that deficits will rise, at least for the first few years. But if tax rates are cut from extremely high levels, they say that the government would eventually recoup the losses.

Let's take an example to show why the impact rises when tax rates begin in the stratosphere. Start with Ronald Reagan in Hollywood facing a 94-percent tax rate. If we cut rates by 50 percent, his new bracket is 47 percent. After the cut, a $100 bonus would get him an additional $53, rather than $6, increasing his incentive to earn by more than eight-fold. Yet if a lowly gaffer on the Warner Bros. set falls into the 10-percent bracket, slicing his rate by 50 percent gets him only an added $5 after a $100 bonus (at a 10-percent rate he would have kept $90; now he gets to keep $95). That's just a 5.5-percent boost to his earning incentive.

No wonder supply-side economics makes more sense when you are starting with higher tax levels. No wonder the current Federal Reserve Board governor Lawrence Lindsey discovered that wealthy Americans shifted their behavior when taxes were cut in 1981.[23] For this same reason, though, critics blast supply-side economics for favoring the rich. In truth, while the incentive impact is greatest on the rich, that is only because they start off in far higher tax brackets. At the end of the day, the federal government ends up collecting more dollars from them, as they switch away from tax shelters and toward more productive activities. Of course, since most of the tax cuts in the 1980s actually went to middle-income Americans, who had weaker incentives to change their behavior, the federal budget deficit grew. This combined with the Reagan administration's inability to reverse the path of federal spending launched the deficit into space.

Though the supply-side debate continues to rumble in the United States, it clearly has inspired other countries to experiment. During the last half of the 1980s, over fifty countries cut their top tax rates. The biggest declines came in such former egalitarian bastions as Sweden, Australia, Italy, and the U.K. Only Luxembourg and Lebanon (did they not have enough trouble?) bumped up their rates. While in the 1990s a few countries, the U.S. and the U.K. among them, have reversed course a bit, note that even SSE's critics do not wish to return to the punitive rates of the 1970s. When President Clinton urged Congress to hike taxes on the rich, he meant moving from a top rate of 33 percent to a top rate of 39.6 percent. Despite his campaign rhetoric blasting the 1980s as a giveaway to country-clubbers and jet-setters, he did not suggest a return to anywhere near the 70-percent level that welcomed Ronald Reagan in 1981 when he moved into the White House.

While the Reaganauts tried to wrestle with the Congress on economic policy in the 1980s, another school of economic thought, public choice scholars, shook their heads and thought the idea of changing Congress's stripes was doomed to fail. With them we come full circle, for of all the modern schools, they best exemplify "dismal economists."

Why do public choice scholars distrust government?

While the rational expectations school begins with the premise that people are smart, public choice economics (PCE) starts with the idea that politicians are creeps. Well, maybe not creeps, but certainly most interested in advancing their careers, prestige, and power. Politics is a kind of business, and politicians are entrepreneurs of a sort. Once you wipe away the fantasies about congressmen and bureaucrats utterly devoted to the public good, you end up with a different view of the government's role in the economy. Public choice scholars, like Will Rogers, tend to view Congress with the same nervousness as a parent does when his baby picks up a hammer.

The roots of the public choice school go back even further than Adam Smith, basically to the first ancient person who ever cursed bureaucrats. The school really took off, though, after World War II, with pathbreaking work on voters and democracy by Nobel laureate Kenneth Arrow and Anthony Downs. Downs's book *An Economic Theory of Democracy* showed that voters are ignorant of policy issues.[24] So far this sounds pretty bland. But here is the clincher: rather than lamenting their ignorance as a junior high school civics teacher would, Downs announces that *they are right to be ignorant!* Spending time and energy to figure out what Congress is doing will probably not get them anywhere, he says. Even if they discover that some program cheats taxpayers out of, say, half a billion dollars, their share of that is about the price of a bag of potato chips. So, why bother? The trouble with being a responsible citizen is that it takes up too many evenings.

Let's take a real-life example. Do you care about honeybees? Probably not, unless they are chasing you. Yet ever since World War II, the U.S. Congress has subsidized honey producers with billions of taxpayer dollars. In the 1980s alone, the U.S. spent about half a billion dollars to buy up surplus honey and store it—in case of nuclear war.[25] The real motive, of course, was not to prepare for war but to give some sweet goodies to the producers, who had found sugar daddies on Capitol Hill willing to protect them. Though Congress finally cut the direct subsidy deal in 1994, the American Beekeeping Federation and the American Honey Producers Association have not given up. They still get access to cheap federal credit, and they have now turned their attention to blocking imported honey from crossing our borders, which they see as a threat to their incomes.

While it does not make much economic sense for any normal citizen to worry about the subsidy, the producers have a deep need to follow the story. Suppose there are a thousand official honeybee raisers in the U.S. The $500 million paid to them during the 1980s translates into $500,000 each. That is a strong incentive to mind your beeswax—and your congressman.

Western economies are riddled with special deals that seem almost invincible because of the "logic of collective action." In a book called *The Rise and Decline of Nations,* Mancur Olson argues that older economies slow down precisely because they eventually become skewered with favors to special interests.[26] A related problem concerns government regulation of industry. Nobel laureate George Stigler pointed out that bureaucrats, like hostages, tend to grow sympathetic to their captors. As a result, the U.S. Department of Transportation coddles maritime unions, and the Department of Energy routinely lobbies the White House to subsidize U.S. oil drillers. Ralph Nader echoed Stigler's argument back in 1970 when he made reference to the allegedly lax regulatory policies of the "Interstate Commerce Omission."

The public choice approach goes a little too far and grows a little too cynical for most economists. Even the strongest critics, though, admit the truth of the school's key lesson: Do not assume that the government will take prudent steps in the face of political or bureaucratic pressures. For the twenty years following World War II, standard textbooks blithely prescribed government action to cure market imperfections like oligopolies and pollution. But they forgot to ask whether the government could accomplish the task, given its own inherent imperfections. Will political forces deliver the wrong dosage and make matters worse? We should be comparing a realistic view of the market economy to a realistic view of the government. For too long, textbooks compared a blemished view of the private economy with a squeaky clean view of government. At long last, we may admit that the only squeak in Washington comes from the subways, not from the Capitol.

CONCLUSION

We've now completed this tour through economics. Perhaps you found that even the shortcut to economic literacy has some bends in the road, some detours and potholes that we swerved by. There is, of course, more to economics than the material we have covered. We have not addressed Third World debt, Marxism, or colonialism, for example. Maybe next time. Even if we had performed an exhaustive review, picking apart every economic theory, we would have missed something.

We would have missed that indefinable, psychological element that often propels economic actors and shapes economic history. Joseph Schumpeter taught that entrepreneurs are the driving force of growth. Their special, psychological need to innovate and create pushes them to shake up the status quo. One of his Harvard colleagues described Schumpeter's romantic entrepreneur as a "medieval knight errant, who rides out in search of exciting adventures, ready to slay the dragons of routine and stagnation."[1] Likewise, Maynard Keynes explained that capitalism must be energized by those active "animal spirits" that excite investors and ignite new business ventures.

While these almost mystical forces are hard to analyze with the economist's standard toolbox, we do know that they thrive in basically free environments. Too many rules, regulations, and taxes can snuff the entrepreneurial spark. Like matter and antimatter, government bureaucrats always seem to be fighting off entrepreneurs and vice versa. While bureaucrats wear only gray, entrepreneurs see only vivid colors. Tribal taboos may also stifle animal spirits. Though modern economies thrive on circulating money through a system where borrowers pay back lenders with interest, the Bible and Koran both condemned it. Schumpeter was almost whipped in Cairo when he insisted a devout Moslem accept an interest payment from him!

Economies need some flux and cannot thrive in perfect order. That was the problem with socialism: by putting everything and everyone in their "proper" place, it prevented things from getting better. Socialist countries could keep the status quo but could not keep up with their neighbors who were not content with the status quo. No wonder Western Europe flew past Eastern Europe after World War II. The Soviet Union fell not because the Kremlin could not keep constant the standard of living, but because that standard of living was stuck in 1917!

This same fear of change, this clutching on to yesteryear inspires the evils that infect even advanced economies like the United States': protecting producers from competition, over-regulating businesses to utterly eliminate risks, and urging investors to take the absolute safest route, even if it cannot give them a high enough return to live on.

The problem with a boring, gray world was best described by Orson Welles in the movie *The Third Man:* "In Italy, for thirty years under the Borgias, they had warfare, terror, murder, and bloodshed, but they produced Michelangelo, Leonardo da Vinci, and the Renaissance. In Switzerland, they had brotherly love; they had five hundred years of democracy and peace—and what did that produce? The cuckoo clock."

Now, no one wants the chaotic world of the Borgias, but a little risk, a little uncertainty, and a little freedom to shake things up make the difference between a dynamic economy with ever new opportunities and that dark day when animal spirits go out with a whimper.

APPENDIX: GREATEST HITS OF ECONOMICS

Editorialists and pundits often lament that Americans have become "innumerate," incapable of performing arithmetic tasks any more complex than figuring out whether they have won the state lottery. Yet we have grown fond of one kind of counting: popularity ratings. From *Consumer Reports*' list of the most dependable automobiles, to *U.S. News & World Reports*' list of top colleges, to *Forbes*' wealthiest 400 people, to *People*'s list of the 10 sexiest men, to David Letterman's top ten, Americans seem obsessed with ranking people and things. In a recent book on economic theory, a noted American economist rather gratuitously decided to point out that the eminent scientist Stephen Hawking was not the world's "leading" physicist. (The author's book galleys had actually stated that Hawking was not "even among the top ten.")

While I refuse to opine on physicists, I happily share my judgment on the greatest hits of economics.

The Top Five Economists

- Adam Smith (1723–1790)—Not the brightest light in the galaxy, but without his colorfully anecdotal master-piece *Wealth of Nations,* the rise of modern econom-ics would have been delayed many decades.
- David Ricardo (1772–1823)—Brainpower and political courage, combined with the talent for building theo-ries that underlie Smith's observations, especially on trade issues.
- Alfred Marshall (1842–1924)—A devoted teacher who basically invented the economics curriculum, Marshall helped to reinvent classical theory by developing mar-ginalism, aided by his wife, economist Mary Paley Marshall.
- John Maynard Keynes (1883–1946)—The great philoso-pher Bertrand Russell said that he was embarrassed by Keynes's phenomenal intellectual superiority. Keynes's work on the government's role in the economy has hit on hard times, but his star still shines.
- Milton Friedman (1912–)—A feisty antidote to Keynes-ian economics, Friedman fought his way into the mainstream by turning everyone else to his direction on macroeconomics.

There are many runners-up, including Joseph Schumpeter, whom I left out of the top five because he unfairly disparaged the work of Smith, Ricardo, and Keynes. Of all the great econo-mists, Keynes is the one you would like to be seated across from at a dinner party, for witty and wise conversation.

The Three Most Important Economic Events Since Adam Smith

- The Industrial Revolution—Before the 1800s, most people in Europe lived as they had back in Roman times, with simple agrarian methods leaving their lives at the mercy of droughts and floods. The rise of industrial capabilities permitted incomes to double in just a few decades, a startling development never seen in human history.
- The Great Depression—With 25 percent of the workforce unemployed, this catastrophic bust has haunted America's memories and undergirded support for government programs to stabilize the economy and insulate working people from extreme hardship. The 1929 depression became "great" when the Fed squashed the money supply, Congress and European parliaments raised tariffs, and overextended businessmen ran for the hills.
- The Computer Revolution—Through most of history, brawn beat out brains in the workplace and in the fields. Steel, grain, and minerals determined gross national product. Now, tiny yet sophisticated components and weightless software algorithms move the economy forward.

The Three Most Important Economic Formuli

- MSB = MSC (Marginal Social Benefit Equals Marginal Social Cost)—A community should decide to do something if the additional benefits at least equal the added costs imposed on society.
- MV = PQ (The Money Supply times Velocity Equals the

Price of All Goods times the Quantity of Goods)—
This formula underlies the actions of central banks all
over the world and tells them that the supply of
money in the system should not overwhelm the ability
of the economy to produce goods, or else prices will
rise (inflation). See chapter 2.

- $Y = C + I + G + (X - M)$—This formula, which comes
from Keynes's model, adds up the contributors to
income, namely, National Income is composed of
Private Consumption plus Private Investment plus
Government Spending plus Exports minus Imports. If
one of these factors falls in value, the others better
make up for it, or else the economy could slip into
recession.

Three Likely Future Nobel Laureates

- Amartya Sen—British-educated Indian scholar who has
written pathbreaking articles on Third World poverty
and the philosophy of economics.
- Martin Feldstein—One of the most innovative thinkers
on public finance since Keynes, Feldstein has men-
tored many of today's top economists.
- Robert Lucas—A founder of rational expectations theory, Lucas remains in the minority, but his views
command respect for their theoretical challenges to
conventional models.

The Five Best Economic Articles

- Hayek's "The Use of Knowledge in Society" (*American
Economic Review*, 1945)—argues that socialism can-

not work because central planners cannot replicate all of the decisions and calculations that private firms make in a market system (see chapter 3).

- Friedman's "The Role of Monetary Policy" (*American Economic Review,* 1968)—explains how he persuaded a skeptical profession to throw out the Phillips Curve apparatus, which depicted a clear trade-off between inflation and unemployment (see chapter 2).
- Robert Solow's "Technical Change and the Aggregate Production Function" (*Review of Economics and Statistics,* 1957)—this MIT-based Nobel Laureate demonstrates that economic growth often stems from technology and education, not just land, capital, and labor, as economists used to think.
- Franco Modigliani and Merton Miller's "The Cost of Capital, Corporation Finance, and the Theory of Investment" (*American Economic Review,* 1958)—"M&M" revolutionized how economists looked at corporate finance, by proving that the value of a firm may be independent of whether it finances its operations by stock or by bonds (see chapter 7).
- Ronald Coase's "The Problem of Social Cost" (*Journal of Law and Economics,* 1960)—Coase invents the discipline of law and economics by showing how property conflicts can be resolved at the bargaining table, rather than in the courtroom.

The Most Successful Government Economic Policy of the Twentieth Century

- The German Economic "Miracle"—After World War II wiped out a huge portion of Germany's workforce, as well as its industrial capability, Bavarian finance minister Ludwig Erhard prescribed a new currency and decontrolling prices to cure shortages and the threat of rampant inflation.

The Most Unsuccessful Government Economic Policy of the Twentieth Century

- Smoot-Hawley Tariff and the Retaliation by Europe—To battle the Great Depression in 1930, President Hoover signed a tariff that boosted import taxes by over 50 percent, leading to a furious round of protectionism in Europe. By closing each other's markets, world trade fell by two-thirds and the industrialized nations sent the world economy even deeper into depression.

Best Forecast of the Twentieth Century

- Keynes in *The Economic Consequences of the Peace* (1919) warned that the punitive German reparations after World War I would so bankrupt the country that it would take up arms again, launching another war even more devastating.

Worst Forecast of the Twentieth Century

- In 1929, shortly before the stock market crash, re-nowned Yale professor Irving Fisher assured investors that stock prices had reached a "permanently high plateau," and one day before Black Friday (October

29), he said that "the only event which can bring about a serious decline in stock value is a severe business slump, which does not seem likely from present indications."

Most Economically Illiterate Maxim

- "If at first you don't succeed, try, try again." Bad advice. First, try to figure out why you've failed, but also make sure the goal is worth the price. Maybe it's time to cut your losses and move on to something else (see chapter 3).

Most Economically Literate Maxim

- "Don't put all your eggs in one basket." Good investment advice. Financial planners dress up this aphorism with phrases like "portfolio diversity," but the Mother Goose–like point remains—you reduce your risk by spreading around your financial exposure (see chapter 8).

NOTES

Chapter 1. The Big Picture

1. Howard Ruff, *Survive and Win in the Inflationary Eighties* (New York: Times Books, 1981). Ravi Batra, *The Great Depression of 1990* (New York: Simon and Schuster, 1987).

2. William Stanley Jevons, *Investigations in Currency and Finance,* ed. H. S. Foxwell (London: Macmillan, 1909) p. 196.

3. Ibid., p. 185.

4. Wesley Clair Mitchell, a University of Chicago professor, wrote the classic text entitled, of course, *Business Cycles* (New York: National Bureau of Economic Research, 1927). Then along with Arthur Burns, who later became chairman of the Federal Reserve Board, Mitchell penned *Measuring Business Cycles* (New York: Columbia University Press, 1946).

5. *Economic Report of the President,* February 1992, p. 103.

6. See, for example, Lawrence H. Summers, *Understanding Unemployment* (Cambridge, Mass.: MIT Press, 1990).

7. John Maynard Keynes, *Essays in Persuasion* (New York: Norton, 1931), p. 77.

8. See the argument in Paul Krugman, *The Age of Diminished Expectations* (Cambridge, Mass.: MIT Press, 1990).

9. Rudiger Dornbusch, "Lessons from the German Inflation Experience of the 1920s" in *Exchange Rates and Inflation* (Cambridge, Mass.: MIT Press, 1988), p. 417.

Chapter 2. Uncle Sam the Debtor

1. Robert Eisner, "Budget Deficits: Rhetoric and Reality," *Journal of Economic Perspectives* 3 (1989): 73–93.

2. See Laurence J. Kotlikoff, *Generational Accounting: Knowing Who Pays and When for What We Spend* (New York: Free Press, 1992).

3. *Economic Report of the President,* 1993, p. 256.

4. Robert J. Barro, "Are Government Bonds Net Wealth?" *Journal of Political Economy* 82 (December 1974): 1095–1117.

5. John Maynard Keynes, *The Collected Writings of John Maynard Keynes,* vol. 21 (London: Macmillan/St. Martin's Press, for the Royal Economic Society), p. 334.

6. Ibid., p. 296.

7. See the work of Nobel laureates Friedman and Modigliani in Milton Friedman, *A Theory of the Consumption Function* (Princeton: Princeton University Press, 1957); and A. Ando and F. Modigliani, "Tests of the Life Cycle Hypothesis of Savings: Comments and Suggestions," *Bulletin of the Oxford University Institute of Statistics* 19 (1957).

8. See Todd G. Buchholz, "What Do You Mean, No Pool Tables?" *Forbes* (February 1, 1993), p. 58.

9. A. W. H. Phillips, "The Relation between Unemployment and the Rate of Chance of Money Wage Rates in the United Kingdom, 1861–1957," *Economica,* no. 2 (1958): 283–99.

10. James Callaghan, quoted in "Keynes is Dead," *Wall Street Journal, Review and Outlook,* January 31, 1977.

11. Lawrence S. Ritter and William L. Silber, *Money* (New York: Basic Books, 1984), p. 11.

12. Quoted in John M. Berry, "The Fed Hunts a Number to Hang a Monetary Policy On," *Washington Post,* June 23, 1994, p. D12.

Chapter 3. The Very Model of a Modern Major Market

1. Thach is quoted in Dan Seligman, "Keeping Up," *Fortune* (February 27, 1989), p. 133. In a survey of U.S. economists printed in the *American Economic Review* (December 1984), 98 percent agreed that capping rents "reduces the quantity and quality" of housing.

2. Robert H. Hazen, *The New Alchemists* (New York: Times Books, 1993), p. 141.

3. F. A. Hayek, "The Use of Knowledge in Society," *American Economic Review* 35 (September 1945): 526–27.

4. Ibid., p. 528.

5. Alfred Marshall, *Principles of Economics,* 9th ed., vol. 1, ed. Guillebaud (London: Macmillan, 1961 [1920]), p. 99.

6. Quoted in J. Siegfried and T. Tiemann, "The Welfare Cost of Monopoly: An Interindustry Analysis," *Economic Inquiry,* journal of Western Economic Association (June 1974).

7. W. J. Baumol, J. C. Panzar, and R. D. Willig, *Contestable Markets and the Theory of Industry Structure,* rev. ed. (San Diego: Harcourt Brace Jovanovich, 1988).

Chapter 4. Applying Microeconomics to Major Markets

1. Len Benham, "The Effect of Advertising on the Price of Eyeglasses," *Journal of Law and Economics* 15 (October 1972): 337–52.

2. Marshall Goldman, "Product Differentiation and Advertising: Some Lessons from the Soviet Experience," *Journal of Political Economy* 68 (1960): 346–57.

3. *Economic Report of the President,* 1992, p. 84.

4. John E. Chubb and Terry M. Moe, *Politics, Markets, & American Schools* (Washington: Brookings Institution, 1990).

5. *Economic Report of the President,* 1993, p. 1653.

6. Ibid., p. 218

7. Joseph A. DiMasi, et al., "The Cost of Innovation in the Pharmaceutical Industry," *Journal of Health Economics* 10 (1991): 107–42.

8. American Medical Association, *Encyclopedia of Medicine* (New York: Random House, 1989), p. 228.

Chapter 5. Border Crossings

1. U.S. General Accounting Office, *Peanut Program: Changes Are Needed to Make the Program Responsive to Market Forces* (February 1993), p. 4.

2. U.S. General Accounting Office, *Sugar Program: Changing Domestic and International Conditions Require Program Changes* (April 1993), p. 3.

3. Gary C. Hufbauer and Kimberly A. Elliott, *Measuring the Costs of Protection in the United States* (Washington: Institute for International Economics, 1994), p. 20.

4. Frédéric Bastiat, *Economic Sophisms* (Princeton: D. Van Nostrand, 1964), pp. 56–57.

5. Quoted in Harry Anderson, Rich Thomas, and James C. Jones, "Carving Up the Car Buyer," *Newsweek,* March 5, 1984, p. 72.

6. Commission of the European Communities, *European Union* (Brussels, 1992), p. 10.

7. See Gary Clyde Hufbauer, Jeffrey J. Schott, and Kimberly Ann Elliott, *Economic Sanctions Reconsidered,* 2 vols., rev. ed. (Washington, D.C.: Institute for International Economics, 1990).

Chapter 6. Money Makes the World Go Round

1. Among the more hysterical screeds was Martin and Susan Tolchin's *Buying into America: How Foreign Money Is Changing the Face of Our Nation* (New York: Times Books/Random House, 1988).

2. "Dukakis-Bentsen-Gephardt," *Wall Street Journal,* October 11, 1988, p. 22.

3. Hans-Werner Sinn, "U.S. Tax Reform 1981 and 1986: Impact on International Capital Markets and Capital Flows," *National Tax Journal* 41, no. 3 (1988): 327–40.

4. *Economic Report of the President,* 1992, p. 205.

5. Ibid.

6. See Milton Friedman's classic "The Case for Flexible Exchange Rates," in *Essays in Positive Economics* (Chicago: University of Chicago Press, 1953).

7. Michael D. Bordo and A. J. Schwartz, eds. *A Retrospective on the Classical Gold Standard, 1821–1931* (Chicago: University of Chicago Press, 1984). *Fortune* 363.

Chapter 7. Going for Broke

1. Jane and Michael Stern, *The Encyclopedia of Bad Taste* (New York: HarperCollins, 1990), pp. 70–71.

2. Franco Modigliani and Merton Miller, "The Cost of Capital, Corporation Finance and the Theory of Investment," *American Economic Review* 48 (June 1958): 261–97.

3. John R. Dorfman, "Luck or Logic? Debate Rages on Over 'Efficient Market' Theory," *Wall Street Journal,* November 4, 1993, p. C1.

4. See Eugene Fama, "Efficient Capital Markets II," *Journal of Finance* (1991): 1575–1617.

5. Chiarella v. United States, 445 U.S. 222 (1980); Quoted in *The Wall Street Journal,* December 16, 1987, p. 29.

Chapter 8. Taking Stock of Personal Investments

1. U.S. Bureau of the Census, *Statistical Abstract of the United States: 1992,* p. 493.

2. John Maynard Keynes, *The Collected Writings of John Maynard Keynes,* vol. 7 (London: Macmillan/St. Martin's Press, for the Royal Economic Society, 1973), p. 156.

3. Tennessee Williams, *The Glass Menagerie.*

Chapter 9. They Shoot Economists, Don't They?

1. See Robert Skidelsky, *John Maynard Keynes,* vol. 2 (New York: Allen Lane/The Penguin Press, 1994), p. 518.

2. See my "Biblical Law and the Economic Growth of Ancient Israel" in *Journal of Law and Religion* 6, no. 2 (1988).

3. Adam Smith, *The Correspondence of Adam Smith,* ed. E. C. Mossmer and I. S. Ross (Oxford: Clarendon Press, 1977), p. 102.

4. Adam Smith, *An Inquiry into the Nature and Causes of the Wealth of Nations,* ed. R. H. Campbell, A. S. Skinner, and W. B. Todd, vol. 1 (Oxford: Clarendon Press, 1976 [1776]), p. 25.

5. Ibid., pp. 26–27.

6. Ibid., p. 456.

7. Ibid., p. 15.

8. William Godwin, *An Enquiry into Political Justice,* vol. 2 (London: 1798), p. 504.

9. Quoted in Patricia James, *Population Malthus* (London: Routledge & Kegan Paul, 1979), pp. 110–11.

10. Jeremy Bentham, *Introduction to the Principles of Morals and Legislation* (New York: Haffner, 1948), pp. 30–31.

11. John Stuart Mill, "Bentham," in *Essays on Politics and Culture,* ed. G. Himmelfarb (Garden City, N.Y.: Doubleday, 1962 [1838]), pp. 85–131.

12. Alfred Marshall, *Principles of Economics,* 9th ed., vol. 1, ed. Guillebaud (London: Macmillan, 1961 [1920]), p. 14.

13. John Maynard Keynes, "Alfred Marshall," in *Essays in Biography,* in the *Collected Writings of John Maynard Keynes,* vol. 10 (London and New York: MacMillan/St. Martin's Press for the Royal Economic Society, 1972), p. 173.

14. Hayek's innovative argument is found in Hayek, *Prices and Production,* 2d ed. (London: Routledge, 1931).

15. Lange's thesis and Hayek's response are both accessible to noneconomists. See Oskar Lange, *On the Economic Theory of Socialism,* ed. B. E. Lippincott (New York: McGraw-Hill, 1964), and F. A. Hayek, "The Use of Knowledge in Society," *American Economic Review* 35 (September 1945).

16. Robert E. Lucas, Jr., "Econometric Policy Evaluation: A Critique," in *The Phillips Curve and Labor Markets,* ed. K. Brunner and A. Meltzer, Carnegie-Rochester Conference Series, no. 1 (Amsterdam: North-Holland, 1976).

17. N. Gregory Mankiw, "Real Business Cycles: A New Keynesian Perspective," *Journal of Economic Perspectives* 35 (Summer 1989), p. 79–90.

18. Robert L. Bartley, *The Seven Fat Years* (New York: Free Press, 1992), p. 44.

19. Arthur B. Laffer and Jan P. Seymour, *The Economics of the Tax Revolt* (New York: Harcourt Brace Jovanovich, 1979), p. 2.

20. Lawrence B. Lindsey, *The Growth Experiment* (New York: Basic Books, 1990), p. 42.

21. Ronald Reagan, *An American Life* (New York: Simon and Schuster, 1990), p. 231.

22. Note that this discussion focuses on tax *rates,* not the amount of taxes paid. That's because tax rates help us figure out what incentive households and firms have for working, producing, or investing *more.*

23. See Lindsey, *Growth Experiment,* pp. 80–92.

24. Anthony Downs, *An Economic Theory of Democracy* (New York: Harper, 1957).

25. Peter Passell, "Economic Scene," *New York Times,* February 4, 1994, p. B2.

26. Mancur Olson, *The Rise and Decline of Nations* (New Haven: Yale University Press, 1982).

Conclusion

1. Alexander Gerschenkron, "Comments," in *The Transfer of Technology to Developing Countries,* ed. Daniel L. Spencer and Alexander Woroniak (New York: Frederick A. Praeger, 1967), p. 84.

SUGGESTED READINGS

In general, if you want to learn more about economics you should faithfully read *The Wall Street Journal* and the business pages of your local newspaper. Columnists like *The Washington Post*'s Robert Samuelson, *The New York Times*'s Peter Passell, and *The Los Angeles Times*'s James Flanigan do an impressive job explaining how public policy intertwines with economics. And despite the scowls that *USA Today* receives from highbrows, the "Money" section is quite good. On television, CNN's "Business Morning" and "Moneyline," CNBC's all-day coverage of Wall Street, and PBS's "Nightly Business Report" keep viewers abreast of the financial markets. Radio fans should tune into public radio's evening "Marketplace" program. For feature writing, the business weeklies—*Forbes, Fortune, Barron's* (especially for those interested in the financial markets), and *Businessweek* (including the "Economic Viewpoint" columns by Gary Becker and Rudi Dornbusch)—can also be illuminating.

Though pathbreaking economic theories usually get developed in dry and dense professional journals, the following writings offer some variety and fairly accessible prose for those who want to delve deeper into economic principles.

Chapter 1. The Big Picture

Alan Blinder. *Hard Heads, Soft Hearts*. Addison-Wesley, 1987.
Martin Feldstein. "The Economics of the New Unemployment." *Public Interest* (Fall 1973).

Douglas North. *Institutions, Institutional Change, and Economic Performance.* Cambridge University Press, 1990.

Herbert Stein. *Presidential Economics.* American Enterprise Institute, 1988.

Lawrence H. Summers. *Understanding Unemployment.* MIT Press, 1990.

Peter Temin. *Lessons from the Great Depression.* MIT Press, 1989.

Chapter 2. Uncle Sam the Debtor

Robert Eisner. *How Real Is the Federal Deficit?* Free Press, 1986.

Benjamin M. Friedman. *Day of Reckoning: The Consequences of American Economic Policy.* Random House, 1988.

Milton Friedman and Anna J. Schwartz. *A Monetary History of the United States, 1867–1960.* Princeton University Press, 1963.

William Greider. *Secrets of the Temple: How the Federal Reserve Runs the Country.* Simon and Schuster, 1987.

Laurence J. Kotlikoff. *Generational Accounting: Knowing Who Pays—and When—for What We Spend.* Free Press, 1992.

Lawrence Lindsey. *The Growth Experiment: How the New Tax System Is Transforming the U.S. Economy.* Basic Books, 1990.

Chapter 3. The Very Model of a Modern Major Market

Walter Adams and James W. Brock. *Antitrust Economics on Trial.* Princeton University Press, 1991.

William J. Baumol, John C. Panzer, and Robert D. Willig. *Contestable Markets and the Theory of Industry Structure.* Harcourt Brace Jovanovich, 1982.

Richard Caves. *American Industry: Structure, Conduct, Performance,* 6th ed. Prentice-Hall, 1987.

Richard B. Freeman and James L. Medoff, *What Do Unions Do?* Basic Books, 1984.

George Stigler, *The Economist As Preacher and Other Essays.* University of Chicago Press, 1982.

———. *Memoirs of an Unregulated Economist.* Basic Books, 1988.

Lester Thurow. *The Zero Sum Society.* Basic Books, 1980.

Chapter 4. Applying Microeconomics to Major Markets

Gary Becker. *Human Capital,* 3rd ed. University of Chicago Press, 1993.

Edward H. Chamberlin. *The Theory of Monopolistic Competition,* 7th ed. Harvard University Press, 1956.

John E. Chubb and Terry M. Moe. *Politics, Markets, and America's Schools.* Brookings Institution, 1990.

Robert W. Crandall, *Controlling Industrial Pollution.* Brookings Institution, 1983.

Alain Enthoven. *Consumer Choice Health Plan: The Only Practical Solution to the Soaring Cost of Medical Care.* Addison-Wesley, 1980.

U.S. Department of Energy, Office of Environmental Analysis. *A Compendium of Options for Government Policy to Encourage Private Sector Responses to Potential Climate Change,* 1989.

Chapter 5. Border Crossings

Jagdish Bhagwati. *Protectionism.* MIT Press, 1988.

Gary Clyde Hufbauer, Jeffrey Schott, and Kimberly Ann Elliott. *Economic Sanctions Reconsidered.* Institute for International Economics, 1990.

Paul Krugman. *The Age of Diminished Expectations.* MIT, 1990.

Robert Z. Lawrence and Robert E. Litan. *Saving Free Trade.* Brookings Institution, 1986.

Michael Porter. *The Competitive Advantage of Nations.* Free Press, 1990.

Chapter 6. Money Makes the World Go Round

Robert Z. Aliber. *The International Money Game.* Basic Books, 1987.

Milton Friedman. "The Case for Floating Exchange Rates." *The Financial Times* (London), December 18, 1989.

Peter Kenen. *EMU After Maastricht.* Group of Thirty, 1992.

Stephen Marris, *Deficits and the Dollar: The World Economy at Risk.* Institute for International Economics, 1985.

Chapter 7. Going for Broke

Peter L. Bernstein. *Capital Ideas*. Free Press, 1992.

Richard A. Brealey and Stewart C. Myers. *Principles of Corporate Finance*, 4th ed. McGraw-Hill, 1991.

Richard A. Posner and Kenneth E. Scott, eds. *Economics of Corporation Law and Securities Regulation*. Little Brown, 1980.

Chapter 8. Taking Stock of Personal Investments

Peter Lynch. *One Up on Wall Street*. Penguin, 1989.

Burton G. Malkiel. *A Random Walk Down Wall Street*, 5th ed. W.W. Norton, 1990.

Peter Passell. *How to Read the Financial Pages*. Warner, 1993.

Chapter 9. They Shoot Economists, Don't They?

Todd Buchholz. *New Ideas from Dead Economists: An Introduction to Modern Economic Thought*. Plume, 1990.

John Maynard Keynes. "Thomas R. Malthus" and "Alfred Marshall," in *Essays in Biography*. MacMillan/St. Martin's Press, 1972.

Ludwig von Mises. *Human Action*, 3rd ed. Regnery, 1966.

Mancur Olson. *The Rise and Decline of Nations*. Yale University Press, 1982.

Thomas Sargeant. *Rational Expectations and Inflation*. Harper & Row, 1986.

Joseph A. Schumpeter. *Capitalism, Socialism and Democracy*. Harper & Row, 1950.

Robert Skidelsky. *John Maynard Keynes*, vols. 1, 2. Penguin, 1983; 1992.

INDEX